ISSUES IN CONTEMPORARY PHILOSOPHY OF RELIGION

STUDIES IN PHILOSOPHY AND RELIGION

Volume 23

Issues in
Contemporary Philosophy of Religion

Edited by

EUGENE THOMAS LONG

Department of Philosophy
University of South Carolina
Columbia, South Carolina, USA

Reprinted from
International Journal for Philosophy of Religion
Volume 50, Nos. 1-3 (2001), Special Publication
on the Occasion of the 50th Volume of this Journal

Kluwer Academic Publishers
DORDRECHT / BOSTON / LONDON

A C.I.P. Catalogue record for this book is available from the Library of Congress.

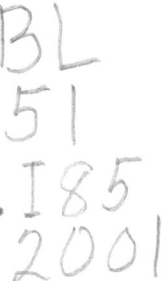

ISBN 1-4020-0167-3

Published by Kluwer Academic Publishers,
P.O. Box 17, 3300 AA Dordrecht, The Netherlands.

Sold and distributed in North, Central and South America
by Kluwer Academic Publishers,
101 Philip Drive, Norwell, MA 02061, U.S.A.

In all other countries, sold and distributed
by Kluwer Academic Publishers,
P.O. Box 322, 3300 AH Dordrecht, The Netherlands.

All Rights Reserved
© 2001 Kluwer Academic Publishers
No part of the material protected by this copyright notice may be reproduced or utilized in any form or by any means, electronic or mechanical, including photocopying, recording or by any information storage and retrieval system, without permission from the copyright owners.

Printed in the Netherlands on acid free paper

Contents

Contemporary philosophy of religion: Issues and approaches
   by Eugene Thomas Long   1

Postmodernism in philosophy of religion and theology
   by John Macquarrie   9

Philosophy – religion – theology
   by Adriaan Peperzak   29

Of miracles and special effects
   by Hent de Vries   41

Religious diversity and religious toleration
   by Philip L. Quinn   57

Theological determinism and the problem of evil: Are Arminians any better off
   by William J. Wainwright   81

The foreknowledge conundrum
   by William Hasker   97

Theology in philosophy: Revisiting the Five Ways
   by Fergus Kerr   115

Process philosophy of religion
   by David Ray Griffin   131

The temporality of God
   by Keith Ward   153

Some reflections on Indian metaphysics
   by Keith E. Yandell   171

Gender and the infinite: On the aspiration to be all there is
   by Pamela Sue Anderson   191

Contemporary philosophy of religion: Issues and approaches

EUGENE THOMAS LONG
University of South Carolina

The following essays are presented in celebration of the publication of the fiftieth volume of the *International Journal for the Philosophy of Religion*. Since the publication of the first volume in 1970, there has emerged a new era in western philosophy of religion characterized by pluralism in content and method.[*] Some philosophers identify themselves as traditional theists, often returning to their roots in medieval philosophy. Others seek either to reconstruct the God of classical theism or in some cases leave it behind altogether. Persons often associate the first with Anglo-American or analytic approaches to the philosophy of religion and the latter with Continental or phenomenological approaches to philosophy of religion. There is some justification for this. It is not unusual to see the work of a contemporary analytic philosopher of religion begin with the declaration that by God he or she means the God of classical theism. By contrast the work of a philosopher of religion in the phenomenological tradition may begin with the declaration that theism in its traditional form has lost its credibility.

The picture given above, however, over-simplifies the situation. First, significant diversity exists in both Anglo-American and Continental approaches to the philosophy of religion. Second, these approaches to the philosophy of religion tell only part of the contemporary story. There are other approaches to the philosophy of religion which cannot be classified easily under these headings. Third, in spite of striking differences among contemporary philosophers of religion, they often share a good bit of common ground. For example, many contemporary philosophers of religion reject the neo-positivist and classical foundationalist approaches to knowledge, and discussions of religious knowledge often center on religious experience or the religious dimensions of experience. There are important differences regarding theories of experience, but few philosophers of religion today limit experience to self-authenticating revelation or the empirically verifiable. There is also a growing awareness of the diversity of human experience and of the historical and interpretive dimensions of experience. These developments

---

[*] I have discussed these developments in more detail in Part Four of *Twentieth-Century Western Philosophy of Religion 1900–2000* (Kluwer Academic Publishers, 2000).

challenge claims to universal truth in religion, send philosophers in search of new conceptions of rationality and in some cases lead to new conceptions of the nature and tasks of the philosophy of religion.

One of the important developments in the philosophy of religion during the last quarter of the twentieth century traces its roots to Martin Heidegger and the phenomenological tradition. One can hardly think of Heidegger and religion without thinking of Rudolf Bultmann and Paul Tillich. Yet Heidegger's emphasis upon interpretation and his understanding of language as the house of being helped prepare the way for what has been called a hermeneutical or linguistic turn in phenomenology. In its more radical form this is called deconstruction or postmodernism and is illustrated in the work of such philosophers as Emmanuel Levinas and Jacques Derrida. Postmodernism is an expression used widely in literature, philosophy and theology during the last decades of the twentieth century to signal a rejection in various degrees of the concept of rationality associated with modern philosophy or the Enlightenment.

The first essay by John Macquarrie, 'Postmodernism in Philosophy of Religion and Theology', provides an analysis of postmodernism and its influence in contemporary philosophy and theology. Macquarrie, whose own approach to philosophical theology is influenced by Heidegger and Bultmann, identifies several characteristics of postmodernism, including the limits of the intellect, the questioning of authority, the rejection of any unified world view, and the emphasis upon difference, the particular, pluralism and desire. From his own point of view he then illustrates and critically evaluates these characteristics in the work of three postmodern philosophers, Levinas, Jean-François Lyotard and Derrida and three postmodern theologians, Mark Taylor, Graham Ward and Jean-Luc Marion.

Adriaan Peperzak, the author of the second essay, 'Philosophy-Religion-Theology', is also indebted to recent continental philosophy. Defining the religious dimension of human existence in a broad way to mean the deepest dimension of human life in which all other dimensions are rooted, Peperzak argues that the religious dimension is a necessary and basic topic of philosophy, that philosophy itself is a kind of faith, and that if philosophy proclaims itself autarchic, it is a religion that must look down upon other religions as deficient forms of its own truth. From this perspective he challenges the modern self-conception of philosophy and argues that other religions can in turn criticize the impossibility of philosophy's faith in its autarchy and the arrogance that follows from it. Peperzak analyzes some relations between faith and thought in philosophy, philosophy of religion and theology and argues for a form of universality different from that professed by modern philosophy.

During much of the twentieth century, religion was relegated by many to the margins of the so-called modern political and intellectual worlds. Religion, however, has emerged on the geopolitical stage of the late twentieth-century as a significant force leading many to challenge an overly simplistic separation of the worlds of the religious and non-religious. In his article, 'Of Miracles and Special Effects', Hent de Vries argues that the narrative of Western 'secularist' modernity has obscured the fact that in most of its historical forms the concept of the political has to some extent always been dependent upon the religious. He is particularly concerned with what he identifies as an intrinsic and structural relationship between religion and the new media, and the transformative changes we are witnessing today. His study of miracle in relation to special effects provides a concrete example to illustrate this. Starting out from a discussion of Jacques Derrida's recent essay, 'Faith and Knowledge', de Vries investigates the structural resemblances and differences between the miracle and the special effect and sketches out the place and function of religion in relation to the new technological media.

Analytic philosophers of religion trace their twentieth century roots to the new realism that characterized much British and American philosophy in the early part of the century. Since the 1960s, however, many analytic philosophers have called into question classical foundationalism and the evidentialist challenge to religious belief in the work of such philosophers as W.K. Clifford, Bertrand Russell, and Antony Flew. Some of these philosophers are classified as moderate foundationalists while others, who are more closely indebted to the later Wittgenstein, are often called anti-foundationalists. Among the leading so-called moderate foundationalists is William Alston. Alston argues that a person may be justified in holding certain beliefs about God based on his or her direct experience or perception of God. Given what appears to be the incompatibility of perceptual religious beliefs formed in different religions, however, questions arise concerning the reliability or rationality of different religious practices and the closely connected issues of religious exclusivism and religious tolerance. In his essay, 'Religious Diversity and Religious Toleration', Philip Quinn discusses the work of Alston and related thinkers and challenges their tendencies towards religious exclusivism. Abstracting arguments from Pierre Bayle and Immanuel Kant, Quinn makes a connection between discussions of religious diversity in religious epistemology and discussions of religious diversity in moral and political philosophy. He argues that religious diversity reduces the epistemic status of religious exclusivism and intolerance, and makes it possible for a person to be justified in aspiring to be religious while living fully within a religiously pluralistic cultural environment.

Many contemporary analytic philosophers of religion are committed to traditional Jewish or Christian theism and this has helped stimulate interest in a diversity of topics associated with theistic faith and belief. The problem of evil has proven to be particularly acute for traditional theists and it has been the focus of much discussion in recent analytic philosophy of religion. In addressing this problem analytic philosophers have often explored medieval and other classical texts. William Wainwright's article, 'Theological Determinism and the Problem of Evil: Are Arminians Any Better Off?', plumbs the work of Jonathan Edwards in an effort to better understand contemporary debates concerning freedom, determinism and the problem of evil. Wainwright maintains that Edwards' theological determinism aggravates the problem of evil in three ways. It appears to make God the author of sin, exposes God to charges of insincerity and raises questions about God's justice. Wainwright argues that Edwards is correct in thinking that Arminianism is exposed to many of the same difficulties, but that his idea of God's justice inflicting infinite punishment upon persons whose actions have been determined by God is indefensible and may not be a difficulty for Arminianism.

The apparent incompatibility between divine foreknowledge and human freedom is another problem that has haunted the theistic tradition for many centuries and has received almost unprecedented attention in recent analytic philosophy of religion. In his article, 'The Foreknowledge Conundrum', William Hasker provides a survey and analysis of several classical and contemporary efforts to solve the problem of the incompatibility between comprehensive, infallible divine foreknowledge and libertarian free will, focusing in particular upon those solutions most actively considered by philosophers during the last three decades of the twentieth century. Concluding that none of the proposed solutions to the problem is fully satisfying, Hasker raises the question, whether theological incompatibilism might be less inimical to traditional theism than some have supposed. In this context he calls attention to 'open theism', a recent movement within evangelical Protestantism which, based upon its revised conception of God and of God's relationship with the world, affirms the incompatibility of divine foreknowledge and free will. While admitting that it is too soon to draw conclusions about the effects of this movement, Hasker suggests that at a minimum it demonstrates that one cannot simply assume that theological incompatibilism is inimical to Biblical faith and traditional Christian theology.

Thomism is the expression applied since the fourteenth century to philosophers whose thinking has its foundation in the thought of St. Thomas Aquinas. The expression Neo-Thomism is sometimes used to refer to the revival of Thomism which began in the middle of the nineteenth century and was later officially endorsed by the Roman Catholic Church. The aim of this revival was not merely a restatement of Thomas' philosophy and theology, but an accurate understanding of the permanent truth of the principles of his thought that could be applied to contemporary thought. This has led to a re-vitalization of the Thomistic tradition as some have brought Thomas' thought into conversation with other contemporary philosophical movements and others have challenged traditional conceptions of how to read his thought. In his essay, 'Theology in Philosophy: Revisiting the Five Ways', Fergus Kerr calls into question what he calls the standard reading of Aquinas' arguments for the existence of God. On the standard view, Aquinas is understood to be a good example of those who think that the existence of God can be inferred from natural features of the world. Kerr challenges this reading of Aquinas and the general conception of philosophy of religion that arises from it. Reading the text in context, argues Kerr, suggests how theologically determined the philosophical arguments are. Thomas' approach in the *Summa Theologiae*, he suggests, may be read not as turning away from the Bible, choosing Aristotle and conducting foundationalist apologetics, but as continuing more than a thousand years of reading the Vulgate in the light of a certain neo-Platonism.

Process philosophy is widely understood today to refer to the kind of realistic metaphysics associated with Alfred North Whitehead and Charles Hartshorne and those influenced by them. Although not limited to American thinkers, its greatest impact in recent years has been in the United States and in particular among those who declare themselves to be neo-classical or process theists. In general process theists are committed to the view that whatever exists in reality should be characterized in terms of processes rather than substances or things, and that we should look for God in the world process itself. They argue for a close relationship between philosophy and the natural sciences and understand God less in terms of timeless perfection and more in terms of temporal becoming. It is not their intention to deny the perfection of God, but to insist that perfect knowledge and love require involvement in the world.

In his article, 'Process Philosophy of Religion', David Ray Griffin summarizes ways in which he has sought to employ process metaphysics to address several topics, including the problem of evil and the relation between science and religion. Process philosophy's panentheistic view of God seeks to combine features of both pantheism and theism. This results in a rejection of *creatio ex nihilo* in the strict sense and a rejection of the traditional idea of God's omnipotence which leads to the traditional problem of evil. Creative power is understood to be inherent in the world as well as God, and God's power is understood to be persuasive rather than coercive. With regard to the question of the relation between science and religion, Griffin argues that the real conflict is not between science and religion as such, but between traditional views of scientific naturalism and religious supernaturalism. He maintains that process philosophy provides a theory of naturalism more adequate to science than traditional scientific naturalism, and a theory of theistic naturalism more adequate to theism than traditional supernaturalism.

Although philosophical reflection on religion can be traced back to the origins of western philosophy, western philosophy of religion in the more strict sense is a modern development indebted in particular to the work of such philosophers as Hume, Kant and Hegel. It is widely understood to be an autonomous discipline devoted to the kinds of issues that arise in western monotheistic traditions. In recent years, however, some western philosophers of religion have challenged this view arguing that it is too narrow in scope, and that philosophers of religion need to extend the boundaries of their discipline to allow them to take into account other religious traditions and issues raised in those traditions. This has led to the development of a variety of approaches to the comparative philosophy of religion, and in some cases to the view that the sharp boundaries often drawn between philosophy, theology and the history of religions are unjustified. Although some roots of this development may be traced to late nineteenth and early twentieth century anthropological and historical studies, it has been stimulated in recent years by the growing recognition that politically and economically persons are in some sense citizens of the world.

Keith Ward's article, 'The Temporality of God', provides an example of the comparative approach to the philosophy of religion. Elsewhere Ward has argued that the comparative approach is important to efforts to develop a more comprehensive view rooted in but not limited to one's own historical tradition. In the article included here Ward argues that, in spite of different philosophical terminology, Semitic and Indian traditions have developed a similar classical concept of God, and that this concept of God should be revised in view of the post-enlightenment emphasis on the irreducible value of the individual and the historical. Ward considers some primary objections to divine temporality and argues that if contingency and autonomy are real characteristics of the universe, divine knowledge and activity must be partly responsive and thus temporal.

Keith Yandell also represents the comparative approach to the philosophy of religion. In his article, 'Some Reflections on Indian Metaphysics', Yandell explores some themes and tensions in the Indian metaphysical tradition beginning with the idea that everything that really exists is everlasting, and the opposite notion that almost all of what exists is radically impermanent. He discusses the notion of substances that are continuants and argues that Indian monotheists should be friendly to the idea of continuants which, in contrast to everlasting continuants, need not be everlasting. Yandell argues that some initially plausible arguments against continuants do not stand up to scrutiny and considers what account of persons is most in accord with reincarnation and karma doctrine when that doctrine is taken to be literally true.

Although feminist philosophy also has roots in the early part of the twentieth century, it is today often associated with a movement that began in the 1960s, building in some cases upon Simone de Beauvoir's book, *The Second Sex* (1949). Feminist philosophy is a way of thinking which insists that female experiences, identities and ways of being and thinking must be considered at least equal to those of the male. It is rooted in a belief that women have been dominated and disadvantaged by a way of being and thinking that is patriarchal in character. Feminist philosophy has made significant strides during the last quarter of the century. In spite of the fact, however, that there are a number of distinguished women philosophers of religion and distinguished feminist theologians, until recently there has been little in the way of feminist philosophy of religion in the more strict sense. This picture is now changing.

Pamela Anderson's article, 'Gender and the Infinite: On the Aspiration to be All That There Is' helps illustrate this new interest in feminist philosophy of religion. Anderson is particularly concerned with the topic of the infinite. She argues that a gender-sensitive approach to the infinite reveals a corrupt striving to become infinite or all there is in both masculinist and feminist philosophy of religion. She calls for a more inclusive approach that would allow instantiating the regulative ideals of truth, love goodness and justice as conditions for an incorrupt craving for infinitude.

Address for correspondence: Professor Eugene Long, Department of Philosophy, University of South Carolina, SC 29208, USA
Phone: (803) 777-3732; Fax: (803) 777-9178

Postmodernism in philosophy of religion and theology

JOHN MACQUARRIE
Oxford

The term 'postmodernism' has been often heard in the closing decades of the twentieth century, first apparently used in the visual arts, then spreading to other areas, including philosophy and theology. It is not easy to give any general definition of 'postmodernism'. Perhaps the end of the twentieth century with its ambiguous record of progress and retrogression has created a *fin de siècle* mentality in which there is rejection of the past and an intense desire to begin anew. Both the hopes and fears engendered at such a time are liable to be exaggerated.

The very word 'postmodern' is a polemical term, for if you claim to be a postmodern artist or theologian or whatever else, you automatically put all your contemporaries out of date. The merely modern has been outstripped by the postmodern, and in a society like ours the word 'postmodern' confers a certain prestige even before we have inquired just what it means. We can do justice to postmodernism only by looking carefully at particular examples as we find them in the work of some leading exponents. But first it will be useful to draw attention to some characteristics which occur in most of those who accept the postmodernist label and which seem to differentiate them more or less sharply from their predecessors. I am going to mention ten contrasts where the postmodernists break with the past. The number 'ten' is arbitrary – it could have been less, because some of my points overlap, or it could have been more, because almost certainly I shall have omitted points which other writers would consider important.

Contrast 1. Postmodernism and modernism

This is the most general of the oppositions to be considered. Modern religious thought has been observant of what might be called the 'canons' of the Enlightenment, that is to say, it has prized rationality, has been respectful toward natural science and critical history, has questioned authority and minimized the 'supernatural' in religion. Rudolf Bultmann would be a good example of a 'modern' theologian, especially in his radically critical historical criticism of the New Testament and even more in his program of 'demythologizing', aimed at removing from Christianity those features which he deemed unacceptable to 'modern man'.[1] Postmodernists cannot simply reject rationalism if they wish to participate in serious dialogue, but they stress the limits of reason, and are at one with the modernists in questioning any authority or privileged opinion.

Derrida stated in an early writing that his philosophical method 'blocks the way to all theology'[2] but seems later to have modified his opinion, and if he has not become a theologian, he could at least be called a philosopher of religion in search of a theology.

Contrast 2. Objectivity and subjectivity

Whereas modernism laid great stress on objectivity, postmodernism seems to lean toward subjectivism. But we have to be careful in assessing this statement. As far as the natural sciences are concerned, I do not think that many postmodernists would urge a return to the view of Bishop Berkeley, that what we call material things are in reality ideas in the mind: *esse est percipi*, 'to be is to be perceived'. In fact, some postmodernists are convinced materialists, for instance, Lyotard. But in the question of history, the subjectivizing tendency is strong. A good example is the quest of the historical Jesus. In the nineteenth century, there was a vigorous attempt to arrive at a picture of Jesus such as we would have seen had we been present in his lifetime. This quest has been renewed quite recently. But the 'objective facts' can never be fully established. We would need to be able to travel back through time, and see Jesus for ourselves. In fact, we can never get beyond reports, and even the earliest gospel (Mark) was written more than thirty years after the crucifixion, and must itself have had its origin in earlier reports, most or even all of them unwritten. So we have to ask, 'Is there anything except interpretation of interpretations ...?' What do we make of Derrida's claim that 'there is nothing outside of the text'?[3] Does postmodernism lead inevitably to skepticism or can the way to theology can be unblocked?

Contrast 3. Fragmentation and totalization

One of the most prominent features of postmodern thinking is its tendency to take apart the unities of thought on the ground that these unities have been subjectively projected on to a reality which is itself disparate and dismembered. Clearly, this is another rejection of the Enlightenment, which sought to work toward a unified view of the world. The natural sciences do aim at overarching theories which bring together apparently unrelated phenomena under one roof. Philosophy was even more ambitious, especially Hegelianism, which earns the disapproval of most postmodernists. Hegel constructed a metaphysical system which embraced just about everything – logic, nature, law, history, art, politics, religion. But do the realities which constitute the cosmos, including the human realities, fit so neatly into the patterns of thought? Here the postmodernists go back of Kierkegaard, who criticized Hegel on the grounds that only God can view the cosmos as a whole.[4]

But one has to ask the postmodernists whether the sciences could have had their successes unless the cosmos has a rational structure of some sort. (Einstein believed that they could not). The situation is more problematic in the case of an all-embracing metaphysic. What about history, which holds special interest for religion? Extrapolating from records of particular periods, some theologians and philosophers claim to see a pattern in history as a whole. No conclusive proofs are available, but many postmodernists believe that history has neither beginning nor end nor overall pattern. But how can a postmodernist know that history is fragmentary and directionless if he denies that there is any access to objective facts?

Contrast 4. Particular and universal

Enlightenment or modernist thinkers have sought universal laws, and have treated the particular as only an instance of something universal. They have minimized difference for the sake of identity or sameness. Hegel, of course, did not deny difference and believed that throughout the universe there is an unending clash of opposites. But his dialectical method resolved these oppositions by bringing them together in a wider synthesis. The difference is 'taken up' (*aufgehoben*) into a new unity. But while this may be gain, it is also loss, for the particular has an excess of content which has to be discarded in the abstractness of a generalizing concept. Kierkegaard is hailed as a forerunner of postmodernism because he championed the particular. The universalizer should allow more weight to the particular in all its concrete richness (it may be nothing short of 'revelation'), but could anyone have recognized the revelation as such unless he had already some general capacity for it? So this contrast has to be left undecided.

Contrast 5. Others and self

The theme of this contrast is closely related to the one we have just considered. The notion of the 'other' and 'otherness', also called 'alterity', are very important in postmodernism. All men and women share a common humanity, yet each one has a certain uniqueness and a unique perspective on the world. Again we can refer back to the nineteenth century contrast between Hegel and Kierkegaard. Hegel took a poor view of Abraham because he chose to live in isolation. Kierkegaard claimed that the individual is a higher category than the community, and praises Abraham for rejecting the universal demands of morality in order to obey what he took to be the voice of God.[5] Postmodernists are divided, not all following Kierkegaard in this matter. Many of them have accepted Buber's criticism of Kierkegaard, that he concentrated too much on individual experience and was oblivious to the fact that every individual is always involved with others. So the other and otherness figure prominently in postmodern philosophies.

It is the notion of otherness that allows some of them to introduce God into their philosophy, perhaps echoing Buber's teaching that every particular 'thou' is a glimpse through to the eternal 'Thou'.[6] We shall also meet the idea that God is the 'wholly other'.

Contrast 6. Relative and absolute

There is a distinctly negative strain in postmodern philosophy, though it does not necessarily lead to nihilism or skepticism. But we have already seen that postmodernists are against authority and tradition, and they question whether human thought can come to grips with any objective reality. And what about God, as Creator and Source of all that exists? Postmodernism has been deeply influenced by Nietzsche as well as by Kierkegaard and Buber, and in particular by Nietzsche's proclamation of the death and God. So most postmodernists agree that there are no absolute foundations or criteria for our beliefs or moral judgements. Are we plunged into complete relativism?

Nietzsche proclaimed the death of God, but he also asked, 'Who gave us the sponge to wipe away the entire horizon? What were we doing, when we unchained the earth from its sun? Whither is it moving now? Whither are we moving? Away from all sums? Is there still any up or down? Are we not wandering as through an infinite nothing? Has it not become colder? Is not night continually closing in on us?'[7] Nietzsche did not enjoy the prospect of utter relativism.

There is no foundation and we are all the time on shifting sands. Our line of questioning has brought us to a point that is no longer academic but touches on the whole of life. But if we say that this is the consequence of atheism, we have to remember that faith too is something like this. In a metaphor beloved of Kierkegaard, faith is like being cast on 70,000 fathoms of water. Faith is indeed like walking on water, yet it is essentially affirmative, and needs something to which to cling.

And what about morality? Is it too undermined, so that right and wrong become a matter of personal preference, something that has happened already in some areas of human conduct? Some people have begun to look for new foundations, though where can they be found if we have taken a sponge and wiped out the entire horizon? For example, having dismissed the Ten Commandments, once supposed to be of divine origin, people now appeal to 'human rights', alleged to have a universal validity. But postmodernists, notably Lyotard, have shown that these rights are themselves relative. We are left with the worrying question raised by one of Dostoyevsky's characters: 'If there is no God, then is everything permitted?'

Contrast 7. Pluralism and uniformity

All the major post modernists agree in approving pluralism as opposed to uniformity. This has been foreshadowed in the preferences already considered. Pluralism implies the recognition of difference and opposes the dominance of any one group and its ideas. Pluralism is not only negative in denying privilege to any one way of thinking but teaches respect for a variety of traditions, believing that society is enriched by such diversity.

However, even a convinced pluralist recognizes that there are limits, or we may end up with an individualism which threatens the cohesion of society. Pluralism came into being in the modern periods, especially with the growth of religious toleration after the Reformation, and is a modern, not a post-modern idea, still struggling for acceptance in our present confused times. No group has a monopoly of prejudice, and the postmodernists are quite frequently guilty of stating a position quite arbitrarily and privileging it above all others. Presumably this may be expected, if there are no final criteria.

Contrast 8. Passion and intellect

Anti-intellectualism is an ever-present danger in human history. It seems that in all human beings, lurking below the surface, there are irrational passions and desires which can break out, bringing chaos and destruction. Examples have not been lacking in our own time, the most frightening being the anti-Semitism which raged through the civilized lands of central and eastern Europe in the middle of the twentieth century. But the problem with 'modernism' is that it glorified intellect to the extent of crushing the passional side of human nature. The natural sciences aimed at being 'value-free', that is to say, concerned only with scientifically established facts and rigorously excluding everything 'subjective', likes and dislikes, moral and religious considerations, and so on. But if we are to remain human, a balance has to be struck between passion and intellect, better than the one bequeathed by the Enlightenment. Human life needs more than knowledge of facts, more than the sciences can supply. We need poetry, music, justice, great art, morality, religion. We need truth, but we need other values as well – love, goodness, beauty, the sacred.

During the whole of the modern period, voices were occasionally raised in protest against a rationalism that was too narrow, for instance, Pascal in the seventeenth century urging that the heart has reasons of which reason knows nothing.

Many postmodernists wish to broaden the basis of human knowledge beyond the intellect. An extreme case was that of Lyotard who, in one phase of his thinking, championed the libidinous instincts of the human person against rational controls. This is extreme, for sometimes the intellect has to control and even deny the impulse of feeling and desire. But the person who is all intellect is less than fully human.

Contrast 9. Ambiguity and clarity

Modern philosophy has aimed at clarity, with each term having its own definite meaning. Wittgenstein went so far as to say that whatever can be said can be said clearly.[8] He was well aware that language is fallible. The postmodernists, however, seem almost to delight in the fallibilities of language. They use extremely obscure and convoluted sentence constructions, they introduce neologisms and love to play with words. Here is an illustration, admittedly translated from the French but equally obscure in either French or English: 'Presence is only possible as an incessant taking up of presence again, an incessant re-presentation. The incessance of presence is a repetition, its being taken up again in an apperception of representation. Representation is not to be described as a taking up again. Representation is the very possibility of a return, the possibility of the *always*, or of the presence of the present'.[9]

I think that in any subject except philosophy, these sentences would be dismissed as gobbledegook. Even if a painstaking exegesis could extract some sense from the passage, would it be worth the effort? A good philosopher should be able to achieve greater clarity. Let me, however, apologize for taking my illustration from Levinas, whom I consider the most outstanding philosopher among the postmodernists.

Postmodernists are fond of playing with words, sometimes rather pointlessly. Heidegger familiarised us with using etymologies to elucidate the understanding of words. But postmodernists appeal also to similarities of sound (often accidental) to make their views persuasive. An example is Derrida's treatment of the Hebrew name for God, *Yahweh*. It is usually supposed to be derived from the verb *haya*, 'to be', and theologians have claimed that the proper name for God is 'Being'. But Derrida connects the first syllable of *Yahweh* with the German word *ja*, meaning 'yes', and from this fortuitous connection, tells us that God is the One who says Yes.[10]

Indeed, this is a suitable place to ask what kind of discourse some postmodernists are using. We find in many texts fragments of philosophy mingled with psychology, sociology, anthropology and even mythology in a heady but not enlightening (!) mixture. Derrida is the one who has gone furthest in insisting on the imperfections of language. But he himself uses a standard language like the rest of us, so he must acknowledge that it is incapable of accurately expressing whatever ideas he is putting across. Must he not undermine himself?

Contrast 10. Opinion and truth

Truth has usually been considered the supreme value for philosophy. To know the truth is undoubtedly a fundamental human desire, but truth should not be isolated from other values. Here our discussion is closely related to the earlier one on passion and intellect. In the early stages of human existence, truth or the knowledge of how things really are, was prized for practical reasons. The desire for truth was subordinate to the more fundamental desire for survival. But with the emergence of the leisured classes, some persons began to pursue truth for its own sake. Yet even today science is harnessed to technology, and the latter is driven by commercial considerations.

When we reflect on truth, we find very quickly that there are several kinds of truth and therefore several criteria for truth. In everyday life and in natural science, we think of truth as belonging to propositions which describe states of affairs in the world. Such propositions are held to be true if they agree or correspond with the state of affairs to which they refer. But the concept of truth applies to other areas as well. If someone claims, for instance, that Marxism is true, or even that Jesus Christ is the truth, quite different tests would be needed to ascertain whether these claims can stand.

Perhaps it will be said that in such cases the word 'truth' should not be used. It should be restricted to the realm of facts, and anything beyond that is matter of opinion. This is the line taken by positivists, but it leaves out some of the most important questions that concern the human mind. There have been respectable thinkers who have claimed truth for their beliefs, but have acknowledged the difficulty or impossibility of providing objective verification. Kierkegaard, for instance, declared that 'an objective uncertainty held fast in an appropriation process of the most passionate inwardness is the truth, the highest truth attainable for an existing individual'.[11] Such a truth cannot be written in or read off from a book. It is experienced, and is perhaps best described in the Greek word for truth, *aletheia*, 'uncoveredness', in meaning something like the religious word 'revelation'. This understanding of truth has been revived by Heidegger, and we find it appearing among the postmodernists, or at least among those of them who are unwilling to accept what appears to be merely an assertion, that no opinion can be privileged above any other. This last view seems to abolish truth outside of narrow limits, but to abolish truth is to cut oneself off from serious discourse. I would say that as soon as we open our mouths to say anything, the very act of saying contains an implicit assertion that what I am saying is true. I am saying that the very use of language implies mutual trust between speaker and listener. We shall find a similar view in Levinas.

An important consequence follows from these remarks on truth. If language presupposes trust, then this explodes the modernist claim, still held by many philosophers and scientists, that the search for truth is 'value-free' or even that the value of truth takes precedence over all other values. Some postmodernists hold that goodness is more ultimate than being and therefore than any truth which confines itself to describing the way things are, truth in the ordinary sense of the word. It makes us reflect again on a passage of Plato: 'The objects of knowledge not only derive from the good the gift of being known, but are further endowed by it with a real and essential existence; though the good, far from being identical with real existence, goes beyond being in dignity and power'.[12] Such a view is truly revolutionary from the point of view of Enlightenment modernism. Spirituality, uncriticized by reason, tends to become a luxuriant undisciplined growth; but truth divorced from justice ('value-free') may easily become inhuman.

Postmodernism's critique of modernism deserves to be heard, and may well have important contributions to make to religious thought. To find out more, we turn to examine some representative thinkers.

Three postmodern philosophers

Emmanuel Levinas (1906–1995) was born in Lithuania and spent much of his teaching life in France. The early influences on his thinking were Husserl and Heidegger, also the Hebrew scriptures and Jewish thought, nor should we leave out Plato. In 1961 he published a major philosophical work, *Totality and*

Infinity. The word 'totality' refers to those philosophies which set up some inclusive concept in relation to which everything else is explained. Hegel's all-embracing philosophy of Spirit (*Geist*) is the chief example. Levinas believed that these inclusive concepts smother difference, and deprive that which is different of its genuine otherness or alterity. Such totalizing philosophies, he alleges, are guilty of a kind of conceptual imperialism. He reminds us that the word 'concept' is derived from the Latin *capere*, 'to take'. The other is not recognized as other in its particularity but is subordinated to a generalizing concept.

Levinas makes a distinction between metaphysics and ontology. The later, he believes, is conceptual and suffers from the defects of conceptualizing. Metaphysics is fundamentally desire or passion for the infinite. This desire is not a need arising from the human being's consciousness of finitude. The idea of the infinite comes from the Infinite itself, encountering us in and through the face of another human person. The face is important for Levinas, it *expresses*. In the face of the other, we perceive the trace of the Infinite, overflowing the image of the other. Levinas does say quite bluntly, 'The idea of infinity is *revealed* (italics his) in the strong sense of the term'.[13] We have seen that the notion of truth becomes problematic in postmodernism, and when it does emerge, it is closer to revelation than to empirical truth. It reminds us of Kierkegaard, and therefore raises the question of whether there can be an inward subjective truth. At any rate, in Levinas a central place is accorded to the concept of revelation, understood as a form of knowing which is given as a gift rather than attained through intellectual striving. Our knowledge of any human neighbor depends on that person opening himself or herself in an act of self-giving. Levinas' argument seems to be this: in knowing another person, one is encountering not just a replica of oneself, but a genuine other, and this otherness is not just his or her otherness, but a trace of the otherness of what is totally other to oneself, namely, the Infinite.

Furthermore, we do not meet the other as an equal. We are already at the other's disposal, under obligation to the other. In a later writing, Levinas says that the word 'I' means 'Here am I' (*Me voici*) in some such sense as 'I am at your service, what can I do?'[14] One recalls Bonhoeffer's phrase, 'the man for others'. Levinas tells us that on meeting the other, one should be at once open to his need, responsible for him, ready to substitute for him in his troubles.

Does God come into this humanistic picture? Yes, but Levinas denies that there is any direct mystical encounter with God. God or the Infinite encounters us in the face of the neighbour and nowhere else. God is therefore understood as one sharing the sufferings of humanity rather than as a celestial monarch. The belief that we should know God through human beings is compatible both with the Jewish teaching that man is made in the image of God and the Christian belief in an incarnation. But I would not want to deny that there may be other ways of encounter and I am doubtful that the experience of meeting other human beings 'inescapably' (Levinas' own word) leads to encounter with God. The divine image in the human face, the trace of a divine origin, has been grievously damaged by sin, and Levinas does not fully recognize this. He and some other postmodernists have not broken free of one of the worst errors of the Enlightenment – the belief in progress, in the innocence and perfectability of the human race by its own efforts. He acknowledges that a 'conversion' is needed, but does not say how it is to be effected. His affirmative view of interhuman relations seems too optimistic.

Jean-François Lyotard (1924–1998), another prominent French postmodernist, was quite close to nihilism in the sense of one who denies all conventional beliefs and institutions and leaves it to others to construct replacements. In a blanket condemnation of both modernity and antiquity, he declares, 'The ideas of western civilization issuing from the ancient, Christian and modern traditions are bankrupt'.[15]

Although Lyotard's interests were mainly in social and political questions, his views encapsulate the major thrusts of postmodernism and have significance, even if indirect, for theology and philosophy of religion. In his best-known book, *The Postmodern Condition*, he criticizes what he calls 'grand narratives', though he uses the word 'narrative' in a very broad sense to include ambitious theories which Levinas called 'totalizations'. The two examples at which Lyotard hammers away are Hegelianism and Marxism (though he himself had been an enthusiastic Marxist). The fault of these grand narratives is that they prize unity and sameness over plurality and difference. But one wonders what grounds Lyotard has for his critique. Was the preference of Marx and Hegel for unity over difference any more arbitrary than Lyotard's reversal of the preference? In fact, Lyotard makes a boast of not seeking to 'legitimate' his opinions. There are (according to him) no final criteria or foundations on which a judgement can be made. As we have noted already, he criticizes the notion of universal human rights. The various declarations of such rights from the French Revolution down to the present have come from very limited groups of people. He asks, 'Who could make such declarations? Who can tell whether the wars of liberation conducted in the name of the universal are wars of liberation or wars of conquest?'[16]

Lyotard's postmodernism denies that there are any sure foundations for our opinions in such matters. In that case, the theories of Marx and Hegel are on an equal footing with the views of Lyotard. But Lyotard allowed for the case in which an idea breaks into our routine thinking with such force that we cannot but accept it. Unlike Levinas, Lyotard does not speak of revelation, but he does speak of the 'sublime', defined by Kant as 'the name given to that which is absolutely great, what is beyond all comparison great'.[17] Lyotard, following Kant, uses the term in the field of aesthetics. But if such an experience is possible in art, why not in religion? Lyotard prizes the sublime chiefly for the negative reason that it interrupts our run-of-the-mill rational thinking, but it has affirmative significance as well.

Critics of Lyotard question whether he does justice to the 'grand narratives'. Gary Browning writes: 'He tends to read their theories as closed, absolutist schemes, but in doing so he does not allow for the variety of ways in which their theories have been interpreted'.[18] We may ask a further questions which apparently troubled Lyotard himself. Did he accomplish the end of grand narratives by a grand narrative to end all grand narratives?

The name that comes most readily to mind when there is a mention of postmodernism is that of Jacques Derrida (1930–). The most controversial of the postmodern philosophers, he was born in Algeria but has spent most of his life in France.

We did note near the beginning of this article that he once claimed that his method 'blocks the way to all theology'. But nearly thirty years later, he was taking about 'my religion, about which nobody understands anything'.[19] At first sight this looks like a more affirmative statement than the earlier one, but it is so apophatic that it needs much teasing out before we can tell whether theology or, at least, some religious discourse is coming to expression. When we remember that most apophatic theologians have found plenty to say, we must not be surprised if Derrida too tells us more than we may have expected. He found a careful and sympathetic interpreter of his religious tendencies in John Caputo to whose insights our own brief exposition is indebted.

But first we must look more closely at two of Derrida's key-terms, 'deconstruction' and '*différance*'. The word 'deconstruction' is a combination of two opposites, 'destruction' and 'construction', so it is already paradoxical and is both a taking apart and a putting together. According to Derrida, descriptions, histories, theories etc. need to be taken apart, because language is riddled by ambiguities. The logical analyst's plea that each word should have only one meaning is impossible to obey. As Derrida says more than once, we live after the Tower of Babel. Every text has a plurality of meanings as soon as it is put into words, and from that point on there are different interpretations. But if that is the negative side of deconstruction, it points to an affirmative task. The work of deconstruction prevents closure, and room is left for new interpretations. Our language never quite coincides with what is talked about. The language overflows, it has an excess of meanings and connotations. Its failure to coincide with what is talked about is called *différance*, a neologism which combines two distinguishable meanings of the French verb *différer*, 'to differ' and 'to defer'. Every text calls for re-writing, and this goes on indefinitely, always with *différance*. It is interesting to note that although Derrida shares the postmodern aversion to Hegel, he declared in an interview that we shall never be finished with reading and refeading the Hegelian text.[20]

Deconstruction forbids closure and there will always be new deferrals. Thus understood, deconstruction can be seen as not merely an intellectual operation but a passionate quest. It is the desire to think the unthinkable, a kind of spur to transcendence. It is at this point that the possibility of theology appears. Some critics claimed that Derrida's philosophy of deconstruction and *différance* resembles a negative or apophatic theology. Derrida neither accepts this nor does he rule it out. When he speaks of the quest for the 'wholly other', could this be a name for God, as it has been in Barth, Otto and other religious thinkers?

The expression 'wholly other' points to an unknown which is not another entity of the same order as those which we encounter within the world, or which we ourselves are. It lies beyond the realm of existent entities, and therefore beyond the range of range of human thought. The 'wholly other' could be an utterly transcendent God, though not the God of Christianity who is in some respects immanent and to that extent accessible.

Whatever we might call the 'wholly other', it would not necessarily be God. It might be some quite neutral being, not Holy Being. We find that Derrida does speak of a mysterious *Khora*, an idea which he gets from Plato's *Timaeus*. It is a region formless and incomprehensible where created things receive their forms. It could be a totally impersonal process, not God in any usual sense of that word. So the wholly other might be God or other-than-God. According to Caputo, when Derrida was questioned about the resemblance of his philosophy to apophatic theology, his answer was typical: 'Yes and No!'

It seems that in course of time the Yes has made an advance against the No. Perhaps his reading of Levinas or a new appreciation of his own Jewish roots have led Derrida toward an eschatological outlook in which the coming of the wholly other (*tout autre*) becomes identified with a desire for a coming righteousness. Caputo claims that Derrida's beliefs are dominated by the word, *Viens*! 'Come!' It is a kind of messianism, but the messiah will never come, for that would mean closure, while faith and hope require an open future.

Caputo asks: 'So then has not deconstruction been driven all along by a passion for God?'[21] That is a possible interpretation, though I suppose that neither Caputo nor Derrida would deny that there are other possibilities. Again, when the word 'God' appears in these discussions, we have to remember that there are different ways in which it is understood. Derrida himself speaks of his private religion, but also says, quoting St Augustine, 'I do not know what I love when I love God'.[22] But it is hard to see how anyone could love, if the object of that love were *wholly* other. The condition of faith seems to be that at least one 'sees through a glass, darkly'. There is at least a minimal awareness through revelation or otherwise of the One who is loved.

Many criticisms can be made of Derrida. Do not his critical methods apply equally to his own arguments? Is he not often quite arbitrary in preferring one point of view to another? Is not his critique of language as universally fissured, ambiguous and liable to slippage, highly self-defeating, for one who has written so many books and articles? These are questions for debate, but we can accept that he is no nihilist and that at some points what he says has significance for religious thought.

Three postmodern theologians

Mark Taylor (1945–) is probably the best-known American postmodernist who has written specifically on theology. His book, *Erring; An A/theology*, is a serious and important work. The word 'erring' in the title is used in its original sense of wandering. There is no fixed progression from a preselected starting-point to a clearly foreseen goal. About the subtitle, 'An A/theology', we are told that it cannot be pronounced but only written. It seems to indicate a writing that could be read in either a theistic or an atheistic way. It reminds us of Heidegger's remark that he is neither a theist nor an atheist. Taylor suggests that we concentrate on the slash.

The point of departure for Taylor's nomadic exploration is the death of God. This is not a point that he chooses, but simply the place where we currently are in western civilization. He appears to take the death of God in a sociological rather than a metaphysical sense – the modern west has (largely) given up its belief in God. Taylor declares quite plainly that his 'erring thought' is neither theistic nor atheistic, and, like Nietzsche, he recognizes that the death of God is not to be understood onesidedly as the emancipation of the human race, but has its tragic downside: 'With the death of God, a dark shadow falls over the light that for centuries illuminated the landscape of the west'.[23]

Taylor offers a brilliant if brief critique of contemporary western society. If God, the 'transcendental signified', is abolished, there is no reliable standard of meaning or signification. Everything becomes relative and transient. In what he calls 'atheistic humanism', the prevailing world-view in our time, the sovereign God has been replaced by the sovereign self. This was believed by some to be emancipation, but in fact it has bred rivalries, envies and resentments. He cites the French Revolution (modernity's 'grand narrative'?) as summing up what has happened. Liberation gives way to the desire for domination, expressing itself in internal conflicts and international wars of aggression, also consumerism. The death of God results in the death of self. As Taylor puts it, 'There is always a serpent in the garden'.[24]

The death of God and the death of man are followed by two more demises – the end of history and the end of the book. These two are related. They both appear to be instances of the ending of 'grand narratives'. History is without beginning or end and is no more than a series of contingent happenings. By the book, Taylor seems to mean attempts to construct a systematic account of the world and its history. Especially he has in mind the 'book' of Hegel.

So far, Taylor has been deconstructing theology, or at least the presuppositions of modern theology. From that, he passes on to 'deconstructive a/theology'.

We are introduced to it by way of writing. The book (in Taylor's restricted sense) is at an end, but it has given way to writing. The book has a beginning, a middle and an end, but writing begins anywhere and moves erratically to no particular end. This concept of 'writing' is central to Taylor's thought, but it is hard to pin down just what is meant. Derrida's influence is strong, and his famous remark that there is nothing outside the text seems to be paralleled by Taylor's claim, 'Writing is not just *about* something, *it is that something itself*'.[25] It seems to me that 'writing' has become what I would frankly call a metaphysical term. Writing is reality.

We now begin to see the shape of an a/theology. Writing or scripture has played a very large part in Christianity. God has become incarnate in the Word, though the Word is more than a written word, and in any case, God was not exhaustively incarnated in the Word. Taylor can also speak of writing as the 'divine milieu' in which we live our lives. This could suggest a pantheistic understanding of God (or not-God). Taylor's ideas are ingenious, and might be acceptable as a very liberal and somewhat heterodox version of Christianity. But one must ask whether this a/theology has not become too attenuated. Has God been reduced to a paper God?

What has happened to the finite self? I like very much Taylor's claim that in his system (if he will permit the use of the word) 'instead of an aggregate of unique individuals, we have discovered a network of codependent subjects'. Such a network would constitute a being-in-communion, a profoundly Christian idea. But how does Taylor arrive at it if, as he says, 'the subject is nothing more than the generative interplay of properties'.[26]

Of course, all this is complicated by the fact that if Christ is in some sense God, then the death of Christ was in some sense the death of God, and that in exalting self-sacrifice, Christ is in some sense calling for the end of self-contained individualism. We shall never be finished trying to interpret these ideas. Taylor's attempt is fresh and affirmative, but it falls short.

Graham Ward (1955–) is perhaps the leading English representative of postmodern theology. He joins with Taylor in a denunciation of modernism's legacy of nihilism and atheism, but believes that the postmodern God can open a way forward. But who or what is this 'postmodern God'? In our examination of postmodern writers, we have found several ideas of God – God as a trace of the Infinite in the face of the other, God as the virtually unknown God called the 'wholly other', God or not-God as the 'divine milieu' of writing and other ideas besides. Are these adequate substitutes for the God of Abraham, Isaac and Jacob? Ward wants to be both orthodox and postmodern, but is this possible?

It is too early to say, for Ward is still in mid-career. He has, however, contributed an interesting essay on Christology to a symposium entitled *Radical Orthodoxy*. The essay bears the title, 'Bodies: The Displaced Body of Jesus Christ'.[27] The starting-point is the actual physical body of Jesus of Nazareth, in its full humanity and particularity. This particularity includes Jesus' maleness and his Jewishness, and whatever else identifies him in the history of the human race. Ward speaks of the 'deferred identity' of Jesus Christ, reflected in the series of titles that were given to him. As each title turns out to be inadequate, it is displaced or, at least, supplemented by another. Ward works through the gospel narratives from the nativity to the ascension. Throughout these narratives, he says, 'Jesus the man is viewed as a man unlike other men (or women)'. Although it is not his main concern in retelling the story, Ward is also seeking to answer the question raised by some feminist theologians, 'Can a male Savior save women?'

The story is told as one of transfiguration. The specific transfiguration of Jesus on the mountain-top is treated as a kind of summary of his whole career. In that incident, the disciples are said to have seen his face shining like the sun. Here we remember that Levinas saw in the human face a trace of God. In the transfiguration, Jesus became in Ward's word 'iconic'. The body is indeed physical, but it is seen in a new depth, the invisible in the visible. Jesus is, in Paul's words, 'the icon of the invisible God'.

A new and different displacement takes place at the Last Supper. Jesus takes bread and says, 'This is my body'. Ward interprets this to mean that the personal body of Jesus begins to withdraw from the narrative. He has handed himself over to the disciples and is at their disposal in the bread, and this is also the time when he hands himself over to the authorities. Jesus has not ceased to be a physical presence with a human body, but his bodily presence now incorporates other bodies as extensions of his own. Then at the crucifixion Jesus' physical body, the original body of Jesus, is broken as foreshadowed in the breaking of the bread. The physical body has died, but there is already coming into being the community of the faithful, the church, as the continuing extended body of Christ. The church is, in Ward's word, 'multigendered', so the question about a male Savior is answered in this displacement.

I shall not pursue the story as it affects the resurrection and ascension, for we have already seen how Ward operates. But where is he taking us? One answer to that question would be to say that he is taking us in the opposite direction from those who are engaged in the quest for the historical Jesus. As Ward sees it, they are looking for an empirical foundation for their faith, but a good postmodernist does not need such a foundation. Ward claims to believe in both the humanity and the divinity of Jesus Christ, and has much that is interesting and instructive to say about the body or bodies of Jesus, but has he not cut us off too quickly from history and left us with a somewhat docetic Christ? He does say, 'What I wish to emphasize is the textuality of these bodies'. I feel myself wanting to ask, 'Is there anybody out there, beyond the texts?' Or is that a silly question?

A French philosopher and theologian, Jean-Luc Marion (1946–) deserves to be noticed, because he is the best-known Roman Catholic to have joined the ranks of the postmodernists. His principal book is entitled *God without Being*, a deliberately provocative title, seeing that Catholic theologians, including St Thomas Aquinas, have made 'Being' central to their understanding of God. Marion claims to be rigorous in his thinking, but I do not think he succeeds, for when he uses the word 'being' he wobbles quite a bit. But he states clearly that when he speaks of 'God without being' he is not joining the 'death of God' lobby. He says, 'We do not mean to insinuate that God is not, or is not truly God'.[28] He goes on to say that God does not fall within the domain of being, he comes to us as a gift. Here we stumble against the ambiguity of the word 'being' and also its French equivalent. It is true that God does not fall within the domain of being if that means that he is another being, a participant in what Thomas called 'common being'. All this was clear to Thomas, but is muddled in Marion. For Thomas, God himself is not an existent, but the Source of existence and existents. Modern writers such as Tillich are clear that God himself is not a being. Failure to recognize this is to ignore what Heidegger called the 'ontological difference' and to slip into what he called 'onto-theology' (a much abused term). God is prior to all beings, the Source from which they flow.

Marion objects to making Being the primary characteristic of God, and prefers the identification with love. God is love. But it is absurd to set being and love over against one another, as rivals claiming to be the defining attribute of God. I say this, because love is possible only between realities which already enjoy some measure of being, and also because God is the One who lets-be, and letting-be is love in its purest non-possessive form. To let someone be is to empower or assist that person to become what he or she has the potentiality to be. In Heidegger's philosophy the ultimate Event or source which lets the beings be is called *es gibt*, a German expression which would normally be translated 'there is'. Heidegger tells us that it is to be taken quite literally as 'It gives' (capitalization his), and when the question is asked, 'Who or what gives?' the answer is 'Being'. Being gives itself. So the ultimate Source is an act of donation, which seems to me not very different from Marion's idea of God's self-giving. St Thomas says something similar: 'The goodness of God is not something different from his substance, his substance is his goodness'.[29]

But this is still some way short of answering Marion's subtle arguments. Like Feuerbach and Barth, he makes a good deal of the human tendency to project our all-too-human imaginings and to call them 'God'. Such imaginings then become idols, extensions or replicas of ourselves, the very opposite of a 'wholly other'. Must we count being among the idols, as Marion seems to claim? Is this the God of the philosophers as distinct from the God of Abraham, Isaac and Jacob? At first sight, the answer seems to be No. The second of the Ten Commandments prohibits the making of a 'graven image'. An image is understood as something sensible and finite. Nothing of that sort arises in our minds when we hear the word 'being'. The word is the sign of a concept which has no image and is not limited to the finite. So if our concepts arise from our own finite minds, must they not be limited, and if applied to God, must they not limit him also? They would exclude the excess and overplus that constitute God's mystery and escape our attempt to grasp them.

But have not human beings for centuries limited God by thinking of him as a being among others, even if they have called him the 'Supreme Being'? Of course they have, but they have also dimly understood what sophisticated theologians from Dionysius to Tillich have more clearly understood, namely, that such language is symbolic or analogical. The language is not to be understood as dragging God into the categorical scheme which applies within the finite order. But if we are denied the use of such language, we shall not be able to say anything affirmative about God at all.

Strictly, God is unthinkable and unsayable, for whatever we say about him would seem to infringe his otherness and mystery. It could be a slide into idolatry. But symbols symbolize something beyond themselves, signs imply a signified. Tillich maintained that the only non-symbolic statement we can make about God is that he is Being or Being-itself. Marion prefers a different language and claims that the only feasible concept is love. I have already indicated that this opposition is a false one. Being and loving can both bring as closer to God. Simply through the wonder of being or existing, we have within us an as yet unthought or unconceptualized apprehension of being, the beginning of the knowledge of God. This is, if you like, an intellectual approach, but it has religious significance, for it bring us to the point of awe and worship. It brings us to the infinity of Being, and, as Levinas claimed, the idea of the Infinite is not derived from a sense of our own limitation, but received in the encounter with the infinite Other.

In some pages of his book, Marion crosses out the word 'God'. This is not meant to indicate the end of God or the death of God but he acknowledgement that God in Christ gives himself in an excess that crosses out or (to use Marion's own word) 'saturates' all our inadequate misunderstandings of God derived from natural theology. Like Barth, Marion lays all the stress on revelation, though he would seem to include in the revelation not only Christ and the New Testament but the dogmas of the Church as well. Indeed, he seems to imply that theology can only be pursued within the Church, perhaps even only within the Roman Catholic Church. He writes (and he puts the sentence into italics for emphasis) *'Only the bishop merits, in the full sense, the title of theologian'*.[30] So he allows no natural theology, no non-Christian theology. Although I accept the idea of revelation, I think we have also to use our natural resources of reason in seeking to validate the revelation so far as we can.

Postmodernism is not going to solve all our problems in theology and religious studies, but it deserves a fair hearing and has some lessons worth learning. The postmodernist story is unfinished.

Notes

1. R. Bultman, *Kerygma and Myth* (London: SPCK, 1953), p. 18.
2. J. Derrida, *Positions* (Chicago: Chicago University Press, 1981), p. 40.
3. J. Derrida, *Of Grammatology* (Baltimore: John Hopkins University Press, 1976), p. 158.
4. S. Kierkegaard, *Concluding Unscientific Postscript* (Princeton: Princeton University Press, 1941), p. 107.
5. Contrast G.W.F. Hegel, *On Christianity: Early Theological Writings* (New York: Harper Torchbooks, 1961), pp. 185–189.
6. Martin Buber, *I and Thou* (Edinburgh, T. & T. Clark, 1958), p. 75.
7. F. Nietzsche, *The Gay Science* (New York: Random House, 1974), p. 181.
8. L. Wittgenstein, *Tractatus Logico-Philosophicus* (London: Routledge, 1992), p. 27.
9. E. Levinas, *Levinas Reader* (Oxford: Blackwell, 1989), pp. 170–171.
10. Quoted by J. Caputo, *The Prayers and Tears of Jacques Derrida* (Bloomington: Indiana University Press, 1997).
11. S. Kierkegaard, *Postscript*, p. 182.
12. Plato, *Republic* (New York: Random House, 1937), §509.

13. E. Levinas, *Totality and Infinity* (Pittsburgh: Duquesne University Press, 1961), p. 63.
14. E. Levinas, *Levinas Reader*, p. 104.
15. J-F. Lyotard, *Postmodern Fables* (Minneapolis: University of Minnesota Press, 1997), p. 235.
16. J-F. Lyotard, *The Postmodern Explained* (University of Minnesota Press, 1993), p. 52.
17. Immanel Kant, *Critique of Judgment* (Oxford: Clarendon Press, 1952), p. 94.
18. G. Browning, *Lyotard and the End of Grand Narratives* (Cardiff: University of Wales Press, 2000), p. 38.
19. J. Derrida, *Circumfession* (University of Chicago Press, 1993), p. 154.
20. Quoted by M. Taylor, *Altarity* (University of Chicago Press, 1987), p. 266.
21. Caputo, *op. cit.*, p. 332.
22. Ibid.
23. M. Taylor, *Erring: An A/theology* (University of Chicago Press, 1984), p. 20.
24. Ibid., p. 71.
25. Ibid., p. 105.
26. Ibid., p. 133.
27. J. Milburn et al., eds., *Radical Orthodoxy* (London: Routledge, 1999), pp. 163–181.
28. J-L. Marion, *God without Being* (University of Chicago Press, 1991), p. 30.
29. Thomas Aquinas, *Summa contra Gentiles* (Notre Dame: University of Notre Dame Press, 1975), bk. 1, ch. 38, §3.
30. J-L. Marion, op. cit., p. 153.

Address for correspondence: Professor John Macquarrie, 206 Headley Way, Oxford OX3 7TA, UK
E-mail: jenny@macquarrie.fsnet.co.uk

Philosophy – religion – theology

ADRIAAN PEPERZAK
Loyola University

This essay is a (meta)philosophical attempt to clarify the theoretical practice called 'philosophy of religion'. It proceeds in stages. (1) Beginning with a very broad definition of 'religion', it claims (a) that the religious dimension is not only a necessary and basic topic of philosophy, but also its source, and (b) that *all* philosophers, in the practice of their life, rely on a basic 'faith'. If this is true, the question arises as to whether they can abstract from their faith in practicing philosophy. (2) The existing 'positive' religions concretize the religious dimension, but it is universally realized and expressed, even in atheistic and agnostic attitudes and convictions. *All* humans rely on a basic faith. (3) The modern self-conception of philosophy rests on the assumption that because it is autonomous it can separate itself from the lived existence from which it springs. This conception is a dream that has not been and cannot be realized. It must therefore be replaced with a metaphilosophy that respects the faith-based essence of philosophy. (4) Religion (the religious dimension and its concretization in faith) is united with philosophy in at least two ways: (a) as its object, and (b) as the basic condition of the philosophical (re)search. (5) Philosophy is a *relatively* autonomous element of the self-aware and critical life of philosophers. Its language is simultaneously particular and universal. As an attempt to think in the name of and for all humans, it continues its traditional task. Insofar as it is done at the service of a religious community, it is a particular faith searching for understanding, both of the universe and of itself. In its latter function philosophy can be called theology; in its universal function, it brackets its theological character, though it neither can nor should repress it. (6) The union of religion, including its faith and theology, and philosophy is guaranteed by all the connections mentioned in (1)–(5). Lacking an Archemedean standpoint, philosophers of religion should concentrate not only on the religions that are their subject, but also on the religious dimension to which they owe their inspiration. Philosophy of religion is one possible mode of being religious, that is, in an enlightened way. It cannot master what it illuminates, but it can express its own mixture of dependence and independence in conceptual language.

Religion

From an existential perspective we can use the word 'religion' to indicate the deepest dimension of human life in which all other dimensions are rooted. This very broad definition of religion points to the basic fact that human individuals and communities feel more or less at home in the world and its history. Instead of 'feeling at home in the universe', we could also say that the religious dimension is the dimension (or the level) where the question of decisive or ultimate meaning is asked and – at least tentatively and in an embryonic form – answered. All living persons accept their existence as somehow and to some degree meaningful, despite the many doubts, frustrations, rejections, and rebellions that may assail them. Insofar as the meaning that is found or presumed in the universe is fundamental, supporting human existence as a whole, it permeates and colors all other dimensions. As such it decides about the meaning of human lives.

The definition of religion proposed here implies that all concrete (or 'positive') religions can be interpreted as symbolic, ritual, and practical enactments of specific modes of being at home in the universe, aware that existence is not absurd, but possibly meaningful. It also implies that modes of inhabiting the world without religion, such as agnosticism or atheism, are likewise 'religious', insofar as their acceptance of the universe expresses (or even confesses) that existence in it must have a meaning. Materialists, biologists, and historicists, for example, may locate meaning elsewhere than in a realm of God or the gods, but they, too, believe in a basic meaning of existence.

The self-awareness that belongs to the deepest dimension of human lives is a pre-predicative and pre-propositional experience with a primarily affective character: the awareness of a fundamental attunement, a basic mood. We feel more or less at home in a specific mood. The universe can inspire awe, admiration, gratitude, anxiety; we can feel threatened, safe, secure, content, frustrated, nostalgic, and so on. Being affected by the phenomena, we react by affectively responding to them. How we respond depends on our degree of openness, receptivity, sensitivity, character and life story, and many other conditions; but so long as we continue to live, there is always some sort of basic consent and trust, even if these are hidden or overwhelmed by anguish and temptations of despair. Somehow we remain attached to our existence and confident that it is better to be than not to be. Even suicide cannot be preferred without, for the time being, approving and using the tools and actions needed to assure one's own disappearance.

Trust, confidence, or 'faith', taken in a sense as broad as the basic concept of 'religion', implies the affirmation that existence (including the entire universe insofar as one has to deal with it) has an overall meaning. Even if it is not *full* of meaning, it must be more meaningful than nothingness. This affirmation is lived, rather than pronounced or thought. It is the element of consent in our moods, the basic mood that grants us the possibility of having a position and an attitude with regard to the universe and our existence in it. It grants us a 'stance'.

To have a stance is not statically fixed. An originary desire keeps humans on the move. As propelled by desire, a stance does not only trust the present (despite all threats), it also tends forward in search of meaning. Although, on this level, a clear answer to the question of life's meaning is not available, desire darkly anticipates that it must be possible to discover it and that it is already operative in the search. 'Faith' is thus linked with hope. If it includes attachment and the will to continue, it is also animated by a basic form of love, which, at this stage, still may be confined to love for oneself.

A reader of the preceding lines may have become suspicious: is this an attempt to read the three 'divine virtues' of Christian theology into the originary dimension of human existence, encompassing even such areligious or antireligious ways of life as atheism or agnosticism? Or is it perhaps an attempt to reduce the Christian religion and its theology to existential categories that fit all human beings so well that religion in any normal sense of the word and the differences between religions no longer matter? Not exactly; but undeniably it attempts to identify a universal dimension, level, or structure that can be found at the core of all forms or ways of life. At the same time it remains well-aware of the impossibility of doing so from a completely neutral, Archemedean perspective. The universality of the religious dimension is always approached from the perspective of a particular attachment (faith, hope, and love). However, such a perspective no more prevents a discussion with different perspectives or approaches than the difference between French and English or Chinese and Russian prevents a dialogue; but it clearly departs from the modern dogmas about universality and autonomy.

Autonomy

By proclaiming its own independence, philosophy has positioned itself as a rival of all moral, religious, literary, and political authorities. No longer a tributary to the authority of dogmas, ancients, or traditions, philosophers had to reinvent the universe on the basis of self-evident facts and principles. Their task was no longer ruled by powers other than thought itself; instead of serving states or churches, a philosopher would from now on speak in the name of humanity and for its benefit.

The modern emancipation necessitated a separation of thought itself from all the particular features of communal, historical, and individual life. None of the contingent, idiosyncratic, or epochal elements involved in human existence should play a role in the constitution of universally valid truth. The great variety of factual religions should either be interpreted as a series of variations on one general 'religiosity' (not a 'positive', but a 'natural' religion) or seen as approximations of one universally valid philosophy, or even as failed attempts to capture the truth, which is in any case the monopoly of philosophy.

Descartes has thematized the necessity of a clear separation between his life in the world and the philosophical abstractions on which he wanted to thoughtfully rebuild the world and his own humanity,[1] but his successors have dedicated little attention to the (im)possibility of the radical split between theory and practice he proposed. They resumed his program of an abstract reconstruction without showing the possibility of a thought that would be wholly free from existential particularities.

The history of modern philosophy has demonstrated with utmost clarity that none of its systems is self-sufficient and that all philosophers have remained heavily dependent on the questions, discussions, conceptual frameworks, methods, and terminologies of predecessors and traditions, even when they succeeded in their revolutions and transformations. The best philosophers appropriated their past in an original way, thus transforming their inheritance into new beginnings, but none of their systems can be understood as a creation founded upon an indubitable evidence and crystalline logic. All of them are rooted in some hidden faith, though these authors were perhaps not always clearly aware of it.

In order to separate their philosophy from their lives as they live them, philosophers must find a free-standing perspective outside their own worldly and historical existence. Only then can they form an objective and universally valid judgment about the universe, including their own functioning within it. This standpoint was sought in thought itself. Thinking thus became the activity of an extra-existential, supra-historical and supra-terrestrial thinker, either in the form of a transcendental consciousness or as a trans- or superhuman subject whose thoughts must be revealed by a human interpreter. As a hermetic or prophetic service to humanity, philosophy had to reduce the entire variety of cultures and stories to general forms and structures that could be verified everywhere. A formal universe was (re)created that had to be filled in by the real diversity of individual lives and communal histories.

Philosophy and religion

How does religion fare in the context of a philosophy that claims to be autonomous?

If religion, like art and morality, is an essential phenomenon, it cannot be excluded from philosophy. For within philosophy all exclusions are arbitrary, or rather, they are impossible because the horizon of philosophy is unlimited or universal. If religion is not a genuine phenomenon, philosophy must show which more genuine dimension hides behind its mask; if it is genuine and irreducible to anything else, philosophy will have to confront the rivalry that emerges from this fact. An autonomous philosophy necessarily submits religion to its own perspective and principles. Either it takes itself to be the highest tribunal for questions of meaning, or it leaves open the possibility that the ultimate judgement can be expected from another, deeper or higher realm. If there is such a realm, philosophy accepts the subordinate, relative, and provisional character of its 'autonomy', whereas in the first case, it is philosophy that knows the meaning of religion *and more*: its truth or falsehood, the reason why religion is meaningful or not, the extent to which different religions represent different degrees of truth and meaning, and so on. Hegel's reduction of the religious phenomenon to an imperfect presentation of philosophical truth is a consummate example of this reduction, while the subordination of philosophy to religion is asserted or assumed by all those philosophers who see themselves as primarily religious.

Is the expression 'primarily religious' a pleonasm? Can one be religious, i.e., attached to and engaged in a religion without being aware that religion *founds and encompasses* the entirety of human existence? Is it inevitable that the thought of religious persons either fits into their faith, or puts this faith to the test, which then might result in turning away from it, modifying it, or reinforcing it with philosophical considerations?

The crucial question is where a thinker stands when observing and thematizing others' or her own religious involvement. Thinking from the stance of religion (which I have called the basis of lived existence) ipso facto relativizes philosophy as a branch that cannot separate itself from the tree it serves. How could the branch claim the final judgment about the meaning of the tree? Thinking from an Archemedean position is either an abstraction – and to that extent only a provisional or hypothetical enterprise until it find its place in the whole of a life – or it is indeed autarchic, but then it expresses another faith: the faith (or the 'religion') that identifies autonomous thinking with the truest and deepest dimension of life. The main task to which existence calls humans is then nothing other than thought, and all other tasks, such as art, morals, sport, and love, are subordinate to it. Philosophy itself is then the true religion. It is not difficult to show that the God of this religion must coincide either with a grounding and all-encompassing thinker whose existence is imaginary as an unrealized ideal, or with a transcendental or transcendent consciousness whose truth is revealed in the finite messages of the philosophers.

If the autarchy of philosophy is in fact rooted in its own philosophical faith, the principle of philosophical autonomy implies a rivalry with concrete religions. An autarchic philosophy necessarily competes with religions for the right to present the basic and decisive answer to the question of ultimate meaning. In the name of its autonomy, philosophers must claim that they presuppose nothing that is not obvious to all people, while looking down on religions as a variety of particular beliefs that are neither empirically nor rationally fully warranted. These beliefs might be interesting (i.e., they might respond to existential interests or even be of interest for an epistemology of the connections between belief and truth), but their meaning is subordinate to the overall interest and the ultimate meaning of the philosophical enterprise. The stance and the faith of philosophy puts the faiths of religions in their place and relativizes their interests.

The claim of autonomy obscures the faith-driven passion of modern philosophy. The pretention that it is led by universal reason alone falsifies its dealings with religion by interpreting its relationship to the latter as a relationship between universality (reason) and particularity (faith). If, on the contrary, philosophy recognized its rootedness in its own faith, it would recognize the particularity of its own bias. This bias does not necessarily preclude the task of speaking in a universally recognizable way, but it entails the awareness that it cannot do this in a non-particular language. Neither natural, nor conceptual languages are universal. All of them are particular perspectives on the universe. Moreover, the individuals who express their thoughts in them give them a personal twist.

Philosophy as religion

Dedicated philosophers are aware of a double impetus: though fascinated by the task of formulating universal truths (e.g., the truth about the religions, their own included), they are primarily interested in their own destiny (and its truth) and that of others. If their existential and their theoretical interests coincide, philosophy is nothing other than the theoretical part of their existential endeavor. Thought and life are then one, though a distinction is still possible to the extent that existence encompasses more than thought. If faith or 'religion', in the broad sense, is fundamental for existence, the religion of a thinker permeates his thinking, but when he speaks to those who do not share his faith, he will look for common ground and shared assumptions in order to make a discussion possible despite any fundamental differences. If we reserve the name 'philosophy' for the level of universally shared assumptions, we abstract from all the real and possible differences in faith. Such a universally valid philosophy does not represent the concrete (and therefore existential) thought of its author, because it is only an abstract element of it.

Modern philosophers have believed that this element could be emancipated and proclaimed as something independent, while denying that such independence presupposes another kind of existential rooting and another kind of trust than the faith from which self-thinking was liberated. This conviction explains why modern philosophy saw itself as the universal and highest perspective; but its faith in itself as the supreme way of finding meaning in the universe puts it beside, not above, other religions. Philosophy, in its modern self-interpretation, is the religion of Enlightenment; it is a 'form of life' rather than an abstract element that, thanks to its abstractness, fits into a more deeply rooted engagement with existence. The real relation between philosophy and religion varies with philosophy's conception of its own practice. If philosophy tries to be autarchic, it is a rival of other religions, claiming for itself the same kind of ultimacy, universality, and authority. However, if it confines itself to being the thinking element within a religion – as the conceptual understanding and clarification of the universally relevant meaning of that religion – it gives up its autarky by adopting a more authentic, if limited, relative, and subordinate autonomy.

The religious character of autarchic philosophy is shown by its appeals to particular traditions and authorities, by the rituals it develops, by the standards and the fora through which it protects its orthodoxy, by the scholasticism of its questions and answers, and by its excommunication of dissidents. Originality and revolutions soon develop into chapels of heterodoxy, if they are not domesticated by integration into the mainstream. The stories that philosophy tells about its past – e.g., in their Kantian, Hegelian, Nietzschean, or Heideggerian versions – are as simplistic as other all-encompassing myths and the practice it recommends is ruled by the law of celebration and repetition. Congresses are dominated by endless monologues and controlled by judges who screen the thoughts of the newly initiated. For those who profess the autonomy of philosophy, there is a Church in which they can feel at home. What is more tempting than the promise of a free, all-judging thought, especially when it is authorized by the fame of stars!

The freedom of the enlightened faith on which modern philosophy thrives necessarily rivals with the inspired freedoms that are enacted in Jewish, Buddhist, Hindu, Christian, or Muslim faith. But rivalry is a kind of enmity, as long as each faith is convinced that it must triumph over the others. Such a triumph can consist in an *Aufhebung* or integration, by which other faiths are judged and subordinated. Hegel's philosophical integration of the religions or Origen's integration of Platonic and Stoic elements are examples of such conquests.

Are hostility or submission the only alternatives or is a friendly coexistence, perhaps even a sort of fraternity, between philosophy and religion possible? If philosophy is an autonomous and secular 'religion', its coexistence with Christian faith (and its theology) is comparable, for example, to the co-existence of Christianity with Judaism, Islam, Buddhism, etc. Peaceful co-existence between religions cannot be established by giving up one's own faith, but only by mutual respect. But how can one maintain a wholehearted adherence to one faith without relativism or syncretism? Respect, on this level of ultimacy, presupposes the recognition of a fundamental and ultimate truth and meaning. How can such a recognition of other faiths avoid relativizing one's own faith insofar as this contradicts the others? Recognition – and the mutual respect that ensues from it – is not possible unless the different faiths, despite the contradictions that seem to make them utterly hostile, are experienced as somehow pointing to and converging on a truth that, though darkly and differently revealed in respectable religions, does not let itself be captured completely by any of them. Such truth must then be deeper and 'more ultimate' than faith and religion themselves.

Even this hypothesis does not undermine the possibility of a firm adherence to one's own religion, because such an adherence does not exclude that other religions, in their aporetic or contradictory way, point toward the same hidden God.

One formulation of the non-relativistic relativity intended here is the Christian conviction, which is part of its faith, that in heaven there are no sacraments or ecclesiastical structures and dogmas. Even religion itself should not be made into an idol; it should always be lived as referring to the first and last itself.

Must the modern project of an autarchic philosophy be saluted by other religions as an alternative way of salvation? Is its *gnosis* one of the religions through which human beings open up to the ultimate truth of their existence? If receptivity, listening, acceptance, thanksgiving, and celebration are characteristic of religion, modern philosophy does not strike us as characteristically religious. Its obsession by the 'I' that thinks and masters, uses, acts, concludes, and enjoys seems too humanistic to allow for much mystery. But perhaps its infatigable questioning and self-critical requestioning betray a genuine desire of something greater than itself, which could grant it another freedom than the narrow one of self-identity. Perhaps even this philosophy points to an inconquerable dimension of absolute transcendence. From where does its passion for the truth come and what justifies its hope? Would it really be satisfied by conceptual transparency or would that put an end to all hopes? Even Descartes desired wisdom more than knowledge; and who would prefer clarity over a good life? If philosophy, even in its modern version, has always been a passionate search for the union of ultimate truth and goodness in the form of a partly given, partly conquered wisdom, it, too, is a religious enterprise. But then it can and must also be understood, evaluated, respected, and dealt with from the perspective of other religions.

The recognition of modern philosophy as one among many religions would restitute its existential seriousness, but at the same time it would rob it of its metaphilosophical monopoly. Philosophy could no longer claim to be the highest court for questions of meaning and truth, because it is only one (respectable, but particular) way of engaging in the essential quest. Even intellectuals could not proclaim its supremacy unless they could demonstrate that its conceptual language is more trustworthy and encompassing than the symbolisms of other religions. If the reverse is true, or if both have their own strengths and weaknesses, a more brotherly or sisterly relationship might be possible, unless one or more religions could correctly claim that it encompasses all true philosophy. But why should the latter be the case? Can't we become what we have to be without conceptual mastery? To see such mastery as the summit of wisdom would make us Hegelian or Spinozist; but it is exactly such kinds of faith that we are questioning.

Philosophy of religion between philosophy and religion

What are the consequences of the (hypo)thesis defended in the preceding pages for the philosophy of religion? If philosophy is autonomous and autarchical, it must summon all (other) religions and judge their identity, structure, truth, and meaning in the name of its own standards, which it regards as the highest and ultimate standards of truth and meaning. The identity and essence of the religions are then *a priori* adjusted to the patterns and restrictions of the judge's logic. All the elements that do not fit with its observational or conceptual network must be considered irrelevant, meaningless, and extrarational. A certain form of contempt then, inherent to all judgmental looking-down, characterizes the philosopher's attitude.

If an autonomous philosophy itself is a kind of religion, the situation is different. Instead of being the highest tribunal before which the other religions must legitimize themselves, it must rather allow other religions to identify and evaluate this philosophy (and its thought about religions both in general and in particular) from their own religious perspective. In the trial that ensures, philosophy must justify its faith in reason and its exclusion of certain elements considered essential by other religions but rejected as irrational, superstitious, irrelevant, or false by any autonomous philosophy. In presiding at the tribunal, a religious judge will question the claimed neutrality and universality of such a philosophy and ask what credentials it has for promising a way to existentially relevant truth, freedom, wisdom, salvation, and goodness.

To be understood, so that philosophy can defend its own endeavors, including its judgment about the religions, the judging religion must speak a language that philosophy can understand. It will therefore borrow thoughts and terms from the philosophers that are available in the culture of the time. Many examples of this procedure can be found in Jewish, Christian, and Muslim thought from the First to the Fifteenth century: while adopting Platonic and Stoic elements of the Greek and Hellenistic cultures, Philo, Origen, Augustine, and many others used them to distinguish their own way of existence from the philosophical forms of life of their epoch. Their appropriation certainly transformed the thoughts that had emerged in another context, but even so they tried to remain comprehensible to differently inspired philosophers. The result of their attempt was a multitude of theologies for which they often used the title *philosophia* to show its affinity with the Greek program. Aware of the impossibility of being and thinking autonomously in a rigorous sense of this word, they tried to translate their faith as much as possible into a renewed kind of philosophical language, while remaining convinced that such an enterprise could never reduce the mysterious character of their faith. At the same time, however, they did not doubt that human reason was enlightened enough to engage in a rational dialogue with the (other) philosophers, many of whom recognized their own religious allegiance.[2]

The relationship between Christian or Jewish or Muslim 'philosophy' on the one hand, and philosophies that claim to be autonomous, on the other, can be transformed from a trial into a dialogue when both the judging and the judged parties agree to deal with one another as respectable partners in a discussion about wisdom and the ultimate meaning of human existence in the universe. Valid observation and logical clarity are necessary conditions for such a discussion, but they are not sufficient, because the radical dimension in which they are rooted and the faith that guides their existential engagement cannot be reduced to conceptual or empiricist claims and arguments.

It is difficult for dedicated philosophers to give up the standpoint from which all things in heaven and on the earth are subjected to a universally valid and final judgment, but it is more authentically religious and truthful to recognize that such a standpoint is either too abstract to be true or too proud to be good. However, a similar judgment is true about theologians who, longing to be modern and respected by secular thinkers, accept the autonomy of philosophy as a principle of their own work. Instead of revering philosophy as a separate realm of universal truth, they should integrate and transform the proper meaning of that realm, which can thus show its theological virtuality. As a limited clarification of faith, theology is a self-conscious philosophy of religion. It tries to understand how its own thinking can throw some light on religions (including modern philosophy as well as the faith from which it emerges or onto which it has been grafted). As a faith in search of understanding, philosophy (even in its explicitly theological version) does not entail a dictatorship, because its arguments should not be mistaken for faith itself, while faith can only be authentic if it is and remains free. The free consent of trust guides both philosophy and theology because neither of them is radical enough to be original. Thus, both are at the service of an orientation that originates and carries them, and this orientation constitutes the essence of human existence.

Universality?

To conclude, just a remark to prevent misunderstanding. What happens to the universality that modern philosophy has loudly proclaimed to be the distinguishing mark of its validity? If philosophy itself is a *faith* in search of understanding, must we then abandon all hope that universally valid truth can ever be found and communicated?

It would be preposterous to claim that such a question can be answered by a supplementary remark. What can be said is that these pages plead for another conception of universality than that of conceptually clear propositions, theses, or theorems. The universality defended here is more similar to the universality that conditions and underlies the sharing of thoughts that are expressed in different languages. All translation presupposes a silent, prelingual commonality. Would this not be a necessary presupposition for human universality? Perhaps the assumption that unity and universality can be grasped and possessed in the form of judgments and an explicit understanding of our own position is itself an idol that we should discard, if we want to be true to religion and the origins of philosophy.

Notes

1. Cf. the third part of Descartes' *Discours de la méthode*, and Adriaan T. Peperzak, 'Life, Science, and Wisdom According to Descartes,' *History of Philosophy Quarterly* 12 (1995): 133–154.
2. That 'philosophy' in Antiquity was a way of life and not an attempt to realize Descartes' program has been proved by the specialists of Greek and Hellenistic philosophy. A summary of their results can be found in Pierre Hadot's *Qu'est-ce que la philosophie antique* (Paris: Gallimard, 1995).

Address for correspondence: Professor Adriaan T. Peperzak, Department of Philosophy, Loyola University, 6525 North Sheridan Road, Chicago, IL 60626, USA
Phone: (773) 508-2309; E-mail: apeperz@luc.edu

Of miracles and special effects[1]

HENT DE VRIES
University of Amsterdam

Though the phenomenon of religion might seem to have become obsolete in the recent intellectual and political history of 'secular' modernity, in late twentieth and early twenty-first century liberal-democratic states and worldwide, it has resurfaced with an unprecedented – and unanticipated – force. This 'return of the religious'[2] at a geopolitical scale conflicts with the self-interpretation of modern states and their citizens. The emergence of a supposedly enlightened and increasingly differentiated public sphere had gone hand in hand with the formulation of ideals of identity and self-determination, individual autonomy and universalist cosmopolitanism, both of which *seem* at odds with the heteronomy and particularism – the authoritarianism or even the violence – commonly ascribed to religious doctrine and its practices.[3]

The uncontested and often self-congratulatory narrative of Western, 'secularist' modernity – whose hegemony has only been reinforced by current tendencies toward globalization and the almost unchallenged appeal of free market capitalism[4] – has from the outset obscured the fact that, in most of its historical formations, the concept of the political had to some extent always been contingent, if not upon the authority or the explicit sanction of a dominant religion, then at least upon a plausible translation and renegotiation of the central categories of this religion's historical beliefs, its central rituals, and their implicit politics. This was true for premodern times and during the first establishment of so-called nation-states. Mutatis mutandis, the same holds true for the so-called new geopolitics that follows in the wake of globalization and its medium, 'informationalism'.[5]

Most analytical and empirically informed studies on the recent transformations of the information based economy, society, and culture, on the one hand, and of the contemporary role of religion in the public sphere, on the other, have a common blind spot. What they fail to see is that it is precisely an intrinsic and structural relationship between the new media and the renewed manifestation of religion that enables a comprehension of the ways in which socio-cultural identity, diversity, a certain commonality and universality as well as adversity and violence, are constructed *and*, so to speak, *diffused*.[6] Turning to a recent essay by Jacques Derrida will help me to address this relationship in a systematic, theoretical or philosophical, mode. But concrete contemporary examples of it abound. A certain *politics of the miracle*, such as the one regularly deployed by the Vatican, is only one of them.[7] By presenting a concrete example (confronting the ancient concept of the miracle and its present day counterpart, the special effect), this article sketches out the place and function of religion in relation to the new technological media. In the understanding of these relatively new phenomena contemporary comparative religious studies find their most daunting task.

Thus far not much has been done to bring these two revolutionary and unanticipated developments – the rise of the new media and the re-emergence of religion – into a single perspective. At a major Harvard conference some years ago, entitled *The Internet and Society*,[8] no one raised the question of religion and even the most interesting studies in media and networks that originate in literary studies, hermeneutics and system theory pass over religion in silence.[9]

Conversely, contemporary discussions in *Religion and Contemporary Liberalism* and *Religion in Public Life*,[10] to cite just a few of the most compelling contributions to the question of democracy, pay little attention to the simultaneous rise of the new media technologies and the relation they may have to the phenomenon of religion and its return as a political factor of world importance. The renewed prominence of the religious and the proliferation of political theologies it entails, on the one hand, and the equally unanticipated revolution in information technologies, on the other, are analyzed as if we were dealing with two totally independent developments. And where a relationship between the phenomena is acknowledged at all, the assumed link is often that of an instrumentalization of the one by the other, as if media formed the mere vehicle of religion or as if the medium could ever succeed in creating religion in its own image. Yet the medium is not secondary, nor is the religious mere epiphenomenon. And this is precisely what even the most promising theoretizations of the contemporary social and cultural world would seem to suggest.[11]

The sole exception to this mutual blindness, it seems, is Derrida's 'Foi et savoir: Les deux sources de la "religion" aux limites de la simple raison' (Faith and Knowledge: The Two Sources of "Religion" at the Limits of Reason Alone), a text that be taken as an reelaboration of certain insights first formulated in the analysis of the postal system in *La Carte postale* (*The Post Card*), a text in which the reference to religion could have seemed virtually absent at a first reading.[12] In Derrida's more recent analysis, the reassessment of the concept and the practice of 'religion' goes hand in hand with that of the new media of communication, the increasingly sophisticated form of teletechnology. The two cannot be separated; inquiry into the first forms an interpretative key to the latter, and vice versa. What is more, their intersection – and virtual interchangeability – have everything to do with a peculiar '*artifactuality*' and '*actuvirtuality*' that is characterized by a singular temporality, a 'deconstructed actuality', of sorts.¹³

As his title indicates, Derrida's whole analysis is driven by certain reticence concerning what seems to be central presupposition of the project of modernity and, perhaps, of the philosophical tradition *in toto* as it seeks to radically distinguish between *muthos* and *logos, phusis* and *nomos, doxa* and *episteme*, faith and knowledge:

> one would blind oneself to the phenomenon called 'of religion' or of the 'return of the religious' *today* if one continued to oppose so naïvely Reason *and* Religion, Critique or Science *and* Religion, techno-scientific Modernity *and* Religion. Supposing that what was at stake was to understand, would one understand anything about 'what's-going-on-today-in-the-world-with-religion' ... if one continues to believe in this opposition, even in this incompatibility, which is to say, if one remains within a *certain* tradition of the Enlightenment, one of the many Enlightenments of the past three centuries (not of an *Aufklärung*, whose critical force is profoundly rooted in the Reformation), but yes, in this light of Lights, of the *Lumières*, which traverses like a single ray a *certain* critical and anti-religious vigilance, anti-Judaeo-Christiano-Islamic, a *certain* filiation 'Voltaire-Feuerbach-Marx-Nietzsche-Freud-(and even)-Heidegger'? Beyond this opposition and its determinate heritage (no less represented on the other side, that of religious authority), perhaps we might be able to try to 'understand' how the imperturbable and interminable development of critical and technoscientific reason, far from opposing religion, bears, supports and supposes it.¹⁴

There is, Derrida maintains, an instrinsic relationship between the mediatic and the religious. Translated into contemporary geo- and theo-political terms, this would mean that one cease to portray, for example, political Islam in an anachronistic way, as the epitome of fundamentalism, '*intégrisme*', and the like:

> the surge of 'Islam' [*le déferlement 'islamique'*] will be neither understood nor answered ... as long as one settles for an internal explanation (interior to the history of faith, of religion, of languages or cultures as such), as long as one does not define the passageway between this interior and all the apparently exterior dimensions (technoscientific, tele-biotechnological, which is to say also political and socioeconomic etc.).¹⁵

This interfacing between the interior and the exterior, to the point where the very distinction collapses (or is, at least, significantly displaced), must have held true for all times, even though the present day and age would seem to have witnessed a generalization and intensification beyond measure of the mode of communication and mediatization: the '*mondialatinization*' of the '*nouvelles nouvelles*', as he has it, but one in whose expansion the sheer quantity of scale and pace reverses – once more almost, albeit it not necessarily dialectically (as Hegel and Adorno believed) – into a virtual qualitative change:

> Like others before, the new 'wars of religion' are unleashed over the human earth ... and struggle even today to control the sky *with finger and eye*: digital systems and virtually immediate panoptical visualization, 'air space', telecommunications satillites, information highways, concentration of capitalistic-medicatic power – in three words: *digital culture, jet*, and *TV* without which there could be no religious manifestation today, for example no voyage or discourse of the Pope, no organized emanation [*rayonnement*] of Jewish, Christian or Muslim cults, whether 'fundamentalist' or not.[16]

Derrida observes that if religion had ever been dead and overcome, surely in its resurrected form it is less predictable than ever before, most manifestly in the 'cyberspatialized or cyberspaced wars of religion [*guerres de religion*]' or 'war of religions [*guerre des religions*]'.[17] And these wars may take on all the forms of radical evil and atrocity and mask themselves behind the most enlightened and most universalist intentions. Indeed,

> it is not certain that in addition to or in face of most spectacular and most barbarous crimes of certain 'fundamentalisms' (of the present or the past) *other* over-armed forces are not *also* leading 'wars of religion', albeit unavowed. Wars or military 'interventions', led by the Judaeo-Christian West in the name of the best causes (of international law, democracy, the sovereignty of peoples, of nations or of states, even of humanitarian imperatives), are they not also, from a certain side, wars of religion? The hypothesis would not necessary be defamatory, nor even very original, except in the eyes of those who hasten to believe [sic] that all these just causes are not only secular but *pure* of all religiosity.[18]

Never before has it been so clear that there can be no such thing as an ultimate – analytical, *de iure*, let alone *de facto* – neutrality of the public sphere. Attention to the new and persistent prominence of religion could counterbalance the phantom of a culturally homogeneous society. And yet, it would be false to identify religion with inevitable resistance with particularistic and idiomatic or even idiosyncratic views alone; religion has opposite, universalizing tendencies as well. What may be needed is a conceptual and empirical analysis of the multiple ways in which religion not only shapes the experience of possible tensions between collective and personal identities – and, perhaps, challenges the very concept of 'identity' – but also affects the conditions under which conflicts can be addressed, worked through, and 'resolved'. The relationship between religion and media sheds light on the question of how cultural identity and difference are constituted, as well as on how they relate to the aims of socio-political integration. Religion, thus interpreted, forms the condition of the possibility *and* the impossibility of the political. Derrida offers a simple 'hypothesis', whose implications are far-reaching:

> with respect to all these forces of abstraction and of dissociation (deracination, delocalization, disincarnation, formalization, universalizing schematization, objectivation, telecommunication etc.), 'religion' is *at the same time* involved in reacting antagonistically and reaffirmatively outbidding itself. *In this very place*, knowledge and faith, technoscience ('capitalist' and fiduciary) *and* belief, credit, trustworthiness, the act of faith will always have made common cause, bound to one another by the band of their opposition.[19]

On the one hand, it is increasingly difficult to deny that hyper-text manifests itself in a quasi-religious manner, in ways that we have, perhaps, not yet begun to comprehend. Indeed, there seems to be both irony and a deep truth in the description of media-produced and media-dependent celebrities a 'icons' and 'idols'.[20] On the other hand, the return of the religious, Derrida points out, concerns a certain resistance toward the abstraction of technological in the name of language and of nation and be it in name of the *lingua franca*, the Latin, of the West:

> if, today, the 'question of religion' actually appears in a new and different light, if there is an unprecedented resurgence, both global and planetary, of this ageless thing, then what is at stake is language, certainly – and more precisely the idiom, literality, writing, that forms the element of all revelation and of all *belief*, an element that ultimately is irreducible and untranslatable – but an idiom that above all is inseparable from the social nexus, from the political, familial, ethnic, communitarian nexus, from the nation and from the people: from autochthony, blood and soil, and from the ever more problematic relation to citizenship and to the state. In these times, language and nation form the historical body of all religious passion.[21]

Yet the force of abstraction around which religion revolves – reactively *and* productively – is at the same time a sine qua non for the universality (indeed, the messianicity) of what Derrida calls a 'democracy-to-come'. The theologico-political seems to stand for an imperative and a mode of belonging no longer – or not yet – limited by the traditional and modern concepts of politicization and democratization modeled on the frontiers of the nation-state. In other words, the theologico-political – the 'mystical foundation of authority' that Derrida sees as the constitutive element of the political and legal order, indeed of any 'force of law' – enables us to 'deterritorialize' the political; that is to say, it allows us to strip it of its preconceptions concerning self-determination and its concern with ascribed, 'acquired', or 'natural' citizenship, based on *jus solis* or *jus sanguinis*. In the wake of recent technological developments, this 'imperative' is 'imposed on us concretely'; for these developments, Derrida hastens to add, constitute a 'chance' and a 'menace' at once; they permit us to entertain a different 'politics of memory' or to 'politicize otherwise'.[22] They enable us to think the political beyond (existing forms of) democracy or, conversely, to think the democracy-to-come beyond the political (as we know it). In both cases, we touch upon the limits of representation, in more than one sense of the word.

So far, I have attempted to situate the 'return of the religious' within the geopolitics of 'secular' modernity and its globalization. Religion 'returns' at the juncture in which the political of 'secular' modernity is recognized to be contingent upon the authority of a dominant religion, if not directly, at least by way of its renegotiation. Yet, it is the contradiction between the premises of a 'secular' modernity that promises autonomy and universalism and the heteronomous and particular nature of religious doctrine which marks a tension within this contingency. In other words, the reorientation of the political that is at work here is a 'curvature of the social space' (Levinas), a process of mediatization, and mediation, in which religion is both private and public.

In order to illustrate this interfacing of the religious and the medium, the theological and the technological, I would like to offer just one example, that of 'miracles' in their relation to 'special effect'.[23] Is a miracle a special effect? Does the special effect – or what is commonly described as such – enter into the tradition inaugurated or legitimized by the invocation of miracles? If so, how? Do special effects summon up the 'wonder of all wonders' (*'das Wunder aller Wunder'*), in Heidegger's words, *'that* beings *are*' (*das Seiendes ist*)[24] or, in monotheistic parlance, *creatio ex nihilo*, the fact that all of a sudden, through a sheer act of free divine will - there was something rather than nothing? Are miracles special effects in their very structure (that is to say, as event) or merely in the perceptual and then psychological effect they have on 'us'? Is there a difference between these two interpretations? Or between the two phenomena? Do the 'miracle' and the 'special effect' resemble each other *formally* or, as it were, *phenomenologically* speaking?

Strictly speaking, in *Webster's* definition, the special effect is nothing but 'an often illusory effect introduced into a motion picture during the processing of the film'. What grounds, then, do we have for connecting this purely technical device to a tradition whose metaphysical presuppositions seem increasingly obsolete?

Confronted with these questions, two hypotheses impose themselves. The first is that we cannot understand the full range of possible meanings of the very phrase 'special effect' and its component elements – namely, reference both to some unanticipated or even non-natural ('special') occurrence and to a peculiar modality of causation ('effect') – without, however implicitly or indirectly, returning to the tradition called the religious. I hesitate to say the 'theological', since the designator 'religious' allows us to indicate a much wider field than that covered by the 'Religions of the Book', their natural or revealed theologies, their ontologies and onto-theologies. The miraculous and the magical – their difference remains a matter of debate – were never the prerogative of Judaism, Christianity, or Islam alone. Reference to the religious can include the most theatrical of its guises, for example, the *deus ex machina* in Greek literature. And in his work *Das Heilige* (*The Idea of the Holy*), subtitled 'Über das Irrationale in der Idee des Göttlichen und sein Verhältnis zum Rationalen [An Inquiry into the non-rational factor in the idea of the divine and its relation to the rational]' – a book that influenced several generations of scholars of religion – Rudolf Otto does not hesitate to describe miracles and the miraculous as constitutive elements of the 'numinous'.[25]

To view the special effect against the foil of the miracle means invoking the concept of divine intervention. Here, the miraculous act – of God or his intermediaries – becomes the paradigmatic case of an event that stands out by its absolute character, its being uncaused or caused by an act of free Will, whose force forms the model for the acts of all finite beings, all of which are portrayed as being created out of nothing. This original scene supposedly determined all the creative acts – indeed, all special effects – that followed in its wake. The word *effect*, from the Latin *effectus*, the past participle of *efficere*, 'to bring about, to accomplish, to effect, to perform', would in effect (that is to say, virtually) come to stand for any event (and for any action) whose structure finds its prime model in the theological – perhaps even theistic – concept of God: the being that has no cause outside itself (hence the most metaphysical of God's names, *causa sui*). On this reading, not even the most artificial special effect could be possible – that is to say, thought or experienced – without some reference to (or conjuring up) of the miracle and everything for which it stands.

Conversely, my second hypothesis is that thinking the miracle was never possible without introducing a certain *technicity* and, quite literally, a *manipulation* of sorts. Human fabrication – or the rumor thereof, in false miracles and in magic – always went hand in hand with the seemingly sure signs and acts of the hand of God. Not only was God seen as the great engineer – the demiurge, as in Plato's *Timaeus*, or the world architect (*Weltbaumeister*), known from all the physico-theological proofs of His existence – those who performed lesser miracles in his name (whether as impostors or not) drew on a certain technical skill. The apostles performed miracles – powerful acts (*dynameis*), signs and wonders (*semeia* and *terata*) – speaking in tongues, healing and exorcising, that accompanied their diffusion of the Word and the spreading of the Spirit and *in so doing* established its authority.

How should we understand the relationship between these two elements – or, as Derrida has it in 'Faith and Knowledge', the 'two sources' – of the miraculous, between their representation or presentation of a supposedly *extraordinary event*, on the one hand, and their *artificiality* and *technicity*, on the other? How do these two features form two sides of the same coin, two aspects of the same phenomenon, whose givenness – and, as it were, 'saturation' – we take for granted, as witnesses, spectators, or viewers? (Lest we forget, the word *miracle* comes from Latin *miraculum* and the verb *mirari*, which means 'to wonder at'.)

In *Religion and the Decline of Magic*, arguably the most comprehensive study of 'popular belief in sixteenth and seventeenth century England' and one the most influential studies on the subject of (Christian) religion and the supernatural, Keith Thomas reiterates an almost unchallenged consensus in modern historical scholarship. This opinion is based on the presupposition of linear modernization and secularization, differentiation and a logic of *disenchantment*,[26] and one that increasingly reveals its empirical and conceptual limits, especially when confronted with the technological and mediatic innovations – the special effects – that interest us here. Thomas writes:

> Nearly every primitive religion is regarded by its adherents as a *medium* for obtaining supernatural power. This does not prevent it from functioning as a system of explanation, a source of moral injunctions, a symbol of social order, or a route to immortality; but it does mean that it also offers the prospect of a supernatural *means* of control over man's earthly environment. The history of early Christianity offers no exception to this rule. Conversions to the new religion, whether in the time of the primitive Church or under the auspices of the missionaries of more recent times, have frequently been assisted by the view of converts that they are

acquiring not just a means of other-wordly salvation, but a new and more powerful magic.[27]

Thomas shows that both the New Testament and Patristic literature stress the significance of miracles in 'the work of conversion'; indeed, in the history of the church, the 'ability to *perform* miracles soon became an indispensable *test* of sanctity'.[28] The prophets and priests of the so-called Old Testament had similarly challenged their counterparts – the 'devotees of Baal' – to work supernatural acts. They did not in principle deny their opponents' capacity to do such things, but merely asserted their own greater *effectiveness* in bringing about these special occurrences. By the same token, in the medieval church, Thomas continues, the 'working of miracles' was seen as 'the most *efficacious means* of demonstrating its monopoly of the truth'.[29] 'By the twelfth and thirteenth centuries the *Lives* of the Saints had assumed a stereotyped pattern. They related the miraculous achievements of holy men, and stressed how they could prophesy the future, control the weather, provide protection against fire and flood, magically transport heavy objects, and bring relief to the sick.'[30]

For Thomas, this 'stereotyped pattern' was the sedimentation of the desire – typical of all religions – *to take control of the natural order by way of the supranatural and vice versa*. Magic, astrology, witchcraft, the belief in ghosts and fairies, are all forms of the desire to negotiate with the transcendent, a desire that would soon undergo successive onslaughts of demystification from the Reformation and the increasing mechanization of early modern views of the cosmos. Both attempted and, Thomas believes, succeeded in *taking the magic out of religion*.

True, there have been times when *official* religion or its greatest minds considered the miracle to be something of the past or mere superstition, pertaining only to *popular*, unsophisticated belief. Though in 1870 the Roman Catholic Church could still maintain, during the third Session of the First Vatican Council, that 'If anyone shall say, that miracles cannot happen, or that the divine origin of the Christian religion cannot properly be proved by them: let him be anathema' (Denziger, par. 1813), by then the battle for the *historical* evidence of Christian faith had long been lost.

As Thomas points out, the eventual condemnation of the miraculous had its roots in early Protestant orthodoxy:

> For those Protestants who believed that the age of Christian miracles was over, all supernatural effects necessarily sprang from either fraudulent illusion or the workings of the Devil. Satan, it was believed, was well acquainted with the secrets of nature and might counterfeit an effect when he could not reproduce it directly. Those persons who sought to

use objects for purposes which nature could not justify were guilty of idolatry, superstition, and at least implicitly of soliciting the aid of the Devil.[31]

But David Hume's critique of authentication by miracles, undertaken in his *Dialogues Concerning Natural Religion, The Natural History of Religion*, and *An Enquiry Concerning Human Understanding*, was especially devastating.[32] The traditional argument ran:

> Granted that both the power of performing miracles (i.e., bringing about events impossible with the natural order) could only be conferred upon a man by God, and that God would not confer such a power upon those misrepresenting him, then any man who performed miracles gave evidence in so doing that he had authority from God to deliver a revelation, and hence that the revelation was true.[33]

Hume's riposte, in section X of the *Enquiry*, entitled 'Of Miracles', consisted simply in raising the suspicion that 'it is more probable that the historical records are in some way inaccurate than that the miracles they relate actually took place'.[34] This argument – like the one propounded by Spinoza in Chapter 6 of the *Tractatus Theologico-Politicus*, entitled 'De miraculis' – anticipated the textual criticism that, from the nineteenth century onward, would treat the Bible as a historical document like any other. In consequence, the prophecies of the Old Testament and the miracles of the New Testament, as a commentator claimed in 1776, would from now on have to 'depend for much of their credibility on the truth of that religion whose credibility they were first intended to support'.[33]

And yet all attempts to undo the continuing significance of the miraculous – hence all effort to set it apart from the essence or the nature of religion, whether natural or rational, and also from reason and knowledge, science and technology – have hardly led to its demise. The miracle has continued to appear unannounced, even where it does not do so *as* miracle, on its own account. But perhaps this self-effacement had always belonged to the structure of the miraculous – and hence, the magical and the religious – as such. The logic of its exception, the saturation – the self-sufficiency and, as it were, in-difference – of its phenomenon, was never that of empirical truth or manifest fact – that is to say, *out there, for all to see*. The mode of its appearance was always unique, comparable only to its functional equivalents – its paradigm and its remainders – such as revelation, epiphany, iconicity, the liturgical, the sacramental, and so on.

No one has analyzed the uniqueness of this event of absoluteness – the absolution of experience or, at least, of the conditions and limitations of its possibility – better than Jean-Luc Marion in *Étant donné: Essai d'une phénoménologie de la donation*. Marion elaborates the possibility – not the reality or 'effectivity'! – of revelation in terms of a paradoxical form of donation whose structure resembles the irruption of the miracle. Speaking of the general structure of the event, he notes that it remains 'undecidable' with respect to the situation – and situatedness – of its occurrence and thus 'without an adequate cause'.[36] In consequence, we could now infer, it occupies the same space (conceptually and ontologically speaking) as the 'illusory effect' introduced into the course of action during the 'processing' of history. *Analytically*, there is no observable difference between true and false miracles, between the icon and the idol, between prayer for the divine name and blasphemy.

In sum, there are not only empirical, historical, and technological but also systematic reasons to doubt that magic and the miraculous could ever be (or have ever been) taken out of religion, just as there are reasons to suspect that religion was never fully taken out of reason, secularization, mechanization, technization, mediatization, virtualization, and so on.

Although there have been various semi-popular discussions of links between religious imagery and technological development (with titles such as *The Religion of Technology* or 'God in the Computer'),[37] to the best of my knowledge Derrida was the first to insist on the opposite need: to re-conceptualize the notion of 'religion' in light of the current development of the newest 'media', especially the multifaceted relationship – or, more precisely, *interface* – between them. We should no longer reflect exclusively on the meaning, historically and in the present, of religion – of faith and belief and their supposed opposites such as knowledge and technology – but concentrate on the significance of the processes of mediation and mediatization without and outside of which no religion would be able to manifest or reveal itself in the first place. In contradistinction to Heidegger's analysis, mediatization and the technology it entails form the condition of possibility of all revelation – of its revealability, so to speak. An element of technicity belongs to the realm of the 'transcendental', and vice versa.[38]

This all too oblique reference brings us back to the two hypotheses with which I started out, namely, the suspicion that the special effect should be understood against the backdrop of the religious tradition, in particular, the miracle, and that the miracle has always been characterized by a certain 'mechanicity' or technicity. To speak of special effects *in terms of miracles* means at least two things. First, it implies that one *generalize* the applicability of the world of religion – its concept and imaginary, its semantic and figural archive – to include almost everything that, at one time or another, had set itself apart from religion (or from which religion had sought to distance itself, in turn). The magical and the technological thus come to occupy the same space, obey the same regime and the same logic.

Second, to speak of miracles *in terms of special effects* means to *trivialize* the meaning and scope not only of religion but also of its supposed counterparts (magic, technology). What good could such a strategy do? For one thing, it would complicate matters, correcting a simplistic opposition between realms we only wish could be kept apart. Doing away with the last and most pernicious of all binary oppositions – indeed, with the very matrix of the binary as such – all this would, perhaps, not work wonders. But it might very well have a salutary effect.

Notes

1. Excerpted from the introduction to *Religion and Media*, edited by Hent de Vries and Samuel Weber, forthcoming from Stanford University Press. Used with the permission of the publishers. Copyright by the Board of Trustees of the Leland Stanford Junior University.
2. See my *Philosophy and the Turn to Religion* (Baltimore and London: The Johns Hopkins University, 1999).
3. See Hent de Vries and Samuel Weber, eds., *Violence, Identity, and Self-Determination* (Stanford: Stanford University Press, 1997) and Hent de Vries, *Religion and Violence: Philosophical Perspectives from Kent to Derrida* (forthcoming from The Johns Hopkins University Press).
4. See, for example, Francis Fukuyama, '10 Years After *The End of History* Its Author Takes on His Critics', in the *International Herald Tribune*, July 6, 1999.
5. On the new geopolitics, see the survey of *The Economist*, July 31, 1999. The term 'informationalism' stems from Manuel Castells (see below). On the origins of the so-called information age, see James R. Beniger, *The Control Revolution: Technological and Economic Origins of the Information Society* (Cambridge and London: Harvard University Press, 1986, 1997); on its legal aspects, see James Boyle, *Shamans, Software and Spleens: Law and the Construction of the Information Society* (Cambridge and London: Harvard University Press, 1997).
6. In *Religion and Violence*, the sequel to my *Philosophy and the Turn to Religion*, I argue that violence inevitably shadows our ethico-political engagements and decisions, including our understandings of identity, whether collective or individual. Violence, I suggest, entails and exceeds any force, justified or illegitimate, exerted by one entity on another. Thus defined, it finds its prime model in key elements of the religious tradition. It is the very element of religion: no violence without (some) religion; no religion without (some) violence. Given this intrinsic relation to violence, I further claim, the recent turn to religion can best be studied by rethinking modern philosophical assumptions concerning ethical and political responsibility in light of what Kierkegaard, in *Fear and Trembling*'s reading of the sacrifice of Isaac, calls *horror religiosus*. This motif belongs to a chain of interrelated notions that must be studied in historical detail and that range from Kant's discussion of radical evil to Eric Weil's understanding of the other of discourse, Emmanuel Levinas's evocation of the sordid neutrality of the 'there is', Walter Benjamin's meditations on divine violence, and Michel de Certeau's interpretation

of divine anger, culminating in Jacques Derrida's sensitivity to the ever-looming possibility of monstrosity, of the worst, of the proximity between hospitality and hostility. Questions that touch upon ethics and politics, I conclude here, can greatly benefit from being rephrased in terms borrowed from the arsenal of religious and theological figures, because the association of such figures with a certain violence keeps moralism, whether in the form of fideism or humanism, at bay. Such an inquiry, then, could pioneer new modalities for systematic engagement with religion and philosophy alike.

7. See Garry Wills, 'Fatima: The Third Secret', in *The New York Review of Books*, August 10, 2000.

8. Donna Woonteiler, ed., *The Harvard Conference on The Internet and Society* (Cambridge and London: O'Reilly & Harvard University Press, 1997).

9. For all their merits, this would seem to hold true of the works of Friedrich Kittler, *Discourse Networks 1800/1900*, translated by Michael Metteer, with Chris Cullens, Foreword by David E. Wellbery (Stanford: Stanford University Press, 1990); idem, *Gramophone, Film, Typewriter*, translated, with an Introduction, by Geoffrey Winthrop-Young and Michael Wutz (Stanford: Stanford University Press, 1999); but also for Avital Ronell, *The Telephone Book: Technology, Schizophrenia, Electric Speech* (Lincoln and London: The University of Nebraska Press, 1989). As to the tradition of hermeneutics, one could think of the relatively unrelated character of two of Gianni Vattimo's most recent writings, especially: *The Transparent Society*, translated by David Webb (Cambridge: Polity Press, 1992), which discusses the prominent role of the communication media at some length, and *Belief*, translated by Luca d'Isanto and David Webb (Stanford: Stanford University Press, 1999), which speaks of a turn to religion, mostly in biographical terms. In systemtheory a recent reference is Niklas Luhmann. *The Reality of the Mass Media*, translated by Kathleen Cross (Stanford: Stanford University Press, 2000). See also idem, *Die Gesellschaft der Gesellschaft* (Frankfurt/M: Suhrkamp, 1997), vol. 1, chapter 2, and idem, *Die Religion der Gesellschaft*, ed., André Kieserling (Frankfurt/M: Suhrkamp, 2000), pp. 15ff. and 187ff.

10. Paul J. Weithman, ed., *Religion and Contemporary Liberalism* (Notre Dame: University of Notre Dame Press, 1997); Ronald F. Thiemann, *Religion in Public Life: A Dilemma for Democracy* (Washington: Georgetown University Press, 1996); Nancy L. Rosenblum, ed., *Obligations of Citizenship and Demands of Faith: Religious Accomodation in Pluralist Democracies* (Princeton: Princeton University Press, 2000); Robert Audi, *Religious Commitment and Secular Reason* (Cambridge, New York: Cambridge University Press, 2000).

11. Interesting exceptions can be found in Lawrence A. Babb and Susan S. Wadley, eds., *Media and the Transformation of Religion in South Asia* (Philadelphia: University of Pennsylvania Press, 1995), and in Bruce David Forbes and Jeffrey H. Mahan, eds., *Religion and Popular Culture in America* (Princeton: Princeton University Press, 2000). The study of the relationship between religion and popular culture and that of religion and media overlaps in part as is clear, for example, from the role played by religion in media-staged events such as American football. See Mark Singer, 'God and Football: The Fight to Keep Prayer in the Stadium', *The New Yorker*, September 25, 2000, 38–42.

12. Jacques Derrida, *La Carte postale: de Socrate à Freud et au-delà* (Paris: Flammarion, 1980); *The Post Card: From Socrates to Freud and Beyond*, translated by Alan Bass (Chicago and London: The University of Chicago Press, 1987).

13. See the interview conducted by Brigitte Sohm, Cristina de Peretti, Stéphane Douailler, Patrice Vermeren, and Émile Malet, 'Derrida, La déconstruction de l'actualité', *Passages*

(September 1993): 60–75; 'The Deconstruction of Actuality: An Interview with Jacques Derrida', trans. Jonathan Rée, in *Radical Philosophy* 68 (Autumn 1994): 28–41.
14. Jacques Derrida, 'Foi et savoir: Les deux sources de la "religion" aux limites de la simple raison', in Jacques Derrida and Gianni Vattimo, eds., *La Religion* (Paris: Seuil, 1996), pp. 9–86, 40–41; trans. Samuel Weber as 'Faith and Knowledge: The Two Sources of "Religion" at the Limits of Reason Alone', in Derrida and Vattimo, eds., *Religion* (Stanford: Stanford University Press, 1998), pp. 1–78, 28.
15. Derrida, 'Faith and Knowledge', 20/30.
16. Ibid., 24/35.
17. Ibid., 24/36 and 30/43.
18. Ibid., 25/37. The reasons why this is impossible are multiple. Derrida introduces the difficulty as follows: 'To determine a war of religion *as such*, one would have to be certain that one can delimit the religious. One would have to be certain that one can distinguish all the predicates of the religious ... One would have to dissociate the essential traits of the religious as such from those that establish, for example, the concepts of ethics, of the juridical, of the political or of the economic. And yet, nothing is more problematic than such a dissociation. The fundamental concepts that often permit us to isolate or to *pretend* to isolate the *political* – restricting ourselves to this particular circumscription – remain religious or in any case theologico-political' (ibid., 25/37–38).
19. Ibid., 2/10.
20. See Willem Frijhof, *Heiligen, idolen, iconen* (Nijmegen: SUN, 1998).
21. Derrida, 'Faith and Knowledge', 4/12.
22. See Derrida and Bernard Stiegler, *Échographies: De la télévision* (Paris: Galilée, 1996), p. 76.
23. The following excursus was also presented as a lecture at a conference on 'Special Effects', Stanford University, February 11–13, 2000.
24. Martin Heidegger, *Wegmarken* (Frankfurt/M: Vittorio Klostermann, 1978), p. 305; *Pathmarks*, edited by William McNeill (Cambridge and New York: Cambridge University Press, 1998), p. 234.
25. Rudolf Otto, *Das Heilige: Über das Irrationale in der Idee des Göttlichen und sein Verhältnis zum Rationalen*, first published in 1917 (Munich: Verlag C.H. Beck, 1997), pp. 82–84, 172; *The Idea of the Holy: An Inquiry into the Non-Rational Factor in the Idea of the Divine and its Relation to the Rational*, translated by John, W. Harvey (London, Oxford, New York: Oxford University Press, 1923, 1958), pp. 63–64, 143.
26. A schema adopted also by Marcel Gauchet, *Le désenchantement du monde: Une histoire politique de la religion* (Paris: Gallimard, 1985); *The Disenchantment of World: A Political History of Religion*, translated by Oscar Burge, with a Foreword by Charles Taylor (Princeton: Princeton University Press, 1997).
27. Keith Thomas, *Religion and the Decline of Magic*, first published in 1971 (London, New York: Penguin Books, 1991), p. 27, my emphasis, HdV.
28. Ibid., my emphasis, HdV.
29. Ibid., my emphasis, HdV.
30. Ibid.
31. Ibid., pp. 304–305.
32. From a different perspective, Karl Barth and Emmanuel Levinas condemn the belief in miracles as religion qua unbelief (*Unglaube*) and as a religion of infants, respectively. This does not prevent Barth from describing faith itself in terms of a miracle: the fourth chapter of Barths *Der Römerbrief, Zweite Fassung, 1922* (Zürich: Theologischer Verlag Zürich, 1989), entitled *Die Stimme der Geschichte*, opens with a section *Glaube ist Wunder*); and,

by the same token, Levinas does not tire to describe the enigma of the responsibility in terms of the 'miracle of the trace', that is to say, as an non-phenomenologizable event that excedes the very order experience or that, paradoxically, may signal the absolute empiricity or *concretissimum* of an 'experience par excellence'. Not unlike the allegorical readings of all ages, both Barth and Levinas could be said to *demythologize* the miracle and to strip it of all of its supernatural and historical content. That is not to conclude that they simply spiritualize its meaning. A different logic is at work here.

33. J.C.A. Gaskin, 'Introduction', to David Hume, *Dialogues Concerning Natural Religion* and *The Natural History of Religion* (Oxford and New York: Oxford University Press, 1993), pp. ix–xxvi, xii.
34. Ibid.
35. Ibid. As recent discussions in the analytical philosophy of religion have shown, Hume's argument in 'Of Miracles' is not as invincible as it has always seemed. See David Johnson, *Hume, Holism, and Miracles* (Ithaca: Cornell University Press, 1999); and, from a different perspective, C.A.J. Coady, *Testimony: A Philosophical Study* (Oxford: Clarendon Press, 1992), chapter 10 on 'Astonishing Reports'.
36. Jean-Luc Marion, *Étant donné. Essai d'une phénoménologie de la donation* (Paris: PUF, 1997), pp. 235 and 236 n. 1. Marion comes at times close here to Alain Badiou's analysis of the singularity of the event, which is forcefully presented with reference to 'religion' in his *Saint Paul: La fondation de l'universalisme* (Paris: PUF, 1997).
37. In a critical review of David Noble, *The Religion of Technology: The Divinity of Man and the Spirit of Invention*, Keith Thomas argues that one must be careful in evaluating the apparent link between religious imagery and technological development. His article, which carries the ironic title 'God in the Computer', *The New York Review of Books* (December 17, 1998): 78–80, cites many examples to drive home this point. Especially for the twentieth century, which saw the advent and spread of the 'special effect', the claim that inventions are secretly guided by a theological program seems inaccurate.
38. No better of example of this than the remarkable short narrative of Walter Benjamin's, entitled 'Rastelli erzählt ...' (Walter Benjamin, *Gesammelte Schriften*, ed. by Rolf Tiedemann and Herman Schweppenhäuser [Frankfurt/M: Suhrkamp, 1980], vol. IV-2, pp. 777–780; 'Rastelli Narrates', translated by Carol Jacobs, in idem, *The Dissimulating Harmony: The Image of Interpretation in Nietzsche, Rilke, Artaud, and Benjamin* [Baltimore and London: The Johns Hopkins University Press, 1978], pp. 117–119). This narration recounts the remarkable story of a juggler whose artful performance with a magic ball was – seemingly – dependant on the active support of an unseen helper, a dwarf inside the ball who made this ball move in miraculous ways. The juggler's career culminates when in the most important and final performance of his life at the court of the Sultan of Constantinopel he unwittingly brings about the unusual acrobatics but now apparently in the physical absence of his invisible assistant, who has fallen ill and has been able to notify his master only after the 'fact'. The special effect of the dancing ball, made possible, quite literally, by a manipulation and thus a certain craftmanship, artificiality and technicity, takes from here on a miraculous quality of its own, and not just in the eyes of the uninformed spectators. Whether the magician operates with and without his invisible helper, there is no observable difference between the fabricated and the, so to speak, genuinely or autonomously performed act. It would almost seem as if the magician's creative force had unwittingly absorbed and internalized his assistant's technique to the point of no longer needing it in the magical object as such. Or, perhaps, the dwarf merely mimicked his master's telekinetic gestures all along? The story leaves the question open. It just suggests that the miraculous presupposes a certain technicity,

even when the latter actually witholds its support. Moreover, that in both cases – in the presence and the absence of the dwarf – technicity on its turn relies on a certain structure of *belief*, namely the perception of the spectators.

It is impossible not to be reminded here of that of another unseen helper, the little dwarf in the automaton of historical materialism, that Benjamin evokes in the first of his 'Theses on the Concept of History', which open with a very similar narrative: 'The story is told of an automaton constructed in such a way that it could play a winning game of chess, answering each move of an opponent with a countermove. A puppet in Turkish attire and wit a hookah in its mouth sat before a chessboard placed on a large table. A system of mirrors created the illusion that this table was transparent from all sides. Actually, a little hunchback who was an expert chess player sat inside and guided the puppet's hand by means of strings. One can imagine a philosophical counterpart to this device. The puppet called 'historical materialism' is to win all the time. It can easily be a match for anyone if it enlists the services of theology, which today, as we know, is wizened [*klein*] and has to keep out of sight' (Walter Benjamin, *Gesammelte Schriften*, vol. I.2, p. 693; *Illuminations*, edited and with and introduction by Hannah Arendt, translated by Harry Zohn [London: Fontana Press, 1992], p. 245). The machine, which is 'transparent' from all sides, must function as if it does without any further manipulation, that is to say, without the invisible efficacy of the invincible dwarf (the almost supra-natural and oblique support of the theological, operating as a silent and oblique force). Yet it is far from certain that if it were to do without the support (of the dwarf, of the theological), it would not continue to make the same moves and follow the same schemes. The fully operative automaton, like the fully internalized technicity of the magician's act, is no less mysterious and no less miraculous than the dual structure of the two-natured cooperation. In a sense, it is its very culmination: its demise and fulfillment. Impossible to tell which is which.

Address for correspondence: Professor Dr Hent de Vries, Department of Philosophy, Faculteit der Geesteswetenschappen, University of Amsterdam, Nieuwe Doelenstraat 15, 1012 CP Amsterdam, The Netherlands
Phone: +20-525-4500; Fax: +20-525-4503

Religious diversity and religious toleration

PHILIP L. QUINN
University of Notre Dame

Awareness of religious diversity is nothing new under the sun. The early Christian martyrs were doubtless aware that others in the Roman Empire did not share their religious beliefs. Yet it is arguable that awareness of religious diversity has recently assumed qualitatively new forms. Among the factors that might account for this transformation is the increased contact people now have with religions other than their own. Modern technologies of travel and communication foster interchanges between adherents of different religions. Modern scholarship has made available translations of and commentaries on texts from a variety of religious traditions, and cultural anthropologists have recorded fascinating thick descriptions of the practices of many such traditions. People who live in religiously pluralistic democracies have ample opportunities to acquire personal familiarity with religions other than their own without leaving home. It now is therefore harder than it once was to hang onto negative stereotypes of or rationalize hostile reactions to the practitioners of religions other than one's own. But many people succeed in doing so; increased contact often enough produces greater friction. News media have bombarded us with the sights and sounds of religious conflict in Belfast, Beirut and Bosnia. In Africa Muslims clash with animists, in India Hindus and Muslims struggle bitterly, and in Europe Catholic Croats go to war with Orthodox Serbs. The city of Jerusalem remains a focal point for religious quarrels among Jews, Christians and Muslims. In the eighteenth century, Kant complained that the history of Christianity could justify Lucretius's exclamation, *tantum religio potuit suadere malorum*![1] At the beginning of the twenty-first century, support for Lucretius comes from several religions and many parts of the world. The religions of the world may be able to understand one another better now than ever before, but their ability to live together in peace still has not yet been secured.

Recent philosophical work that is responsive to the contemporary challenge of religious diversity has centered in the areas of epistemology and political philosophy. In epistemology, the main issue has been whether or not, given what we now know about religious diversity, exclusivism remains a defensible position. Exclusivism is the view that one religion is basically correct and all the others go astray in one or more ways. It has several dimen-

International Journal for Philosophy of Religion 50: 57–80, 2001.
E. Th. Long (ed.), Issues in Contemporary Philosophy of Religion
© 2001 *Kluwer Academic Publishers. Printed in the Netherlands.*

sions. Doctrinal exclusivism is the view that the doctrines of one religion are mostly true while the doctrines of all the others, where there is conflict, are false. Soteriological exclusivism is the view that only the path proposed by one religion leads securely to the ultimate religious goal, salvation or liberation. And experiential exclusivism is the view that the religious experiences typically enjoyed by the adherents of one religion are mostly veridical and conflicting experiences typical of all the others are nonveridical. It is, of course, entirely consistent to accept exclusivism in one of these dimensions while rejecting it in another. For example, some Christians who are doctrinal exclusivists hold that salvation is available to devout members of other religious traditions, though such Christians often insist that, unbeknownst to those outside Christianity, their salvation comes through Jesus Christ. Starting from the observation that, as far as we can tell empirically, all the world religions are more or less equal in their salvific efficacy, that is, their ability to transform their practitioners from being self-centered to being centered on a transcendent reality, John Hick has mounted a powerful attack on exclusivism in all three dimensions. While admitting that religious diversity does, or at least can, undermine the epistemic credentials of experiential or doctrinal exclusivism to some extent, William P. Alston and Alvin Plantinga have replied with arguments aimed at showing that Christian exclusivism of some sort continues to enjoy an epistemic status high enough to make it a rational option even when religious diversity is taken into account. And other philosophers have added their voices to the discussion of this issue.[2] In my opinion, the debate on this topic has more or less reached a stand off. The positions that are live philosophical options have been fairly thoroughly mapped out, and the main arguments for and against each of them have been developed in some detail. I doubt that there is a realistic prospect of the issue which divides exclusivists from their philosophical opponents being decisively settled or even moved appreciably closer to a resolution by additional arguments.[3]

One might think of exclusivism of another kind as the chief problem addressed by the response to religious diversity within contemporary political philosophy. In this case, exclusivism is the view, advocated by several liberal political philosophers, that religion ought to be excluded from the public square in modern liberal democracies. More precisely, political exclusivists hold that religious arguments should be excluded from the public political discourse of religiously pluralistic democratic societies on certain fundamental questions.[4] Robert Audi has argued vigorously for a version of exclusivism that includes a prima facie obligation not to advocate or support any law or policy that restricts conduct unless one has and is willing to offer adequate secular reason for such advocacy or support. Appealing to grounds of fairness, Nicholas Wolterstorff has challenged Audi's position and forcefully criticized the general exclusivist point of view of which it is an instance.[5] The most nuanced liberal exclusion of the religious so far developed is contained in the political philosophy of John Rawls. According to its ideal of public reason, which imposes a duty of civility, we are not to introduce into public political discourse on constitutional essentials and matters of basic justice reasons drawn from comprehensive doctrines, religious doctrines all being understood to be comprehensive, unless we satisfy the proviso that we do so in ways that strengthen the ideal of public reason itself.[6] My impression is that, unlike the debate about exclusivism in epistemology, this dispute remains in flux to some extent and has not yet reached a stand off. Confirming evidence for this impression may be derived from the fact that Rawls has modified his position to allow that reasons drawn from comprehensive doctrines, religious or nonreligious, may be introduced into public political discussions at any time subject to the proviso that in due course reasons in compliance with the ideal of public reason are presented to support whatever the comprehensive doctrines were invoked to support.[7] To be sue, the modified view still has a proviso attached, but it is more permissive than the proviso of the original view and so is less likely to raise the hackles of religious citizens of a democracy.

I confess I find it a bit odd that the main response to religious diversity in recent liberal political philosophy has focused on the issue of whether or not religious argument should be excluded from public discourse. Given the widespread religious conflict mentioned previously, I cannot help thinking that religious toleration is a more urgent global political issue and that the rather narrow focus on religious discourse in liberal democracies is a bit parochial. I have some ideas about factors that may contribute to explaining the narrow focus, though they are somewhat speculative. One factor is fear of divisiveness. It would be natural to search for moral grounds for constraints on the use of religious arguments in the public square if one were afraid that in a religiously divided society their use would be likely to be destabilizing. Jeffrey Stout expressed such fear not so long ago. Arguing against Basil Mitchell's proposal that traditional theism be employed in order to revitalize public discourse, Stout claims that 'the risks of reviving religious conflict like that of early modern Europe are too great'.[8] I myself reckon that the probability of reigniting the Wars of Religion by including religious arguments in public political discourse is quite low, and so I think that such fear, however real it may be, is unrealistic. It seems to me that, even if the practice of religious toleration in Western democracies is no more than a modus vivendi, it is supported both by the settled habits of religious citizens and by the weight of their traditions to a degree that lends it great robustness. Another factor that may play an explanatory role is complacency about the historical achievements of political philosophy. It would be understandable if people saw no need for new arguments to clinch the case for religious toleration because they thought conclusive arguments were already available in the classic works of liberal political philosophy. One might, for example, look to John Locke's work as a source of arguments for religious toleration.[9] According to Locke, religious persecution is bound to be ineffective and hence is irrational because its goal is to get people to adopt different religious beliefs and people do not have direct voluntary control over their religious beliefs. However, as Jeremy Waldron has recently shown Locke's case for this position falls apart under critical scrutiny, and there is no way to reconstruct it to meet the objections.[10] Or one might look to John Stuart Mill for an argument for religious toleration that at least is successful by utilitarian standards.[11] But David Lewis has shown that Mill will lose his case if he argues against a clever utilitarian religious Inquisitor.[12] So complacency about the justification of religious toleration is, I think, unwarranted.

My main aim in this paper is to broaden the focus of the discussion of religious diversity in political philosophy to include arguments against religious intolerance. I shall not try to refurbish the arguments of Locke or Mill; indeed, I shall depart altogether from the British historical tradition of liberal thought. I shall instead exploit the historical resources of a continental tradition of liberal thought by examining arguments against religious intolerance developed by Pierre Bayle and Immanuel Kant. I choose these particular arguments for scrutiny because they enable me to reach a secondary goal, which is to bring the discussion of religious diversity in political philosophy into contact with the discussion in epistemology and to try to establish some connections between them. The idea that there should be such connections has been rendered intuitively vivid by Avishai Margalit. He draws attention to the parable of the three rings, made famous in Lessing's play *Nathan the Wise*. In Margalit's version of the story, a king leaves a legacy of three rings in his three sons; one of the rings is of great value while the other two are no more than good imitations. The religious analogy is clear. The king is God; the real ring is revealed truth; and the three sons are Moses, Jesus and Muhammad. Reflecting on the parable, Margalit points out that, apart from the king, 'no one else knows for certain which ring is the real one. This doubt should lead to an attitude of "respect and suspect", because it is possible that the truth is in another religion'.[13] It is precisely the connection Margalit sees between epistemic uncertainty and the relatively tolerant attitude of respect and suspect that interests me. I propose to explore that connection and to try to clarify what its implications are through an examination of the arguments of Bayle and Kant. I do not pretend to return a final verdict on the general line of philosophical thought to which those arguments are meant to contribute.

In this paper, I shall ignore some of the issues that have been prominent in other recent treatments of toleration in political philosophy. I am not going to investigate the topic of whether ordinary language marks a conceptual distinction between toleration and tolerance. Nor do I plan to take a stand on whether it is a necessary truth that one can only tolerate things one views as bad or evil. I do not have a definition or an analysis of toleration to offer. I shall work with an intuitive notion of religious intolerance that has within its extension behaviors such as killing people for heresy or apostasy, forced conversions and preventing people from engaging collectively in worship. My interest here is restricted to the fairly specific topic of the ethical or moral status of such intolerant behaviors.[14]

The remainder of the paper is divided into three part. In the first, I rehearse arguments about the negative epistemic consequences of religious diversity. The other two parts address the question of what impact the conclusions of such arguments might have on further arguments against intolerance. The second part subjects to critical analysis an argument by Bayle; the third does the same to an argument of Kant.

1. Alston and others on religious diversity

William P. Alston acknowledges that religious diversity gives rise to an epistemological problem for his view that experience of God confers prima facie justification or beliefs about how God is manifested to the experiencer. He defends this view from within the perspective of a doxastic practice approach to epistemology.[15] A doxastic practice is a practice of forming beliefs together with a series of possible overriders for the prima facie justification a belief derives from having been generated by the practice. Doxastic practices are to be evaluated, from an epistemic point of view, in terms of their likelihood of producing true beliefs, that is, in terms of their reliability. Basic doxastic practices, for example, sense perception, are socially established practices whose reliability cannot be established in a noncircular manner. Alston thinks it rational to grant prima facie acceptance to all basic doxastic practices that are not demonstrably unreliable or otherwise disqualified from rational acceptance. In other words, basic practices are innocent until proven guilty. He also observes that a practice's claim to rational acceptance is strengthened if it enjoys self-support. When he turns his attention to the religious realm, he supposes that each of the major traditions has within it a practice of forming beliefs about how Ultimate Reality, whatever it may be, manifests itself in or through religious experience. As he divides up the pie, different religions have different experiential practices because the systems of possible overriders vary so much from one religion to another. Among them is the Christian practice (CP). For Alston, CP is a basic practice that is not demonstrably unreliable and derives self-support from, for instance, the way in which its promises of spiritual development can be seen, from within the practice, to be fulfilled in the lives of some of its practitioners. However, he allows that other religious doxastic practices are basic too, are also not demonstrably unreliable, and enjoy as much self-support as CP does. In short, CP has rivals that are on an epistemic par with it, and this is why religious diversity creates an epistemological problem for it. And, needless to say, each of these rivals is in the same situation; CP's problem is also a problem for Buddhist practice (BP), Hindu practice (HP) and so forth. Does this disqualify CP and its rivals from rational acceptance?

Alston thinks not. He does admit that religious diversity decreases the justification its practitioners have for engaging in CP, but he denies that it does so to such a degree that it is irrational for them to engage in it. His main argument for this denial deploys an analogy with a counterfactual scenario involving rival sense-perceptual doxastic practices. Imagine that there were, in certain cultures, a socially established 'Cartesian' practice of construing what is visually perceived as an indefinitely extended medium more or less concentrated at various points, rather than, as in our 'Aristotelian' practice, as made up of more or less discrete objects scattered about in space. Further imagine that there were, in yet other cultures, an established 'Whiteheadian' practice in which the visual field is taken to be made up of momentary events growing out of one another in a continuous process. Suppose that each of these three practices served its practitioners equally well in their dealings with the environment and had associated with it a well-developed physical science. Suppose also that we were as firmly wedded to our 'Aristotelian' practice as we in fact are but were unable to come up with any non-question-begging reason for regarding it as more accurate than either of the others. Alston concludes that, absent any non-question-begging reason for thinking that one of the other two practices is more accurate than my own, 'the only rational course for me is to sit tight with the practice of which I am a master and which serves me so well in guiding my activity in the world'.[16] But the sheerly hypothetical sense-perceptual scenario is precisely parallel to our actual situation with regard to CP and its religious rivals. Hence, by parity of reasoning, the rational thing for a practitioner of CP to do is to sit tight with it and continue to form beliefs making use of it. And, again by parity of reasoning, the same goes for practitioners of BP, HP and other uneliminated rivals of CP.

Alston's critics have argued that he has not established his conclusion. Though he concedes that it is pragmatically rational for its practitioners to sit tight with CP, William J. Wainwright contends that Alston has not shown it to be epistemically rational for them to do so. The fact that CP is socially established, significantly self-supporting and not demonstrably unreliable is, he grants, a good reason for regarding it as prima facie reliable. However, the existence of rival religious experiential practices that are also prima facie reliable is, he claims, a good reason for thinking that CP is prima facie unreliable. It is epistemically rational to engage in CP if the good reason for viewing it as prima facie unreliable neither counterbalances nor outweighs the good reason for viewing it as prima facie reliable. It is not epistemically irrational to engage in CP if the good reason for considering it prima facie unreliable does not outweigh the good reason for considering it prima facie reliable. According to Wainwright, the most Alston's argument shows is that the good reason for thinking that CP is reliable is not outweighed, in which case engaging in it is not epistemically irrational. It does not show that it is not counterbalanced, and so it does not show that engaging in CP is epistemically rational. Wainwright therefore thinks the most Alston establishes is that engaging in CP 'is pragmatically rational, and not epistemically irrational'.[17]

My objection to Alston's conclusion can be traced back to a disagreement between us about the lesson to be derived from his sense-perceptual analogy. As I see it, one way to explain the success of the three sense-perceptual practices in the analogy is to suppose that each of them is reliable with respect to the appearances the physical environment presents to its practitioners, but none is reliable with respect to how the physical environment is in itself. Hence it would be rational to modify the Aristotelian practice from within so that the new outputs are beliefs about the appearances the physical environment presents to its practitioners rather than beliefs about how the physical environment really is independent of the practitioner. And, of course, this Kantian turn would be equally rational for Cartesian and Whiteheadean practitioners. So while I grant that sitting tight would be a rational option, I deny Alston's stronger claim that it would be the rational thing to do. By parity of reasoning, then, I conclude that, though it would be rational for practitioners of CP to continue to engage in it, it is not the only rational course of action for them in light of the facts of religious diversity. It would also be rational for them to revise CP in a Kantian direction and to make efforts to get the modified practice socially established. And, again, the same goes for practitioners of BP, HP and other religious experiential doxastic practices.[18]

Despite their disagreements on points of detail, Alston and his critics concur in thinking that religious diversity has a negative impact on the justification for engaging in CP or its rivals such as BP and HP. At least for those who are aware of it, religious diversity seriously diminishes the justification for continuing to form beliefs in any of these ways. What remains in dispute is whether justification decreases to the extent that there are rational alternatives to sitting tight with CP, for example, taking the Kantian turn, or even to such a degree that it is epistemically not rational or irrational to continue engaging in CP. In what follows I shall make use of the shared agreement that justification for engaging in CP or any of its rivals is substantially decreased by religious diversity; I shall not appeal to any of the disputed claims about the exact extent of the decrease. Of course, experiential doxastic practices are not the only sources of support for the systems of belief of the world religions. As Alston reminds us, Christianity also purports to derive support from other sources such as the arguments of natural theology, tradition and revelation, which he takes to include divine messages to prophets, divine inspiration of oral or written communications and divine action in history. However, though additional sources may mitigate the epistemic problem of religious diversity, they clearly cannot eliminate it. After all, some of the other sources confront their own problems of religious diversity. The conclusions of the metaphysical arguments of natural theology conflict with the conclusions of impressive metaphysical arguments in nontheistic religious traditions. The claims of the texts and traditions Christians take to be religiously authoritative must be set against conflicting claims derived from the texts and traditions to which non-Christians grant religious authority. And, as Hume's essay on miracles reminds us, Christian claims about divine action in history compete with the claims of other religions about which historical events have decisive religious significance. Moreover, as Alston insists, the various sources of Christian belief are supposed to provide one another with mutual support and to contribute to a cumulative case for Christianity. So when religious diversity decreases the justification for relying on one of them, it also weakens the others it is supposed to support as well as the cumulative case that rests on all of them. Using a familiar metaphor, Alston summarizes his position this way: 'Though each of these considerations can itself be doubted and though no single strand is sufficient to keep the faith secure, when combined into a rope they all together have enough strength to do the job'.[19] Fair enough, but by the same token, when one or more stands is weakened or cut due to the problem of religious diversity, the rope is weakened and its ability to keep the faith secure is diminished. Thus, absent a special reason to think otherwise, I shall assume that religious diversity has a negative epistemic bearing not only on the beliefs that are outputs of CP but also on other parts of the total system of Christian belief and that the same goes for rivals such as BP and HP and the total religious belief systems for which they are sources.

It is worth noting in passing that even Alvin Plantinga, who is more intransigent than some other defenders of Christian exclusivism, acknowledges that awareness of religious diversity can and often does have a negative epistemic impact on religious beliefs.[20] According to his account of warrant, which is what, when enough of it is added to true belief, yields knowledge, warrant is directly proportional to level of confidence in, or degree of strength of, belief. Awareness of religious diversity therefore can and often does decrease warrant by acting directly to reduce confidence in or strength of belief. Indeed, it can even deprive one of knowledge. It is possible, Plantinga thinks, that someone who would have had religious knowledge in the absence of an awareness of religious diversity lacks knowledge in its presence because of the reduction of confidence and hence warrant produced by that awareness. However, Plantinga goes on to claim that this loss of confidence need not happen and, even if it does happen, need not be permanent. As he sees it, then, the reduction of warrant produced by an awareness of religious diversity can be counteracted simply by a return of the confidence whose loss gave rise to the reduction. Whether Plantinga is right about this last point depends, of course, on whether his account of warrant is correct. Since his development of that account is spread out over three rather large volumes, I cannot in this paper even begin to address the issue of its correctness with the attention to detail that would be needed to settle it.[21] So I will leave it an open question whether the negative epistemic impact to which awareness of religious diversity gives rise can be counteracted in the simple way Plantinga thinks it can.

2. Bayle in defense of religious toleration

Born in 1647, Pierre Bayle was raised a Protestant in predominantly Roman Catholic France. Both his father, Jean, and his older brother, Jacob, were ordained ministers. When he went to study at the Jesuit Academy at Toulouse in 1669, Pierre converted to Catholicism, but he returned to Protestantism after eighteen months. Fearing persecution on account of his relapsed status, he fled in Geneva in 1670. In 1675 he became a professor of philosophy at the Protestant Academy of Sedan. The Academy was closed by royal decree in 1681, and he moved to Rotterdam, where he lived for a quarter of a century. Persecution of Protestants by Catholics grew worse during these years. Jean Bayle died in March 1685. On June 10, 1685, Jacob Bayle was arrested and imprisoned. Pierre learned that he had indirectly caused his brother's arrest. Angered by criticism Pierre had published, the French authorities were treating his brother as his surrogate because they could not reach him in Rotterdam. Jacob was tortured, and his health was broken in an unsuccessful attempt to compel him to renounce his religious loyalties. On October 22, 1685, the Edict of Nantes was revoked, and the persecution of Protestants in France thereafter increased in intensity. On November 12, 1685, Jacob Bayle died in prison. The following year Pierre published his most impassioned and sustained defense of religious toleration.[22]

Its full title is *Commentaire philosophique sur ces paroles de Jésus-Christ, 'Contrain-les d'entrer'* (*Philosophical Commentary on These Words of Jesus Christ, 'Compel Them to Come In'*).[23] The words of Jesus referred to in its title come from the Parable of the Great Dinner in the Gospel of Luke. In the story, when the invited guests make excuses for not coming to the dinner and even poor folk brought in from the neighborhood do not fill all the places, the angry host says to his servant: 'Go out into the roads and lanes, and compel people to come in, so that my house may be filled' (Luke 14:23). Starting at least as far back as Augustine, Christians used this verse as a proof-text to provide biblical warrant for forced conversions. The first part of Bayle's *Philosophical Commentary* contains nine arguments against interpreting the verse according to what Bayle describes as its literal sense, by which he means the sense in which it can be used to serve this intolerant purpose. Though it bills itself as a reply to objections to the arguments of the first part, the second part also sets forth some of Bayle's positive views on religious toleration, including his historically influential doctrine of the rights of an erring conscience.[24] The nine arguments of the first part cover a lot of territory. For example, one of them is a clever *ad hominem* (or, perhaps, *ad ecclesiam*) argument. Bayle points out that if Christians who think Luke 14:23 justifies them in making forced conversions were honest about their intentions, the rulers of non-Christian peoples such as the Chinese would have reasonable grounds for excluding Christian missionaries from their realms. Another should strike a sympathetic chord in the minds of readers of scripture who reject the practice of proof-texting. After arguing that Luke 14:23 should be interpreted in the light of its context, Bayle tries to show that interpreting the verse in a way that supports forced conversion 'is contrary to the whole tenor and general spirit of the Gospel' (p. 39). However, the argument of greatest philosophical interest is one which combines morality and epistemology. I shall concentrate on that argument.

According to Bayle, the general principle on which the argument rests is '*that any particular dogma, whether advanced as contained in Scripture or proposed in any other way, is false, if repugnant to the clear and distinct notions of natural light, principally in regards to morality*' (p. 33). As the reference to clear and distinct notions of natural light suggests, Bayle is working with a Cartesian epistemology in which the epistemic status of deliverances of the natural light is sufficiently high to guarantee their truth. Examples he gives of deliverances of the natural light of reason that come from outside morality are such truths as '*that the whole is greater than its parts; that if from equal things we take away equals, the results will be equal; that it's impossible that two contradictories be true; or that the essence of a subject actually subsists after the destruction of the subject*'

(p. 28). We should, of course, view the last of these examples with suspicion. It is tantamount to the thesis, which is in dispute between Platonists and Aristotelians, that properties can exist uninstantiated. Still, in philosophy three out of four is not a bad record, and the other examples make it clear enough what sorts of propositions are supposed to be deliverances of the natural light. So I think we should grant Bayle the principle that if a doctrine is contrary to the natural light, then it is false.

At the beginning of the second chapter of the first part, Bayle tells us how he proposes to make use of this principle. He says: 'The literal sense of these words is contrary to the purest and most distinct ideas of natural reason; it is therefore false. The business now is only to prove the *antecedent*, because I presume the consequence was sufficiently demonstrated in the foregoing chapter' (p. 35). His argument will thus have the following form:

(1) If the words 'Compel them to come in', interpreted literally, yield a proposition contrary to the natural light, that proposition is false.
(2) The words 'Compel them to come in', interpreted literally, do yield a proposition contrary to the natural light.
(3) Hence that proposition is false.

We are committed to allowing Bayle to assume (1), because it is an instance of the principle we have already granted him. So if he establishes (2), as he has promised, he will be in a position to infer (3) from (1) and (2) by modus ponens.

The argument for (2) has four steps. I shall quote the first and last of them in full because I want to comment on each of them at some length. Bayle first claims 'that by the purest and most distinct ideas of reason, we know there is a being sovereignly perfect who governs all things, who ought to be adored by mankind, who approves certain actions and rewards them, and who disapproves and punishes others' (p. 35). His next point is that we also understand by the natural light that the principal worship we owe to the supreme being consists of inner acts of the mind. It would be as silly to suppose that God would be pleased by mere external behavior, Bayle remarks, as it would be to imagine that a king would regard as homage a situation in which the wind posed statues in deferential postures by knocking them over whenever he happened to pass by. It follows, Bayle then observes, that even when worship involves exterior signs it must also include inner mental acts. His fourth and final point is this:

> It is evident then that the only legitimate way of inspiring religion is by producing in the soul certain judgments and certain movements of the will in relation to God. Now since threats, prisons, fines, exile, beatings, torture, and generally whatever is comprehended under the literal signification of compelling, are incapable of forming in the soul those judgments

of the will in respect to God which constitute the essence of religion, it is evident that this is a mistaken way of establishing a religion and, consequently, that Jesus Christ has not commanded it (p. 36).

What are we to make of this argument?

I think that, as it stands, it is a mess. Consider first Bayle's first step. It is plausible to suppose he thinks that a Cartesian ontological argument is the source of our knowledge of God's existence from the purest and most distinct ideas of reason (*'les plus pures et les plus distinctes idées de la raison'*).[25] But, unlike Descartes, we do not believe that the premises of a Cartesian ontological argument are deliverances of the natural light. Indeed, even if, unlike Kant, we think there is a valid ontological argument whose premises are rationally acceptable, we do not believe they have an epistemic status as high as the law of noncontradiction or other things that are supposed to be known by the natural light.[26] Cosmological arguments for the existence of God are in the same boat.[27] And so too, it seems to me, are all other known arguments of natural theology. So I think Bayle's first step is already a misstep. It insures that he will not get to a conclusion, guaranteed by the natural light, to which the interpretation of Luke 14:23 he wants to reject is a contrary.

Consider now Bayle's final step. He asserts that compulsive measures are incapable of forming in the soul the judgments of the will in respect to God, whatever they may be, that constitute the essence of religion (*'ne peuvent pas former dans l'âme les jugements de volunté, par rapport à Dieu, qui constituent l'essence de la religion'*).[28] We may be sure, I think, that if compulsion really cannot produce the internal acts of mind that are essential to true worship, then Jesus has not commanded compulsion, at least not for this purpose. But is it evident by the natural light that compulsion in incapable of producing those interior acts? It seems not. It may be that religious beliefs, for example, are not under the direct control of the will so that people threatened with religious persecution cannot simply become converts by deciding to do so. But even if compulsion is incapable of producing converts in the short run, it may be effective in the long run in the manner imagined in the distopian fiction of the twentieth century. Or perhaps Pascal was right when he advised the libertine wagerer to attend mass and use holy water, thinking that outward practice would eventually generate inward belief. If so, compelling outward practice would be a rational means to the end of inducing belief. Issues about whether or not various techniques of brainwashing will produce changes in belief are empirical; we would not expect them to be settled solely by the natural light of reason. Like Locke, Bayle is vulnerable to empirical confutation on this point.

After having raised similar objections to Locke's view, Waldron remarks that 'what one misses above all in Locke's argument is a sense that there is anything *morally* wrong with intolerance, or a sense of any deep concern for the *victims* of persecution or the moral insult that is involved in the attempt to manipulate their faith'.[29] This suggests that we would be doing Bayle a favor if we substituted explicitly moral considerations for claims about the efficacy of compulsion at this point in his argument. Even if compulsion of certain sorts turns out to be effective in causing the inner mental acts that are essential to religion, it may nevertheless be wrong to use it for that purpose. We know that Bayle means to appeal to moral considerations sooner or later. Near the beginning of the first chapter of the first part, he announces that he is 'relying upon this single principle of natural light, *that any literal interpretation which carries an obligation to commit iniquity is false*' (p. 28). So maybe Bayle's best bet is simply to insist that it is morally wrong to use compulsion to produce the inner acts that are essential to religion. If he does, he has available to him the following argument. According to the literal interpretation of Luke 14:23, Jesus has commanded the use of compulsion to produce those inner acts. This command carries with it an obligation to use compulsion for that purpose, since commands of Jesus are divine commands and so impose obligations. But the obligation to make such a use of compulsion is an obligation to commit an iniquity, because it is morally wrong to use compulsion thus. Hence the literal interpretation of Luke 14:23 is false, and so Jesus has not commanded the use of compulsion to produce the inner acts essential to religion. This argument has the merit of giving Bayle the conclusion he wants at the fourth step of his larger argument.

However, next we must ask about the epistemic status of the moral principle we have allowed Bayle to assume for the sake of this argument. Is it evident by the natural light that it is morally wrong to use compulsion to produce the inner acts that are essential to religion? I doubt it. What is more, I think Bayle himself could not consistently even hold that this principle is true unless it is qualified by a *ceteris paribus* clause. This is because he allows that God 'may dispense with His own laws in certain cases' (p. 121). Indeed, he believes that God can dispense from the Decalogue's prohibition on homicide. There are, he affirms, circumstances that 'change the nature of homicide from a bad action into a good action, a secret command of God, for example' (p. 171). And he goes on to claim that such circumstances are sometimes actual, that God sometimes does dispense from this precept (*Dieu dispense quelquefois de ce précepte*).[30] The cases Bayle has in mind are, of course, the biblical stories in which God commands homicide. The most famous of them is the *akedah*, the binding of Isaac, recounted in Genesis 22; according to that story, which serves as the basis for Kierekegaard's teleological suspension of the ethical, God commanded Abraham to slay his son.[31] Since Bayle is prepared to make exceptions even to the prohibitions of the Decalogue in such cases, he has left a loophole open to religious persecutors. He cannot consistently deny at least the possibility that they are right if they claim they have been dispensed from the principle that it is morally wrong to use compulsion to make converts or claim they have received a secret divine command to employ compulsion for this purpose. Proving a negative is often very difficult, and I think the present case is one of the hard ones. I do not see how Bayle could hope to prove that the religious persecutors have not, in fact, been thus divinely dispensed or secretly divinely commanded.

In my opinion, though at this point I am going beyond anything to be found in Bayle's text, the best strategy for the defender of toleration is to conduct the argument entirely in epistemic terms and not to make any dubious appeals to the Cartesian natural light. The epistemic credentials of two conflicting claims are to be assessed and then compared. One is a moral principle to the effect that intolerant behavior of a certain kind is wrong; the other is a conflicting religious claim about that intolerant behavior. The applicable epistemic principle is that, whenever two conflicting claims differ in epistemic status, the claim with the lower status is to be rejected. If it can be shown that the epistemic status of the moral principle is higher than the epistemic status of the conflicting religious claim, then the epistemic principle licenses an inference to the conclusion that the religious claim is the one to be rejected. It is fortunate for the defenders of toleration that the strategy depends only on qualitative judgements of comparative epistemic status, for it seems likely that we are incapable of discovering a precise quantitative account of levels of epistemic status. It would be nice for the defenders of toleration if all our moral principles to the effect that intolerant behavior of a certain kind is wrong had the very highest epistemic status possible. But since there may be few if any moral principles about the wrongness of intolerant behavior with this status, it is again fortunate that the strategy still has a chance of success even if it uses a moral principle with a somewhat less exalted epistemic status. Yet the strategy does not guarantee success, because it does not preclude the possibility that in some cases a religious claim supporting intolerant behavior will turn out to have a higher epistemic status than a conflicting moral principle. Hence the strategy does not beg the question against advocates of religious intolerance, though the defenders of toleration will naturally hope that it may serve at least to limit the scope of epistemically respectable intolerance. And the epistemic consequences of religious diversity may have a role to play, at least in some cases, in applications of the strategy that yield successful arguments for religious toleration of one kind or another. It may happen that a religious claim supportive of a certain sort of intolerance has a lower epistemic status than a conflicting moral principle favoring toleration entirely or in large part due to the decrease in the religious claim's status resulting from an awareness of religious diversity.

To help fix ideas, let us return briefly to the issue that vexed Bayle. A valid argument parallel to the one he offered that employs the strategy outline above has the following shape:

(4) If the moral principle that using compulsion to produce the inner acts essential to religion is wrong has a fairly high epistemic status and the religious claim that using compulsion for this purpose is obligatory because Jesus commanded it has a lower epistemic status, then the religious claim is to be rejected.

(5) The moral principle that using compulsion to produce the inner acts essential to religion is wrong does have a fairly high epistemic status.

(6) The religious claim that using compulsion for this purpose is obligatory because Jesus commanded it does have a lower epistemic status.

(7) Hence, the religious claim is to be rejected.

The proposition expressed by (4) is an instantiation of the strategy's governing epistemic principle. Let us suppose, for the sake of argument, that the moral principle cited in (5) does have a reasonably high epistemic status but falls short of being evident by the natural light, absolutely certain or anything similar. It is an intuitively plausible principle. And even if, strictly speaking, it needs to be qualified by a *ceteris paribus* clause to handle things like secret divine commands, the possibility of a violation of such a clause is not at issue in the present context. Debate can then focus on the epistemic status of the religious claim cited in (6). Some of Bayle's own arguments in the *Philosophical Commentary* bear on this question. If he is correct in thinking that this religious claim is contrary to the tenor and spirit of the Gospels, this consideration will do something to decrease its epistemic status. But the religious claim is not without a certain amount of support. It has behind it the authority of a tradition of Christian thought and practice in which it is entrenched. I think considerations of religious diversity can play a valuable role in defeating the epistemic authority of this tradition. They do so indirectly by diminishing the epistemic rationality of the whole Christian package or worldview of which the tradition is a part. And, since Christianity itself is internally complex and contains competing traditions, some of which are more tolerant than the Augustinian tradition that endorses compulsion, such considerations also operate more directly to decrease the epistemic status of that tradition in particular and hence of the religious claim about what Jesus commanded embedded in it. By my lights, the total evidence strongly support (6), and so I think the argument of which it is a premise is sound.

In a couple of ways, it is of course a weak argument. Even if it is successful, it eliminates only one ground for the use of compulsion by the religiously intolerant. However, if we are committed to the project of trying to persuade the intolerant by arguments, it may be practically desirable to be able to argue against their grounds for intolerance one at a time. In addition, the argument does not aspire to eliminate the grounds of all forms of religious intolerance at one fell swoop. But, again, it may be of practical importance to be in position to argue against various form of intolerance piecemeal, starting with the worst. The strategy I have outlined and illustrated can be used repeatedly provided enough moral principles of fairly high epistemic status can be mobilized for inclusion in the premises of its multiple implementations. So my illustrative argument should be understood as part of a cumulative case against religious intolerance.

3. Kant on conscience and inquisitors

The argument by Kant I wish to consider is set forth in the fourth section of the second part of the fourth book of his *Religion within the Boundaries of Mere Reason*. In that section, he presents a doctrine of conscience. As he defines it, '*conscience is a consciousness which is of itself a duty*'.[32] The definition poses for Kant the question of how a state of conscious awareness can be an unconditional duty. In attempting to answer his question, Kant starts from the moral principle, which he says needs no proof, that we '*ought to venture nothing where there is danger that it might be wrong (quod dubitas, ne feceris*! Pliny)' (pp. 202–203).[33] He takes it to be a consequence of this principle that I have an unconditional duty to be aware that any action I want to perform is morally right. I do not have to know, with respect to human actions generally or with respect to all possible actions, whether they are right or wrong. But concerning any action I propose to perform, 'I must not only judge, and be of the opinion, that it is right; I must also be *certain* that it is' (p. 203). Kant contrasts his view with probabilism, which he defines as 'the principle that the mere opinion that an action may well be right is itself sufficient for undertaking it' (p. 203). As I see matters, the probabilist thinks that I may go ahead with an action I propose to perform if I am aware that it is probable that it is right. Holding us to a higher standard, Kant insists that I may go ahead with an action I propose to perform only if I am aware that it is certain that it is right. The comparison thus forces us to view the certainty at stake in Kant's claim as epistemic rather than merely psychological. I may not go ahead with my proposed action if all I am aware of is strongly believing or being utterly convinced that it is right. In short, I have a duty to be aware that it is epistemically certain that an action I propose to perform is morally right before I perform the action. If I act in the absence of this awareness, I act unconscientiously and hence violate this duty, even if the action I perform is, in fact, right and so I violate no further duty in performing it. The demands of conscience are therefore very strict according to Kant.

Kant supplements his brief and abstract treatment of his general views on conscience with an application of his doctrine to a particular case of some interest to the defenders of religious toleration. He asks us to imagine an inquisitor whose exclusivist faith is so firm that he is willing to suffer martyrdom for it, if need be, and who must judge the case of someone, otherwise a good citizen, charged with heresy. If the inquisitor condemns the heretic to death, Kant wonders, should we say that the inquisitor acted in accord with an erring conscience or should we say instead that he acted with a lack of conscience and hence consciously did wrong? Kant allows that the inquisitor acted with firm conviction and for a reason. He builds it into the case that the inquisitor 'was indeed presumably firm in the belief that a supernaturally revealed divine will (perhaps according to the saying, *compellite intrare*) permitted him, if not even made a duty for him, to extirpate supposed unbelief together with the unbelievers' (p. 203).[34] Could such an inquisitor get off the hook by pleading to the lesser charge of acting in accord with an erring conscience and so, as Bayle thought, acting within his rights. Kant thinks not. His famous argument for this negative conclusion deserves to be quoted in full. Kant says:

> That to take a human being's life because of his religious faith is wrong is certain, unless (to allow the most extreme possibility) a divine will, made known to the inquisitor in some extraordinary way, has decreed otherwise. But that God has ever manifested this awful will is a matter of historical documentation and never apodictically certain. After all, the revelation reached the inquisitor only through the intermediary of human beings and their interpretation, and even if it were to appear to him to have come from God himself (like the command issued to Abraham to slaughter his own son like a sheep), yet it is at least possible that on this point error has prevailed. But then the inquisitor would risk the danger of doing something which would be to the highest degree wrong, and on this score he acts unconscientiously (pp. 203–204).

In *The Conflict of the Faculties*, Kant returns to the case of the *akedah*, which is alluded to in the second parenthetical remark in the passage quoted above, in order to say more about Abraham's epistemic situation. He there insists that 'Abraham should have replied to this supposedly divine voice: "That I ought not to kill may good son is quite certain. But that you, this apparition, are God – of that I am not certain, and never can be, not even if this voice rings down to me from (visible) heaven." '[35]

According to Kant, then, Abraham cannot be epistemically certain that the voice he hears comes from God. Hence he cannot be aware that it is certain that killing his son is right or even obligatory. If he proceeds to kill his son, he violates the duty of conscience to have such an awareness and so acts unconscientiously. He thus displays a lack of conscience because he consciously violates this duty. Moreover, Abraham can be certain that killing his son is wrong unless, allowing for the most remote possibility, God commands it. If he proceeds to kill his son, he also runs the very great risk of wrongly doing so. Therefore if Abraham proceeds to kill Isaac, he surely violates a duty to act conscientiously and most likely also violates a duty not to kill his son. Similarly, Kant's inquisitor cannot be epistemically certain that scripture actually records a divine command to eliminate unbelievers along with their heresies. So if he condemns the person accused of heresy to death, he surely violates a duty to act conscientiously and most likely also violates a duty not to kill people on account of their religious faith.

It is, I think, illuminating to view Kant as working with the epistemic argumentative strategy I outlined in my discussion of Bayle. The inquisitor can be almost certain that it is wrong to kill people on account their religious faith; he falls short of complete certainty only because he allows for the remote possibility of a divine command to do so. But the inquisitor cannot be anywhere close to certain that it is right or even obligatory to kill unbelievers because God decrees it, since he cannot achieve anything close to certainty that scripture expresses such a divine command. Hence the claim that it is right or even obligatory to kill unbelievers is to be rejected. In order to keep the subsequent discussion simple, let us set aside the complications that Kant's doctrine of conscience would introduce into this picture of the basic argumentative strategy.

Difficulties with Kant's use of this strategy are similar to those that arise in the case of Bayle. Kant has a very optimistic view of the ability of human cognitive faculties to deliver epistemic certainty about principles of moral wrongness. Those of us who live in societies that are, morally speaking, less homogeneous than his was may well reasonably be less optimistic than he was on this score. It seems to me no accident that his examples, killing one's good son or killing people on account of their religious faith, are among the most favorable cases for his position. Ignoring the remote possibility of special divine commands, I am willing to grant that it is certain that killing people for their religious faith is wrong. But I doubt that the principles of wrongness that cover the full range of intolerant practices to which I am opposed can all achieve the lofty status of epistemic certainty, though of course I believe they are all true. Consider, for instance, exile, which in a passage quoted above Bayle offers as an example of compelling. Is it really epistemically certain that sending people into exile or, more generally, expelling or excluding them from a political community because of their religious faith is morally wrong? Is it certain that the magistrates of Calvin's Geneva would have done wrong if they had expelled Roman Catholics from the city under conditions in which the exiles were compensated for lost property? Is it certain that the elders of a contemporary Amish farming community would do wrong if they excluded non Amish from their community? Living in a religiously homogeneous community can realize some very important values. It does not seem certain to me that it is always wrong, even apart from special divine commands, to endeavor to defend or preserve such values. Hence I think the argumentative strategy I am discussing will not rule out all the forms of intolerance I oppose if it can only be successfully employed with principles of moral wrongness that are epistemically certain or nearly so.

However, another difficulty becomes urgent if we envisage making use of the strategy with principles of moral wrongness that fall a good deal short of epistemic certainty. As traditionally conceived, God is omnipotent or, at least, very powerful. It would thus seem to be within God's power to communicate to us a sign that transmits to the claim that God commands some intolerant behavior, such as issuing threats to heretics, a fairly high epistemic status. Kant, to be sure, would not have found this idea congenial. Speaking rather dismissively, he insists: 'For if God should really speak to a human being, the latter could still never *know* that it was God speaking. It is quite impossible for a human being to apprehend the infinite by his senses, distinguish it from sensible beings, and *be acquainted with* it as such'.[36] Suppose we concede to Kant that one who hears a booming voice resounding from the visible heaven cannot be absolutely or apodictically certain that it is God speaking, because, as the quoted remark suggests, some alternative possibilities cannot be conclusively eliminated, so that one cannot *know*, in some emphatic sense, that it is God speaking. It does not follow that hearing such a voice cannot confer on the claim that God has commanded what it is taken to command a fairly high epistemic status. Therefore it seems possible for even sense-perceptual experience to bestow on the claim that an intolerant act is obligatory because it is divinely commanded an epistemic status higher than that of a conflicting principle of moral wrongness that falls a good deal short of certainty, in which case, according to the argumentative strategy under consideration, it is the moral principle that is to be rejected. What is more, if philosophers such as Alston are correct, as I think they are, then divine commands can also be communicated to us by means of a kind of religious perception that is distinct from, though analogous to, sense perception. And, other things being equal, this perceptual source can also contribute to raising the epistemic status of the claim that an intolerant action is obligatory because divinely commanded to a level in excess of a conflicting principle of moral wrongness that is less than certain. So if we apply the argumentative strategy in question to cases in which the moral principle we appeal to has an epistemic status appreciably less than certainty, we cannot guarantee that it will not lose out in competition with a conflicting religious claim about an obligation imposed by divine command that has achieved a higher epistemic status. In short, there is no good reason to deny that claims about divine speech, communicated to us by means of sense perception or by means of a distinctively religious sort of perception, can acquire a fairly high epistemic status in some cases, other things being equal, a status elevated enough to exceed that of conflicting moral principles.[37]

It is at this point, I think, that the epistemic consequences of religious diversity can do something to advance the cause of religious toleration. The existence of religious diversity will reduce the epistemic status of claims that God has commanded and thereby made right or obligatory intolerant behavior to a level below that which they would occupy were there no epistemic consequences of religious diversity. So when the argumentative strategy we are examining is applied to moral principles that are less than certain, it is likely to succeed more often, given the epistemic consequences of religious diversity, than it would otherwise. It is probably impossible to say with precision how many cases of success will be the result of this factor. And there is no guarantee that, even with its assistance, the strategy will be successful for all the cases in which the champions of religious toleration would like to have strong arguments against intolerant individual actions and social practices.

What is the upshot? I have tried to show that there is an epistemic strategy for arguing against various forms of religious intolerance to be found in the neighborhood of arguments actually offered by Bayle and Kant. The strategy involves attempting to establish that moral principles which support toleration have a higher epistemic status than conflicting religious claims which support intolerance. My objection to both Bayle and Kant is that they were excessively sanguine about the epistemic prospects of moral principles. In light of our greater experience with the reasonable moral disagreements of modernity, it is not plausible for us to suppose that all the moral principles needed to develop a case for a doctrine of religious toleration that is broad in scope using the strategy will be evident by the natural light or apodictically certain. But when the strategy is employed in cases of moral principles with a lower epistemic status, it may well turn out, other things being equal, that religious claims which support intolerance have a higher epistemic status than such moral principles do. Recent work in religious epistemology becomes relevant at this point in the discussion. The negative epistemic impact of religious diversity reduces the epistemic status of religious claims supporting intolerance below what it would otherwise be. It thereby can contribute to improving the success rate of the strategy when it is applied to construct piecemeal arguments against religious intolerance of various kinds. Religious diversity thus both creates the need for toleration and contributes to its epistemic grounds.

I do not claim to have exhausted the contributions Bayle or Kant can make to contemporary philosophical discussions of religious toleration. It seems to me their work is of lasting importance not only on account of its high quality but also because they address the topic from within a broadly Christian religious perspective. Their arguments can speak on behalf of religious toleration in a way religious believers may find sympathetic or, at any rate, so I hope. In expressing this hope, I am clearly disagreeing with those who regard Bayle and Kant as hostile to Christianity and to religion generally, skeptics at best and unbelievers at worst. In this controversy, I side with those who have argued that Bayle and Kant were believers, though not orthodox Christians by various traditional standards.[38] I think they were exploring, in ways from which we still have something to learn, possibilities for religious existence within modern pluralistic societies. If religious people today ignore what they have to teach, they run the risk, as Robert M. Adams puts it, of blinding themselves 'to permanently important possibilities of religious life'.[39] Since I share with Adams the aspiration to be religious while living fully within a religiously pluralistic cultural environment, I consider it valuable to look to thinkers such as Bayle and Kant for lessons about how this might be accomplished.[40]

Notes

1. 'Religion has been able to persuade to such great evils!' Lucretius, *De Rerum Natura* 1, 101. Quoted in Immanuel Kant, *Religion within the Boundaries of Mere Reason*, in Kant, *Religion and Rational Theology*, trans. Allen W. Wood and George di Giovanni (Cambridge: Cambridge University Press, 1996), p. 159.
2. Some of the important contributions to this discussion, including presentations of their view by Hick, Alston and Plantinga, have been collected in Philip L. Quinn and Kevin Meeker, eds., *The Philosophical Challenge of Religious Diversity* (New York and Oxford: Oxford University Press, 2000). See also Jerome I. Gellman, *Experience of God and the Rationality of Theistic Belief* (Ithaca and London: Cornell University Press, 1997), especially Chapter 4 whose title is 'God and Religious Diversity'.
3. For confirmation of this doubt, see the inconclusive exchange involving Hick, Alston, Plantinga and others in *Faith and Philosophy* 14 (1997) and the discussion of some of the contributions to it in the introduction to the collection edited by Quinn and Meeker cited in note 2 above.

4. I cast a critical eye on political exclusivism in my APA Central Division Presidential Address, 'Political Liberalisms and Their Exclusions of the Religious'. The Address was originally published in *Proceedings and Addresses of the APA* 69 (1995), pp. 35–56, and has been reprinted in *Religion and Contemporary Liberalism*, ed. Paul J. Weithman (Notre Dame, IN: University of Notre Dame Press, 1997), pp. 138–161.
5. Audi and Wolterstorff debate the issues on which they disagree in Robert Audi and Nicholas Wolterstorff, *Religion in the Public Square* (Lanham, MD: Rowman and Littlefield, 1997). See also their contributions to the volume edited by Weithman cited in note 4 above.
6. See John Rawls, *Political Liberalism* (New York: Columbia University Press, 1993), especially Lecture 6 whose title is 'The Idea of Public Reason'. The proviso is introduced on p. 247.
7. John Rawls, 'The Idea of Public Reason Revisited', *The University of Chicago Law Review* 64/3 (1997): 765–807. The new proviso is set forth on p. 784.
8. Jeffrey Stout, *Ethics After Babel* (Boston: Beacon Press, 1988), p. 223.
9. John Locke, *A Letter concerning Toleration*, in *Works*, Vol. 5 (London: G. and J. Rivington et al., 1824). This volume of the *Works* also contains Locke's second letter concerning toleration and his third and fourth letters for toleration.
10. Jeremy Waldron, 'Locke: Toleration and the Rationality of Persecution', *Justifying Toleration*, ed. Susan Mendus (Cambridge: Cambridge University Press, 1988), pp. 61–86.
11. John Stuart Mill, *On Liberty*, ed. Gertrude Himmelfarb (Harmondsworth: Penguin, 1982).
12. David Lewis, 'Mill and Milquetoast', *Papers in Ethics and Social Philosophy* (Cambridge: Cambridge University Press, 2000), pp. 159–186. After criticizing Mill, Lewis goes on to set forth an ingenious argument for toleration of his own. It deserves the kind of detailed examination I do not have space enough in this paper to give it.
13. Avishai Margalit, 'The Ring: On Religious Pluralism', *Toleration: An Elusive Virtue*, ed. David Heyd (Princeton, NJ: Princeton University Press, 1996), p. 148. Christians who accept the traditional doctrine of the Incarnation will doubtless hasten to point out the disanalogy between Jesus, who by their lights is God, and Moses and Muhammad, who are not.
14. The papers collected in the volume edited by Mendus that is cited in note 10 above and in the volume edited by Heyd that is cited in note 13 above provide a good indication of the range of issues covered in recent philosophical discussions of toleration. A brief survey that connects some of these issues to theistic religions is contained in Edward Langerak, 'Theism and Toleration', *A Companion to Philosophy of Religion*, eds. Philip L. Quinn and Charles Taliaferro (Oxford: Blackwell, 1997), pp. 514–521.
15. My summary of the defense in based primarily on William P. Alston, 'Religious Diversity and Perceptual Knowledge of God', *Faith and Philosophy* 5 (1988): 433–448. This paper is reprinted in the volume edited by Quinn and Meeker that is cited in note 2 above. I have also made use of William P. Alston, *Perceiving God* (Ithaca and London: Cornell University Press, 1991), especially Chapter 7 whose title is 'The Problem of Religious Diversity' and Chapter 8 whose title is 'The Place of Experience in the Grounds of Religious Belief'.
16. Alston, *Perceiving God*, p. 274.
17. William J. Wainwright, 'Religious Language, Religious Experience, and Religious Pluralism', *The Rationality of Belief and the Plurality of Faith*, ed. Thomas D. Senor (Ithaca and London: Cornell University Press, 1995), p. 188. A part of this paper is reprinted, with the title 'Religious Experience and Religious Pluralism', in the volume edited by Quinn and Meeker that is cited in note 2 above.

18. I spell out the argument summarized in this paragraph in Philip L. Quinn, 'Towards Thinner Theologies: Hick and Alston on Religious Diversity', *International Journal for Philosophy of Religion* 38 (1995): 145–164. This paper is reprinted in the volume edited by Quinn and Meeker that is cited in note 2 above.
19. Alston, *Perceiving God*, p. 306.
20. My summary of his position is based on Alvin Plantinga, 'A Defense of Religious Exclusivism', *The Rationality of Belief and the Plurality of Faith*, ed. Thomas D. Senor (Ithaca and London: Cornell University Press, 1995), pp. 191–215. This paper is reprinted in the volume edited by Quinn and Meeker that is cited in note 2 above. Basically the same view is repeated in Alvin Plantinga, *Warranted Christian Belief* (New York and Oxford: Oxford University Press, 2000), pp. 456–457.
21. The book by Plantinga cited in note 20 above, *Warranted Christian Belief*, is the third volume in the trilogy. Its predecessors are Alvin Plantinga, *Warrant: The Current Debate* (New York and Oxford: Oxford University Press, 1993) and Alvin Plantinga, *Warrant and Proper Function* (New York and Oxford: Oxford University Press, 1993).
22. For a useful overview of Bayle's philosophical thought, see Charles Larmore, 'Pierre Bayle', *Routledge Encyclopedia of Philosophy*, Vol. 1, ed. Edward Craig (London and New York: Routledge, 1998), pp. 672–677.
23. Pierre Bayle, *Philosophical Commentary*, trans. Amie Godman Tannenbaum (New York: Peter Lang, 1987). Page references to this work will be made parenthetically in the body of my text. This volume also contains a lengthy interpretive essay by the translator that contains helpful historical background information.
24. For thorough discussion of this doctrine, see John Kilcullen, *Sincerity and Truth* (Oxford: Clarendon Press, 1988), especially Essay II whose title is 'Bayle on the Rights of Conscience'. For reflections on the limits of Baylean toleration, see John Christian Laursen, 'Baylean Liberalism: Tolerance Requires Nontolerance', *Beyond the Persecuting Society*, eds. John Christian Laursen and Cary J. Nederman (Philadelphia: University of Pennsylvania Press, 1998), pp. 197–215.
25. Pierre Bayle, *De la tolérance*, ed. Jean-Michel Gros (Paris: Presses Pocket, 1992), p. 98. I have used this French edition of the *Philosophical Commentary* to check the English translation where necessary.
26. For discussion of the epistemic status of the premise of a clearly valid ontological argument, see Alvin Plantinga, *The Nature of Necessity* (Oxford: Clarendon Press, 1974), especially Chapter 10 whose title is 'God and Necessity'.
27. For discussion of the epistemic status of the premises of a clearly valid cosmological argument, see William L. Rowe, *The Cosmological Argument* (Princeton, NJ: Princeton University Press, 1975), especially Chapter 6 whose title is 'The Cosmological Argument as a Justification for Belief in God'.
28. Bayle, *De la tolérance*, p. 99.
29. Waldron, op. cit., p. 85.
30. Bayle, *De la tolérance*, p. 320.
31. For a recent discussion of the *akedah* within the context of a divine command theory of obligation, see Robert M. Adams. *Finite and Infinite Goods* (New York and Oxford: Oxford University Press, 1999), especially Chapter 12 whose title is 'Abraham's Dilemma'. And for the classic presentation of the teleological suspension of the ethical, see Søren Kierkegaard, *Fear and Trembling*, trans. Walter Lowrie (Princeton, NJ: Princeton University Press, 1968), especially Problem 1 whose title is 'Is There Such a Thing as a Teleological Suspension of the Ethical?'

32. Kant, *Religion*, p. 202. Hereafter I shall make page references to this work parenthetically in the body of my text.
33. 'What you doubt, do not do!' As an editorial note points out, Kant is quoting Pliny out of context and fails to represent his thought accurately.
34. Kant's inquisitor thus turns out to be, so to speak, among the targets of Bayle's arguments, since *compellite intrare* is, of course, Latin for the 'compel them to come in' of Luke 14:23.
35. Immanuel Kant, *The Conflict of the Faculties*, in Kant, *Religion and Rational Theology*, trans. Allen W. Wood and George di Giovanni (Cambridge: Cambridge University Press, 1996), p. 283. Actually, though Wood and di Giovanni are responsible for all the other translations in this volume, the translation of *Conflict* is by Mary J. Gregor and Robert Anchor.
36. Kant, *Conflict*, p. 283.
37. For arguments in support of the conclusion that there is an actual case in which someone was epistemically entitled to believe God had spoken to her, see Nicholas Wolterstorff, *Divine Discourse* (Cambridge: Cambridge University Press, 1995), Chapter 15 whose title is 'Are We Entitled?'
38. On Bayle, see Elisabeth Labrousse, *Pierre Bayle*, 2 vols. (The Hague: Martinus Nijhoff, 1963–1964), especially the second volume whose subtitle is *Hétérodoxie et Rigorisme*. On Kant, see John E. Hare, *The Moral Gap* (Oxford: Clarendon Press, 1996), especially Chapter 1, Section c, whose title is 'The Christian Seriousness of Kant'.
39. Robert M. Adams. 'Reading the Silences, Questioning the Terms', *Journal of Religious Ethics* 28/2 (2000): 282.
40. Was Kant influenced, directly or indirectly, by Bayle's work on toleration? Karl Ameriks, the expert I consulted on this question, has not been able to provide me with an answer, which inclines me to the belief that the answer is not known.

Address for correspondence: Professor Philip Quinn, Department of Philosophy, University of Notre Dame, Notre Dame IN 46556, USA
Phone: (219)631–6471; Fax: (219)631–8209

Theological determinism and the problem of evil: Are Arminians any better off?

WILLIAM J. WAINWRIGHT
University of Wisconsin – Milwaukee

One of the more striking features of the revival of analytic philosophy of religion that began in the 1960s has been a renewed interest in the scholastics and in seventeenth and eighteenth century philosophical theology. Norman Kretzmann's, Eleonore Stump's, and Scott MacDonald's work on Aquinas, Alfred Fredosso's and Thomas Flint's discussions of Molina, William Rowe's use of Samuel Clarke, and Robert Adams' examination of Leibniz are examples. There appear to be two reasons for the new interest in our predecessors. The first was the discovery that issues central to the debates of the 1960s and 1970s had already been examined with a depth and sophistication missing from most nineteenth and early twentieth century discussions of the same problems. The impact of the recovery of Ockham and Molina on the freedom-foreknowledge debate is an important and well known example. The second is this. A significant number of analytic philosophers of religion are practicing Christian or Jewish theists. Anselm, Aquinas, Maimonides, Malebranche, Leibniz, or Clarke are important models for these theists both because of the broad similarity between their approaches to philosophy and that of contemporary analytic philosophers of religion and because they were self-consciously Jewish or Christian. A conviction of the truth and splendor of Judaism or Christianity pervades their writings.

My own work on Jonathan Edwards is part of this trend. In what follows I shall elucidate and critically examine Edwards' views on an important contemporary problem. By doing so, I hope both to add to our understanding of America's greatest philosophical theologian and to contribute to contemporary debates.

Edwards' theological determinism aggravates the problem of evil in three ways. It appears to make God the author of sin, exposes Him to charges of insincerity, and raises questions about His justice. I shall focus on the first two of these problems, arguing that, while Edwards' response to them isn't fully adequate, he is right on one very important point. Arminians are exposed to much the same sort of difficulties that Calvinists are.

I

The Arminians argue that if there is 'a sure and infallible connection between' God's actions and forbearances and sinful human actions, then 'God is the *author* of sin'.[1] Edwards responds to this objection in three ways.

A

Edwards' first point is that God does not cause sin in virtue of any '*positive agency* or *efficiency*' but only by '*permission*'. An example illustrates the distinction. The sun is the positive or efficient 'cause of the lightsomeness and warmth of the atmosphere, and brightness of gold and diamonds' but, while 'darkness and frost, in the night' are 'necessarily consequent' on the sun's withdrawal, the sun 'is not the proper cause, efficient or producer of them'. Similarly, sin is an inevitable consequence of God's withdrawal; it necessarily 'arises from the withholding of his [gracious] action and energy'. Nevertheless, God is not sin's *positive* or *efficient* cause. It is therefore misleading to say that He is sin's author (FW 403-4). The doctrine of original sin, for instance, doesn't make God 'who is the *Author* of our nature ... the *author* of a sinful corruption', for our corruption is not due to 'some *positive influence*', to something '*infused*' into human nature, to 'a *taint, tincture,* or *infection*' but, rather, 'to the withdrawing of a special divine influence' which leaves the 'natural principles of self-love, natural appetite, etc., ... without the government of superior divine principles'.[2]

It isn't clear that this will do. 'A permitted B to do x' not only entails that A's non-interference was a necessary condition of B's doing x. It also entails that A's actions and forbearances weren't *causally sufficient conditions* of B's doing it.[3] Now Edwards believes that God's actions and forbearances are both a necessary *and* causally sufficient condition of sin. If he is correct, God does more than (merely) permit sin. Edwards accuses his opponents of misusing the expression 'author of sin'. Arminians can reply that he misuses 'permits'.

Yet even if it is misleading to say that God only permits sin, it may still be inappropriate to describe God as sin's *author* if God isn't its *positive* or *efficient* cause. And this seems to be Edwards' point: x is the author of y's being P only if x brings about y's being P by acting on y, or bringing some positive influence to bear upon y. Forbearance, inaction, and so on, aren't 'proper causes' since they do not involved 'positive agency or efficiency'. 'If the sun were the proper *cause* of cold and darkness, it would be the *fountain* of these things, as it is the fountain of light and heat: and then something might be argued from the nature of cold and darkness, to a likeness of nature in the sun'. But it is absurd to argue that 'because it is always dark when the sun is gone, and never dark when the sun is present, that therefore all darkness is from the sun, and that his disk and beams must needs be black'. Similarly, 'it would be strange arguing indeed, because men never commit sin, but only when God leaves 'em *to themselves* ... that therefore their sin is not *from themselves*, but from God, and so, that God must be a sinful being' (FW 404).

Edwards' comparison is specious, however. If the sun were a *voluntary agent* which deliberately chose to withdraw its beams, then it *would* be appropriate to conclude that the sun is the author of cold and darkness, and that they are from the sun, that is, from its preference for, or inclination toward, cold and darkness (in certain places at certain times). For a voluntary agent is the author[4] of those things that it knows causally depend upon its choices for their existence or non-existence. Given Edwards' premises, Judas's betrayal of Jesus depends entirely upon God's choice. That He effects the betrayal by withholding influences rather than exerting them seems irrelevant. Furthermore, Edwards believes that choosing something involves liking it, or loving it, or being inclined toward it in some respect or other. A person's choices express her desires, inclinations, and preferences and so provide some indication of her nature.[5] Given Edwards' premises, then, it *does* seem appropriate to argue from sin's existence to the nature of its divine cause.[6]

B

At one point, Edwards suggests that 'God is the author of sin' can be construed in two ways: (1) as 'God is "the sinner, the agent, or actor of sin, or the *doer* of a wicked thing",' or (2) as 'God is the permitter ... of sin; and at the same time a disposer of the state of events, in such a manner, for wise, holy and most excellent ends and purposes, that sin, if it be permitted ... will most certainly and infallibly follow' (FW 399).

God is indeed sin's author in the second sense. But 'author of sin,' 'is apt to carry' the first sense 'by use and custom' and, in *that* sense, He is not its author (FW 399). Why not?

To be an author of sin in the first sense one must meet two conditions. One must be the '*agent*' or '*actor*' or '*doer*' of the deed, and one's performance of that deed must be sinful. Edwards doesn't clearly distinguish the two but it is important for him to do so. For consider Judas's betrayal of Jesus. Edwards believes that God decreed the betrayal for wise and holy ends. As an occasionalist, he also believes that God is the only true cause. It is thus difficult to see how Edwards can avoid concluding that God is the real agent or actor or doer of Judas's deed. (Suppose that John steals money from the petty cash drawer. We later discover that he was acting under the influence of a master hypnotist who had implanted the desire and intention to steal in John's psyche. Wouldn't we be tempted to say that the real author or perpetrator of the theft was *the hypnotist*? And wouldn't it be *reasonable to say this*?) Edwards can argue, however, that God's 'deed' isn't sinful or wicked because He 'permits' the betrayal for wise and holy ends. That is, given Edwards' premises, God appears to be the author of Judas's act of betrayal[7] and in that sense, 'the agent, or actor of sin, or the doer of a wicked thing'. Nevertheless, because what God does is not wicked, God isn't '*the sinner*'.

But isn't it *wrong* for God to 'commit thefts', 'deceive', and so on, even though He may perform these actions to maximize good? Not clearly. For an action to be sinful, 'there must be one of these things belonging to it: either [1] it must be a thing *unfit* and *unsuitable* in its own nature [such as a lie or act of injustice]; or [2] it must have a bad tendency', that is, it must, when viewed together with its attendant circumstances and consequences, be bad all things considered; 'or [3] it must proceed from an *evil disposition*, and be done for an evil end' (FW 410). Judged by these standards, God's ordination of evil isn't sinful. 'If we consider only those things which belong to the event [the crucifixion] as it proceeded from his murderers, and are comprehended within the compass of the affair considered as *their* act, *their* principles, dispositions, views and aims; so it was one of the most heinous things that was ever done . . .: but consider it, as it was willed and ordered of God, in the extent of *his* designs and views, it was the most admirable and glorious of all events' (FW 406, my emphasis).

In view of the crucifixions's 'circumstances and consequences', it is best, all things considered, and so is 'not of a *bad tendency*' (FW 412). In addition, God orders events so that the crucifixion will occur because 'he certainly knows it would, all things considered, be best' that it should occur (FW 411). Since 'what is aimed at is good', God's act does not proceed '*from any evil disposition or aim*' (FW 412).

Is it intrinsically unfitting ('a thing unfit and unsuitable in its own nature') for God to permit evil that good may come? Edwards thinks not. 'Permit evil that good may come' may be an inappropriate or evil maxim for those who are deficient in wisdom and goodness and are therefore liable to misjudge the consequences of their actions or be misled by their corrupt dispositions, or for beings who *are* wise and good but lack appropriate authority. Neither is true in God's case. God is infinitely wise and perfectly good. He is also the world's lord and owner. There is no reason, then, to suppose that it is intrinsically unfitting *for God* to act on the maxim (and thus order things so that the crucifixion occurs).[8]

C

Edwards' most interesting contention is that Arminians who accept foreknowledge face the same sort of difficulties that he does since, in their view, 'God does determine beforehand to permit all the sin that does come to pass', and 'certainly knows that if he does permit it, it will come to pass'. In other words, they too believe that God has taken steps which He knew would inevitably lead to sin. There is therefore neither more nor less reason to suppose that God is the author of sin upon the Reformed view than upon that of the Arminians. I believe that Edwards is party right about this and partly mistaken.

If libertarianism is true, God can't determine what agents will freely do, and so cannot determine the truth of subjunctive conditionals which describe how those agents would freely act if they were created.[9] Because Judas was free with respect to his betrayal of Christ, God could neither make it true that Judas would freely betray Christ if both he and Jesus were created, nor could He make it true that Judas would freely refrain from doing so if both were created. It is contingently true that Judas would freely betray Christ if he and Jesus were created. But this fact is given. God doesn't constitute it, or bring it about. It is true that, in creating Jesus and Judas, God knowingly brought about a world in which Christ was freely betrayed by Judas. Whether God could bring this world about, however, depended on a fact over which He had no control, namely, that if Jesus and Judas were created, Judas would freely betray Christ. Given the truth of this subjunctive conditional, God could either bring about a world in which 'Judas's free betrayal of Christ' is exemplified or a world in which it isn't. He could bring about the first by creating Judas (and Christ). He could bring about the second by not creating Judas or not creating Christ. If 'Judas will freely betray Christ if he and Jesus are created' had been false, however, God could not have brought about a world in which 'Judas's free betrayal of Christ' is exemplified. By contrast, in Edwards' system, God *determines* the truth of 'If Judas and Jesus were created, Judas would betray Christ'. That Judas will do so if he and Jesus are created is not a given over which God has no control, and which limits His options. It is a fact that God constitutes and could have constituted otherwise.[10] In Edwards' universe, God is *fully* in control of what persons do. In the Arminian's universe, He isn't.

In Edwards' system, God 'permits' sin by withholding gracious influences from persons whose sin is causally inevitable if those influences are withheld. In these circumstances, God's forbearance is a causally sufficient condition of sin. (Just as when I remove a lamp from a room in certain familiar circumstances, darkness is causally inevitable; my action is a causally sufficient condition of the ensuing darkness.)

In the Arminian's system, God permits sin by refusing to limit the freedom of persons whom He foresees will, if they remain free, choose to sin. Given that the persons in question will freely sin if He refuses to interfere, God's permission is a *sufficient* condition of their sinning. But it is not, I think, *causally* sufficient. It seems wrong to say that God has *produced* their sin, and misleading to say that he has *brought it about*.

Suppose someone constructs a machine which randomly turns on either a green or red light. (So that the light is, for example, first red, then green, then green again, then red once more, then green, and so on. The order is genuinely random. Nothing in the machine's mechanism guarantees that the light will flesh in a particular order.) Suppose further that, having consulted a clairvoyant, I learn that if I were to turn the machine on at t1, the light would flash green. I turn it on at t1 and the light flashes green. Since it is true that if anyone were to turn the machine on at t1, the light would flesh green, my turning the machine on at t1 is a sufficient condition of the light's flashing green. Nevertheless, it seems wrong to say that my action was a *causally* sufficient condition of the occurrence, or that I *produced* it. For this suggests that the light's flashing green was not genuinely random but the inevitable outcome of a chain of causes initiated by my action. Although one *could* say that I brought the occurrence about, it would be less misleading to say that I brought about a state of affairs consisting in the machine's being turned on at t1 which I knew would be followed by the state of affairs consisting in the light's flashing green. (This is less misleading because the first state of affairs isn't a [sufficient] *cause* of the second.)

What is at issue is the truth of

(A) If a person does x or brings about x (is the 'author' of x) and knows that x is a sufficient condition of y, then he does y or brings about y (is the 'author' of y).

(A) is plausible when x is a causally sufficient condition of y, that is, when doing x or bringing it about is (when taken together with boundary conditions) the first member of a chain of causally sufficient conditions eventuating in y. It is less plausible when doing x or bringing it about is the first member of a chain of conditions which are causally necessary but not causally sufficient for y's occurrence. It is least plausible when y is a random occurrence or contra-causally free decision. For authorship implies *control*, and breaks in the causal chain diminish an agent's control over the outcome.[11]

Since the Gods of the Calvinist and Arminian differ with respect to the amount of control they exercise over human behavior, their situations relevantly differ. As a result, it isn't clear that if the former is the author of sin, so too is the latter.

D

Is the dispute over authorship significant? It might seem that it isn't. I have argued that the God of the Calvinists is the author of sin while the God of the Arminians is not. Edwards is nevertheless right about one very important thing. A person is responsible or accountable for events of which she is not the author if she was able to prevent their occurrence and knew that they would occur if she did not interfere. It follows that since God knew that Judas would betray Christ if he and Jesus were created, and created them, He is responsible or accountable for Judas's betrayal even if he isn't the author of that betrayal. That God isn't the *author* of sin doesn't absolve Him of *moral responsibility* for it.

Yet isn't something significant at stake in this dispute after all? Compare someone who commits a murder with someone else who could have prevented it but did not do so. Although *both* are responsible, and *both* are guilty, we tend to regard the murderer as more blameworthy.[12] That a person isn't the *author* of an action for which she is (partly) responsible seems to reduce her culpability. If it does, Arminians may have an easier time exonerating God of blame than Calvinists.

But does it? The idea that it is less blameworthy to permit evils that one could prevent than to initiate them is closely tied to the doctrine of double effect. According to this doctrine, there is a morally relevant difference between the harmful consequences of our actions which we intend and those we merely foresee.[13] The distinction is notoriously hard to draw with precision but, by examining two representative versions, I shall attempt to show that the Principle of Double Effect (PDE) is of dubious help to the Arminian.

The version that derives from Aquinas asserts that actions with mixed good and evil effects are permissible provided:

(1) 'That the action itself from its very object be good or at least indifferent;
[2] That only the good [or "first"] effect and not the evil [or "second"] effect be intended;
[3] That the good effect be not produced by means of the evil [or "second"] effect'; and
(4) 'That there be a proportionally grave reason for permitting the evil effect'.[14]

More recently Phillipa Foot has argued 'that there is a morally significant difference between agency of type (i) and agency of type (ii):

(i) initiating or sustaining a harmful causal sequence [setting it in motion or keeping it going "when it would otherwise have stopped"]
(ii) (a) allowing or enabling a harmful causal sequence to run its course [doing "nothing to stop it when one is in a position to do so" or "removing an obstacle that would stop it"]

(b) diverting a harmful causal sequence [by, e.g., "changing the direction of a flood"].'

When forced to choose between actions of type (i) or between actions of type (ii), it is morally permitted to choose the least harmful action. If one is forced to choose between a type (i) and type (ii) action, however, one is 'morally required' to choose the latter even when doing so results in more harm.[15]

It might seem that the PDE can be used to show that the Arminian's God is less blameworthy than that of the Calvinists, for the latter *initiates* a harmful chain of events by (for example) *decreeing* that Adam falls. In the Arminian view, however, Adam is contra-causally free. Furthermore, God knows that, if He doesn't interfere, Adam will freely sin. The alternatives facing Him are therefore these:

(A) To respect Adam's autonomy by not interfering, thus allowing Adam to sin
(B) To prevent Adam from sinning, thus forestalling both the sin and its harmful consequences.

What should God do? Action A is a type (ii)(a) action. What about B? B *initiates* a harmful causal sequence by preventing Adam from exercising his freedom, thus destroying (or at least undermining) Adam's autonomy. Therefore, given Foot's view, God is morally required to choose A over B. (And, by extension, is less blameworthy if He does so than Calvin's God who, in similar circumstances, *initiates* a harmful causal chain).

A similar result can be obtained by using Thomas's version of the principle. For, arguably, action B uses the destruction of Adam's autonomy as a *means* to the prevention of sin and its harmful consequences. In action A, on the other hand, the sin resulting from God's permission isn't directly aimed at (isn't an *end* of God's action). Nor is Adam's sin a means to the good aimed at (the preservation of Adam's freedom). Given that the good aimed at is great enough, so that there is a 'proportionally grave reason for permitting the evil effect', A is permitted while B is not.

I suggest that considerations like these have tempted Arminians to believe that their God is less blameworthy than the God of the Calvinists. I shall now argue that this reasoning is defective.

In the scenario I have just described at least one contra-causally free agent (namely, Adam) *already exists*, and the alternatives confronting God are: allow Adam to exercise his freedom (in which case he sins) or interfere with its exercise (thus impairing his autonomy). But these aren't the relevant choices.

What are they? The alternatives God confronts when deciding what sort of world to create. Suppose that the Arminians are right. If they are (1) libertarianism is true; (2) there are true subjunctive conditionals describing how possible autonomous agents would freely behave if they were created; (3) these 'counterfactuals of freedom' include 'If Adam were created, Adam would freely sin'; and (4) God knows all true propositions (and hence all true counterfactuals of freedom). Under these conditions the relevant choices are (very roughly) these:

(A) Not to create free beings (by either not creating rational agents at all or not creating rational agents that are free in the libertarian sense)
(B) To create free beings knowing that at least some of them will freely sin
(C) To create a set of free beings every member of which is such that it would not freely sin if that set were instantiated.[16]

Now Arminians think that God has chosen B. Assuming that more overall good is produced by choosing B, is B permissible? It might seem so. (1) The creation of contra-causally free beings who can respond to God's love by freely loving Him in turn is, arguably, good 'from its very object'. (2) The harmful effect (sinful actions) isn't directly aimed at (isn't the end God has in view in creating free agents). (3) Nor are sinful actions *means* to the existence of free beings. Finally, (4) in the Christian view, at least, the good effects of God's action vastly outweigh its harmful ones. Given that the latter are necessary by-products of an overwhelming good (the creation of this world),[17] there is a 'proportionally grave reason for permitting' them. So is the Arminian, then, better off than the Calvinist? It is not clear that he is.

To see this consider how the Calvinian God's creative decree fares when assessed by the same criteria. The creation of rational agents who are (only) free in the compatibilist's sense is good (or at least indifferent), if only because their existence is necessary for that of the elect. So the first condition is met. But so too, apparently, are the third and fourth. Sinful actions aren't a *means* to the existence of rational agents with compatibilist freedom (or to the existence of the elect). And, in the view of Edwards and other Calvinists, the good consequences of God's decree swamp the harmful ones. The second condition is *not* met, however, for, in Edwards' version of Calvinism, at least, everything, including Adam's sin, is an immediate effect of divine volition. Of course sin is not aimed at for its own sake but only as a necessary ingredient in the best of all possible worlds. The fact remains that it is intended. And this suggests that, in spite of appearances, the third criterion isn't really met either. For while sin isn't a means to the existence of rational creatures with compatibilist freedom or to the existence of the elect, it *is* a means to something else God directly aims at, namely, the existence of the best possible world.

But isn't something similar true of the Arminian's God? Sinful free choices aren't a means to the existence of contra-causally free beings capable of responding to God's love or to the existence of contra-causally free beings who actually do so (the elect). But if God's ultimate aim includes the redemption of the world through Christ's atonement, as at least some Christians believe, then sin *is* a means to *that* end,[18] and not just an unfortunate by-product of something else God aims at. The same result follows if (as many theodicists assume) God's aim is the existence of the best creatable world, and that world contains contra-causally free agents who sometimes freely sin. Since sinful free choices are *part* of that world, it is difficult to see why God's creation of free agents whom He knew would sin if they were created shouldn't be regarded as a deliberately chosen means to its existence. If it is, then neither the second nor third conditions for morally permissible actions with mixed effects are clearly met. Or, to use Foot's language, in creating free agents whom He knows will freely sin if they are created, God knowingly 'initiates a harmful causal sequence' in order to satisfy His desire to instantiate the best creatable world. Isn't this so near to Edwards' Calvinism as to make no difference?[19]

Be this as it may, there is another and greater difficulty. In the Arminian's scenario, God's options included not creating contra-causally free agents and (probably) creating a world containing contra-causally free agents which, while less good than our own, is such that its inhabitants never abuse their freedom. That is, two courses of action were open to God which, while producing less overall value than the consequences of the action he has taken, had no harmful effects.[20] Since the PDE comes into play only when all alternatives involve harmful consequences, the Arminian can't appeal to it to show that God's permission of the sinful choices which He knew would occur is morally permissible.

I conclude that the PDE can't be used to support the intuition that the Arminian's God is less blameworthy than the God of the Calvinists. Unless the intuition can be supported on other grounds, Edwards is right on the main point. The Arminian isn't much better off than the Calvinist with respect to God's alleged authorship of human sin.

II

There seems to be a 'repugnance in supposing it may be the secret will of God, that his ordination and permission of events should be such that it shall be a certain consequence, that a thing never will come to pass; which yet it is man's duty to do, and so God's *preceptive* will, that he should do'. God appears to be insincere in commanding, 'counseling, inviting and using persuasions' in cases in which He has disposed things so that what He counsels and commands will not come to be pass. (FW 415) Edwards responds to this objection in two ways.

He first point out that God's 'disposing will' and 'preceptive will' are consistent because they have different objects. The object of God's disposing will is what most effectively contributes to the good of the whole and is thus best all things considered. Commands, 'counsels and invitations [on the other hand] are manifestations of God's preceptive will, or of what God loves, and what is in itself, and as man's act, agreeable to his heart' (FW 415). God can consistently 'love' (or approve of) a sinful act considered together with its consequences and attendant circumstances, and yet 'hate' (or disapprove of) it considered in itself. The first attitude expresses itself in the decrees by which God brings things into being and disposes the course of events, the second in God's commandments.

But the 'main seeming difficulty in the case is this: that God in counseling, inviting and persuading, makes a shew of aiming at, seeking and using endeavors for the thing exhorted and persuaded to; whereas 'tis impossible for any intelligent being truly to seek, or use endeavors for a thing, which he at the same time knows most perfectly will not come to pass' (FW 416). The difficulty, in other words, is this:

(1) An end, or aim, or point is built into the description of certain activities (fighting a war, for example, or playing chess, or writing a book). In particular, an end, or aim, or point is built into our understanding of commanding, counseling, and exhorting. The point of commanding someone to shut the door is to get her to shut it, and the point of moral commands, counsels, and exhortations is to incite those to whom they are addressed to 'repentance and holiness of life'.

(2) Someone who engages in activities of this type for some other reason but does not make it clear that she is doing so, and thereby knowingly misleads others, is guilty of deception or insincerity.

(3) If a person knows that an end will not to be achieved by an activity, she cannot engage in that activity for that end.

(4) God knows (for example) that He has disposed things so that the commands, counsels, and exhortations that He addresses to Judas will to be ineffective, but

(5) God did not reveal this to Judas. It follows that

(6) God cannot address commands, counsels and exhortations to Judas in order to incite him to repentance and holiness of life (from 3 and 4), and

(7) Judas (and others) reasonably assumed that these commands, counsels, and exhortations were addressed to him for this purpose. (From 1 and 5.) Therefore,

(8) God can to be accused of deception or insincerity. (From 2, 6, and 7.)

Edwards responds to this objection by arguing that the Arminians are also exposed to it. Although they believe that God doesn't determine sinful actions, they do think He foreknows them and therefore commands, counsels, invites, and exhorts some whom He knows will not respond to His commands, counsels, invitations, and exhortations. If the Calvinist's God is exposed to charges of deception, then so too is the God of the Arminians.

An Arminian might reply to Edwards by distinguishing between

(3a) If a person knows that E *will* not be achieved by doing x, he cannot do x in order to achieve E, and

(3b) If a person knows that E *cannot* be achieved by doing x, he cannot do x in order to achieve E,

and arguing that whereas 3a is false, 3b is true. Now, Edwards is committed to the proposition that God knows that (given His own decrees), Judas *must* die in mortal sin. He is thus also committed to 6. Arminians, on the other hand, are only committed to the claim that God knows that Judas *will* die in mortal sin. Hence, they aren't committed to 6. So while the Calvinist is exposed to the difficulty articulated by our argument, the Arminian is not.

Is the Arminian's response sound? There are several reasons for thinking that it isn't. In the first place, Edwards can reply that it was *not* impossible in the 'vulgar' (that is, ordinary) sense for Judas to respond to God's call.[21] It thus was *not* necessary that Judas die in mortal sin, and so God did not *know* that Judas must die in mortal sin. The Arminian is therefore mistaken in claiming that Edwards' commitment to the necessity of Judas's sinning commits him to 6.

But second, and more important, it is not clear that 3a *is* false. Of course, I sometimes *say* things like 'Although I know she won't take my advice, I will attempt to persuade her'. But I can do this, I think, only because I am not *certain* that she will disregard my advice – because I believe that there is at least an outside chance that she will heed it, and therefore do not really *know* that she won't. Since 3a appears to be true, and the Arminian believes that God knew that Judas would die in mortal sin, he is as exposed to our argument's conclusion as the Calvinist is.[22]

Yet can't the Arminian claim to be better off than the Calvinist in at least one respect? The most serious problem, he might say, is not created by the fact that God employs means which he knows will prove ineffective. It is created by the fact that, in the Calvinist's view, God sometimes commands, counsels, invites, and exhorts while at the same time *determining* that the person whom He commands, counsels, invites and exhorts will not respond to His call. For suppose that I not only offer good moral advice to my daughter knowing that it will be futile but have also knowingly brought her up in a way that makes it certain that she will not take it. I will be accused of deception and worse. And yet, on Edwards' premises, this is precisely how God acts. *This* problem is not a problem for the Arminians but *is* one for the Calvinists.

Arminians *are* faced with a similar problem, however. For suppose that even though I haven't shaped my daughter's character in a way that ensures she will ignore my advice, I not only offer good moral advice to her knowing that it will be futile but have placed her in a situation in which I knew she wouldn't heed it. Even though I don't *determine* that she won't heed my advice, isn't my conduct in this case, too, deceptive or worse? Yet Arminians believe that God's conduct is similar[23] since they think that He has deliberately created Judas in circumstances in which He knew that His advice, exhortations, and so on, would be futile. The Arminians' problem may be somewhat less severe than the Calvinists' (for, in their view, God doesn't determine Judas's failure to repent). Even so, it is similar and serious.

III

Calvinism appears to imply that God is the author of sin and that His counsels, exhortations, and commands are sometimes deceptive. I have argued that Edwards is correct in thinking that Arminianism has similar implications. Edwards' theological determinism creates a third problem, however, which may not be a difficulty for Arminians. Like other traditional Christians, Edwards thinks that God justly inflicts an infinite punishment upon those who die unrepentant. Theological determinism makes this claim especially problematic. In Edwards' view, God inflicts infinite punishment on persons whom He has *made* wicked. Edwards is therefore forced to defend not only the claim that infinite punishment is a fitting recompense for human wickedness but also two further claims – that those whom God has made vessels of wrath are genuinely accountable, and that one can justly punish a person for an offense which one has deliberately caused him to commit. I have discussed the first claim elsewhere.[24] The second will only be acceptable to compatibilists who (like Edwards) believe that determinism and human freedom are consistent. Edwards' third claim is indefensible. Not only is it counter-intuitive, there are no good arguments in its favor.[25] It is particularly important to notice that Edwards' second claim does not entail his third. If those whom God has made wicked are responsible and guilty, they can be justly punished. It does not follow that they can be justly punished *by God*.

Notes

1. *Freedom of the Will*, ed. Paul Ramsey (New Haven: Yale University Press, 1957) hereafter FW, p. 398.
2. *Original Sin*, ed. Clyde A. Holbrook (New Haven: Yale University Press, 1970), hereafter OS, pp. 380–381. There may be a problem here. If humanity's natural and 'innocent'

principles inevitably lead to sin when supernatural principles are withdrawn, then it would seem that, *regardless of the fall and its consequences*, human nature is bad or at least flawed. This casts doubt upon the goodness of God's creation. The most obvious way to avoid this conclusion would be to suppose that supernatural and divine principles are not superadded gifts but an intrinsic component of humanity's original nature. But Edwards refuses to take this route. The divine principle is 'above those principles that are essentially implied in, or necessarily resulting from, and inseparably connected with, *mere human nature*' (OS 381f). As he explains in a footnote, although a divine principle is 'necessary to the perfection and well being of the human nature', it is not necessary 'to the constitution of it' or 'to its being' (OS 381n). It is useful to remember that 'essence' can be understood in two ways: (1) as those features that are logically necessary and sufficient for being a certain kind of thing, and (2) as those features that are logically necessary and sufficient for being a good thing of that kind. (The second includes the first, since it is impossible to be a *good x* without being *an x*.) In the Platonic tradition, 'essence' is understood in its second sense. (A thing's essence is more or less equated with its Idea or form, and an Idea or form is both a universal *and model*.) In that sense, supernatural principles are part of our essence. Edwards, however, understands 'essence' in the first (and modern) sense and, in that sense, supernatural principles are *not* part of our essence. Although one must be governed by supernatural principles to be a good human being, one needn't be governed by them to be human.
3. 'Entails' may be too strong. Nevertheless, it is misleading to use a weaker description when a stronger is appropriate. (Thus, I mislead my hearers if I see a man lurking in the bushes but respond to the question 'What's making that noise?' by replying 'There's an animal in the shrubbery'.) If we have reason to believe that A's behavior was a causally sufficient condition of B's doing x, it is misleading to say that A permitted B to do x instead of saying that he *caused* B to do x. Even if 'A permitted B to do x' doesn't *entail* that B's decision was also necessary, it contextually implies it.
4. Or one of the authors. (Cf. 'I am one of the authors of her misfortune since I failed to prevent it when I could have done so'.)
5. *Only* an indication, however. People sometimes act out of character. Even when they don't, the significance of a single act, or a few isolated actions, can be misinterpreted. A person's behavior must be judged as a whole.
6. Though not necessarily to a *likeness* of nature.
7. But is He the *betrayer* (as the master hypnotist is the real thief)? Not clearly. It is true that (by means of Judas) God leads Jesus into the hands of his enemies. Yet, unlike Judas, He isn't *disloyal* to Jesus.
8. Doesn't this defense presuppose a consequentialist ethic? It does not. That Edwards thinks that certain actions are intrinsically fitting or unfitting isn't sufficient to show that he isn't a consequentialist since consequentialists can include these actions in their list of goods to be maximized and evils to be minimized. But neither is the fact that divine and human virtue is essentially true benevolence, a disposition to maximize the good, sufficient to show that he is a consequentialist. For the goodness of the disposition is not determined by the consequences of its possession or exercise but, rather, by its intrinsic excellence. Edwards' ethics is, in fact, a virtue ethics.
9. If God could determine that if A were created, A would freely do x, then, since God can determine that A is created, God could determine that A will freely do x – which is incoherent if libertarianism is true. That there are true subjunctive conditionals of this kind (so-called 'counterfactuals of freedom') is, of course, controversial. The knowledgeable reader will also notice that I am oversimplifying since the relevant antecedents must

include not only references to A's creation but to the circumstances in which he finds himself at the moment he is called upon to freely decide to either do x or not do it. The argument that follows does not depend upon this simplification, however.
10. He constitutes it by making its antecedent and consequent true in both the actual world and in the possible worlds that are relevantly similar to the actual world.
11. In my first example, the relevant outcomes are the state of affairs consisting in the room's darkness and the state of affairs consisting in the room's illumination. The agent's action determines which of the two relevant outcomes will occur. In my second example, there are *three* relevant outcomes – the state of affairs consisting in the machine's not being turned on at t1, the state of affairs consisting in its being turned on at t1 and the light's flashing green, and the state of affairs consisting in the machine's being turned on t1 and the light's flashing red. The agent's action determines that one or the other of the last two outcomes will occur but even though he *knows* that the second will occur, *whether* the second or third occurs is determined by the random operations of the machine, not by the agent.
12. But just *why* do we do this? Because the murder is somehow more directly or immediately connected with the murderer's intentions, or character, or inner being? Because, unlike the murderer, the other person is only partly responsible for what took place? And even if these things *are* true, why should they be thought to imply that the latter is less blameworthy? Even if the murderer is more to blame *for the murder*, is he more *to blame*? (Is permitting a murder that one could [easily] prevent any less reprehensible than committing it? And, if it is, *why* is it?)
13. Consequentialists reject this distinction but I shall ignore this since most Christians (including Edwards – see note 8) are not consequentialists.
14. Mangan, J.T., 'An Historical Analysis of the Principle of Double Effect', *Theological Studies* 10 (1949): 43.
15. Rickless, Samuel C., 'The Doctrine of Doing and Allowing', *The Philosophical Review* 106 (1997): 556–557. See Foot's 'The Problem of Abortion and the Doctrine of Double Effect', in her *Virtues and Vices and Other Essays* (Berkeley: University of California Press, 1978), 'Killing and Letting Die', in *Abortion: Moral and Legal Perspectives*, ed. Jay Garfield (Amherst: University of Massachusetts Press, 1984), and 'Morality, Action, and Outcome', in *Morality and Objectivity*, ed. Ted Honderich (London: Routledge and Kegan Paul, 1985).
16. I am assuming that, as a matter of contingent fact, there is such a set, i.e., that, given the counterfactuals of freedom that actually obtain, some creatable (and not merely logically possible) combination of free agents and circumstances is such that sin is always freely avoided. In other words, I am assuming that the free agents God can create aren't all tainted with what Alvin Plantinga calls 'transworld depravity'. (An agent is tainted with transworld depravity if it would, as a matter of contingent fact, freely sin in any world in which God can in fact place it.) I find this plausible although my argument doesn't depend upon it.
17. Remember that both Arminians and Calvinists believe that the history of the world is (as Edwards says) a history of redemption, a manifestation in time of God's eternal glory.
18. Since the atonement is impossible without sin.
19. I am assuming that, in this instance, the part-whole relationship is relevantly similar to a means-end relationship. For consider this. (1) I can intend to bring about a whole without intending to bring about each of its parts if (a) I am not cognizant to each of its parts or (b) the parts in question aren't essential to the whole. But neither of these conditions is met here. God is omniscient. Furthermore, each part of a possible world is essential to it.

So, since creatable worlds are a subclass of possible worlds, each part of a creatable world is essential to it. (2) In the case of products, the part-whole relation does seem relevantly similar to a means-end relationship. I produce a brick wall by producing each of its parts. And it would be odd to say that I intended to produce the wall but didn't intend to produce its parts.
20. Assuming, as non-consequentialists would, that the mere absence of a greater good isn't, in general, a harm.
21. Whether the vulgar sense *is* the relevant sense is, of course, moot. But Edwards is a compatibilist. Judas is free provided that his repentance is consistent with the laws of nature, he isn't prevented from repenting by some internal or external impediment, and so on.
22. There is another possibility, however. I can sincerely proffer advice, issue commands, and so on, which I *know* will be ineffectual when it is my *duty* to do so. And certain roles involve duties of just this sort. Examples are counselor, platoon leader, parent, and so forth. So one might argue that, because God's position as the world's sovereign and 'moral rector' involves duties of this kind, He can't be accused of insincerity or deception when he offers advice or issues commands which He knows will go unheeded. If this is correct, then neither Arminians *nor* Calvinists have a problem here.
23. More accurately, is similar if God knows all true counterfactuals of freedom.
24. 'Jonathan Edwards and the Doctrine of Hell', plenary session, *Society of Christian Philosophers*, Marquette University, Milwaukee, Wisconsin, March 1999.
25. More accurately, there are no good arguments in its favor if there are no good independent arguments both for theological determinism and for God's justice. If there are, then we may simply have to bite the bullet and accept the counter-intuitive consequence.

Address for correspondence: Professor William J. Wainwright, Department of Philosophy, University of Wisconsin – Milwaukee, P.O. Box 413, Milwaukee, WI 53201, USA
Phone: (414) 229-4719; Fax: (414) 229-5022; E-mail: wjwain@csd.uwm.edu

The foreknowledge conundrum

WILLIAM HASKER
Huntington College

The apparent incompatibility between divine foreknowledge and human freedom, which has been recognized as a problem since the early days of the Christian Church, was examined with unprecedented energy and thoroughness during the last third of the twentieth century. This examination formed an integral part of the application of the techniques of analytic philosophy to the principal divine attributes, but it was triggered by a pair of seminal articles by Arthur Prior and Nelson Pike.[1] This essay will present the foreknowledge conundrum and consider the principal responses to it that have emerged during this period.

1. Appreciating the problem

Before plunging into technicalities it will be helpful to have before us a brief, intuitive but non-technical, presentation of the problem. It has become customary, in the discussion of this problem, to consider it as applied to a concrete (though arbitrarily chosen) example. For present purposes, we adopt Thomas Flint's example concerning a certain Cuthbert who, on a given occasion, is deliberating about the purchase of an iguana.[2] Suppose Cuthbert decides to make the purchase. It follows from the doctrine of divine foreknowledge that God has always known that Cuthbert would purchase the iguana. But if so, we must ask, could Cuthbert have refrained from making the purchase? On the face of it, it would seem that, if Cuthbert had refrained, God's belief that Cuthbert would purchase an iguana would have been *false* – that this belief would not have been an instance of knowledge, but rather of mistaken belief. But according to the doctrine of divine infallibility, this is impossible. But then, it must have been impossible for Cuthbert to refrain from purchasing the iguana. If, however, this was not possible, then Cuthbert was not *free* in making the purchase. And since similar reasoning can be applied to any human choice whatsoever, it follows that human freedom is purely an illusion.

Apparently simple and straightforward though this argument is, it has met with an astonishing variety of objections and refutations. It is not clear, however, how this situation should be assessed. Conceivably, the abundance of replies could be an indication that the argument is flawed many times over – that in spite of its surface plausibility, it is a Rube Goldberg-like contraption built out of multiple fallacies spliced end to end. But another response is possible. It may be that the multiple refutations are actually a sign that the problem is extremely tenacious and resistant to solution, and that most, if not all, of the refutations are themselves suspect or at best unsatisfying. It is interesting that Linda Zagzebski, who in the end regards the argument as unsound, nevertheless seems to concur in the latter assessment. She writes, 'The divine foreknowledge dilemma is so disturbing, it has motivated a significant amount of philosophical work on the relation between God and human beings since at least the fifth century. A really good solution should lay to rest the gripping worries that have motivated all this work. Sadly, none of the solutions I have proposed in this book really do that, and I have never heard of one that does'.[3]

Our task in this essay is to assess the solutions, but in order to do that it will be helpful to have before us a more detailed statement of the argument, one that makes explicit the assumptions that are implicit in the informal version given above. The following version is borrowed from Linda Zagzebski, modified only by the insertion of Cuthbert and his iguana:

Let three moments of time be ordered such that $t_1 < t_2 < t_3$.

(1) Suppose that God infallibly believes at time t_1 that Cuthbert will purchase an iguana at t_3. (*premise*)

(2) The proposition *God believes at t_1 that Cuthbert will purchase an iguana at t_3* is accidentally necessary at t_2 (*from the principle of the necessity of the past*)

(3) If a proposition p is accidentally necessary at t and p strictly implies q, then q is accidentally necessary at t. (*transfer of necessity principle*)

(4) *God believes at t_1 that Cuthbert will purchase an iguana at t_3* entails *Cuthbert will purchases an iguana at t_3*. (*from the definition of infallibility*)

(5) So the proposition *Cuthbert will purchase an iguana at t_3* is accidentally necessary at t_2. (2–4)

(6) If he proposition *Cuthbert will purchase an iguana at t_3* is accidentally necessary at t_2, it is true at t_2 that Cuthbert cannot do otherwise than purchase an iguana at t_3. (*premise*)

(7) If when Cuthbert does an act he cannot do otherwise, he does not do it freely. (*principle of alternate possibilities*)

(8) Therefore, Cuthbert does not purchase an iguana at t_3 freely. (5–7)[4]

Some of the key terms employed in this argument will be discussed later on in this essay. It will be helpful, furthermore, to adopt one additional bit of terminology: *Theological compatibilism* is the view that comprehensive, infallible divine foreknowledge is compatible with libertarian free will for human beings, and *theological incompatibilism* denies this.[5] Accordingly, the argument given above may be termed the *argument for theological incompatibilism*, or more briefly the *TI-argument*.

2. Some minor solutions

We begin by considering some solutions that are 'minor', not because they lack adherents (though they have lost some of their following among philosophers of late), but rather because they do not address directly the contentions of the argument for theological incompatibilism given above. Instead, they seek by various means to avoid or evade that argument. The minor solutions are as follows:

God's foreknowledge does not cause our actions. This solution goes back to Origen, and has always been the most popular response. It goes as follows: Our freedom is destroyed (only) if there is a prior cause over which we have no control. But divine foreknowledge does not cause our actions, so it poses no threat to free will.

It is noteworthy that this response is strictly irrelevant to the TI-argument, since it does not address that argument or contradict any of the argument's premises. The response seems to be vulnerable to Jonathan Edwards' retort that, even if divine foreknowledge doesn't *make* our actions necessary, it *shows* that they are necessitated, which is just as bad for (libertarian) free will.[6] (Edwards was a theological incompatibilist but a causal compatibilist, since he thought all our actions were efficaciously decreed by God.) This reply, while still popular with the general religious public, has lost a good deal of its following among philosophers – though, as we shall see, it is now enjoying something of a revival.

Theological incompatibilism is just fatalism, and, like fatalism, fallacious. The argument for logical fatalism proceeds as follows. All (non-tensed) propositions that are true, are true at all times, thus it has always been true that (for example) Cuthbert purchases an iguana at t_3. But the past is inalterable, and so the truth that Cuthbert purchases an iguana at t_3 is also inalterable, and Cuthbert cannot do otherwise than purchase an iguana at t_3. This argument is generally conceded to be fallacious. But the TI-argument is essentially the same argument, with the incidental addition of the claim that God knows what Cuthbert will do. So that argument is fallacious as well.[7]

Undeniably there is a parallel between the arguments for logical fatalism and theological incompatibilism. But there is also a crucial difference which means that objections to the former argument need not carry over to the latter. The argument for logical fatalism claims, in effect, that *all* propositions that are true at a given time are accidentally necessary at that time – a claim that is quite implausible and is fairly easily refuted. The TI-argument, however, asserts that *one particular kind* of propositions is such that, if true at a time, they are accidentally necessary at that time – the kind in question being propositions about God's past and present beliefs about future states of affairs. This assertion is not based on the general claim made by logical fatalists, which would in fact be rejected by most theological incompatibilists. For these reasons, most philosophers now realize that this solution cannot suffice as a refutation of theological incompatibilism.

God's knowledge is timeless, not temporal. This solution is very old, going back to Boethius, and has also been extremely popular. It may, in fact, reflect a recognition that the first solution noted above is unsatisfactory. Those who embrace the eternity solution may be theological incompatibilists, and many are. That is, they agree that divine *foreknowledge* of actions would render those actions unfree. However, God's knowledge is *not*, strictly speaking, *fore*knowledge but rather, as Boethius said, 'knowledge of a never changing present'. So the first premise of the incompatibilist argument is rejected – and just as my seeing you sitting, in the present, does not necessitate your sitting, so neither does God's knowledge, in the 'eternal present', of your actions necessitate those actions.

It is actually quite unclear whether this solution is successful. In order for God to be timelessly omniscient and humans free, the following proposition must be true: *It is now possible that God's knowledge is timelessly a certain way, and also possible that God's knowledge is timelessly another way, and it is, right now, in the power of human beings to determine what God's knowledge shall timelessly be.* Such a power would seem quite remarkable, and it is not at all clear that the friends of timeless knowledge are willing to embrace it. Furthermore, as Marilyn Adams has observed, 'if the necessity of the past stems from its ontological determinateness it would seem that timeless determinateness is just as problematic as past determinateness'.[8]

This solution, like the first two, has lost ground in recent decades – not, however, because of the doubts expressed in the preceding paragraph. Rather, there has been a general decline, among analytic philosophers of religion, in the willingness to embrace divine timelessness, though it still has stalwart defenders. In any case, our concern in this essay is with the issue of temporal foreknowledge and free will.

3. The major solutions

We now turn to what have been, in the period under consideration, the most important solutions to the problem of divine foreknowledge and human freedom, those most actively considered and discussed among philosophers. Each of these solutions, unlike the first two solutions considered above, denies one or more premises of the TI-argument.

God's beliefs are 'soft facts' about the past. Shortly after the publication of Pike's seminal article, Marilyn Adams raised the question, 'Is the Existence of God a 'Hard' Fact?'[9] In raising this question she was reviving a proposal originally due to William Ockham, and one that has played a major role in the recent debate. Subsequently, a vast amount of energy and ingenuity has been expended in the attempt to determine whether facts about God's past beliefs are 'hard facts' or 'soft facts' about the past. This dispute is perhaps best seen as a refinement of the argument over logical fatalism discussed above. Both sides in the dispute recognize that the past is in some sense 'necessary' – it is now fixed, settled, and unable to be affected by anything anyone can now do. An example of such a 'hard fact' about the past might be the fact that Julius Caesar was the first Roman emperor. Other facts, though represented in the past and present by true propositions, are 'soft' – they are not, as yet, fixed and determinate, but are capable of being affected by choices that are still waiting to be made. Consider the proposition, *The U.S. President elected in 2040 will be a member of the Democratic Party.* This proposition, let us assume, is either true or false now, in the year 2000.[10] But its truth or falsity, we are inclined to think, is *not* fixed and settled, and unable to be affected by subsequent human decisions. (At least, this is what we will think absent special considerations about divine foreknowledge, divine decrees, and the like.) Propositions of the former sort are said to be 'accidentally necessary';[11] those of the latter sort are not. The difficulty, however, lies in the task of delineating in a general way the conditions under which a proposition is accidentally necessary, and in determining whether accidental necessity attaches to propositions about God's past beliefs. The present slution, then, denies premise 2 of the TI-argument, the premise which states, 'The proposition *God believes at t_1 that Cuthbert will purchase an iguana at t_3* is accidentally necessary at t_2'.

It is an unfortunate but undeniable fact that this controversy has failed to reach a satisfactory resolution. There have been numerous proposals, some of them clearly flawed but others that, so far as is now known, may well be correct.[12] But no proposal has come close to winning the general approbation which would be required in order for it to be used to resolve the dispute between theological compatibilism and incompatibilism. What conclusion should be drawn from this impasse? According to Edward Wierenga, the failure to arrive at such a criterion effectively destroys the force of the TI-argument. In his own formulation of the argument, a crucial role is played by the criterion in question, and if such a criterion cannot be provided the argument fails.[13]

It can be argued, however, that precisely the opposite assessment is the correct one. According to Alfred J. Freddoso (himself a theological compatibilist), 'The past hopes, fears, beliefs, desires, predictions, etc. of historical agents are clearly unalterable elements of our past and must be counted as part of our history'[14] Similarly, Linda Zagzebski (also a theological compatibilist) states, 'Most people have strong intuitions about the necessity of the past in a large variety of cases, the past spilling of milk being the most common folk example. Past beliefs of persons would automatically be put in this category if it were not for the foreknowledge dilemma. If this intuition is strong enough, it may be reasonable to maintain it independently of an account of accidental necessity and, in fact, this might be seen as a constraint on any such account'.[15] These quotations make the point effectively: Our intuitions seem to support the claim that truths about God's past beliefs are accidentally necessary, and in the absence of a successful (and widely accepted) criterion of accidental necessity, the 'soft fact' defense cannot be considered a success.

Accidental necessity is not closed under entailment. This solution has not been as widely adopted as some others discussed in this section, but is included here because of its historical and systematic importance. It was originated by the sixteenth-century Jesuit Luis de Molina, who devised the theory of divine 'middle knowledge',[16] and has been adopted by Alfred J. Freddoso and perhaps by some other contemporary Molinists. This solution, of course, denies premise 3 of the TI-argument, which states, 'If a proposition p is accidentally necessary at t and p strictly implies q, then q is accidentally necessary at t'. And without this premise, the argument fails.

On the face of it, this proposal is extremely puzzling, not to say paradoxical. It is undeniable, given divine infallibility, that *God believes at t_1 that Cuthbert will purchase an iguana at t_3* entails *Cuthbert will purchase an iguana at t_3*. But if so, how can it be possible that the truth of the former proposition is now fixed, settled, and beyond anyone's control, while that of the latter is not? It's just not possible that Cuthbert's decision about the iguana will come out some other way, while at the same time God's belief *cannot* come out differently. The 'solution' seems to make no sense.

Thomas Flint, however, has suggested a way in which we might be able to make sense of Molina's proposal.[17] Suppose we define the accidentally necessary as 'that which no one can cause to be false'. Then God's past beliefs will be accidentally necessary (no one can cause events in the past), but future actions – in this case, Cuthbert's purchase of an iguana – will not be, since (according to theological compatibilists) Cuthbert *can* cause *Cuthbert will purchase an iguana at t_3* to be false, although he will not in fact do so.

It is not clear, however, that this resolves the basic dilemma. How *can* Cuthbert have the power to cause *Cuthbert will purchase an iguana at t_3* to be false, when its truth is immutably fixed and guaranteed by the truth of *God believes at t_1 that Cuthbert will purchase an iguana at t_3*? So long as we lack an explanation of this, the present solution must be judged unsatisfactory.

We have counterfactual power over God's past beliefs. This solution, originally proposed by Alvin Plantinga, has attracted a considerable following.[18] The solution denies that we can *cause* God to have had a different belief than he did have. But, it is claimed, we do have the power to act in such a way that, were we to act that way, God would have had a different belief. We do not have *causal power* over the past, but we do have *counterfactual power* over the past. And because of this, God's foreknowledge does not compromise human freedom.

It is not immediately clear which premise of the TI-argument this solution means to deny. Conceivably, the intent could be to deny that accidental necessity is closed under entailment, as in the preceding solution. If so, however, this solution would be open to the same objection mentioned above – how can Cuthbert have the power to cause *Cuthbert will purchase an iguana at t_3* to be false, when its truth is immutably fixed and guaranteed by the truth of *God believes at t_1 that Cuthbert will purchase an iguana at t_3*? So long as we lack an answer to this question, we are no further forward.

It is more in accord with Plantinga's own intention to see him as denying the second premise of the TI-argument, and as holding that God's past beliefs are not accidentally necessary. But what is the basis for the latter claim? In 'On Ockham's Way Out', Plantinga proposes the following definition of accidental necessity:

> p is accidentally necessary at t if and only if p is true at t and it is not possible both that p is true at t and there exists an agent S and an action A such that (1) S has the power at t or later to perform A, and (2) if S were to perform A at t or later, then p would have been false.[19]

So, since Cuthbert has the power at t_2 to refrain from purchasing the iguana, and if he were so to refrain the proposition *God believes at t_1 that Cuthbert will purchase an iguana at t_3* would have been false, that proposition is not accidentally necessary.

It is clear that Plantinga's proposed criterion for accidental necessity meshes neatly with the rest of his treatment of the foreknowledge problem. The proposition ascribing to God the belief that Cuthbert will purchase the iguana is *not* accidentally necessary (it describes a 'soft fact') just in case Cuthbert has the power in question – which is to say, just in case he is free not to purchase the iguana. So far, all is in order. On the other hand, Plantinga's criterion gives us no help at all in *deciding* whether Cuthbert has this power or lacks it. So how do we go about deciding this?

Plantinga asserts that Cuthbert has the power to act in such a way (namely, by refraining from purchasing the iguana) that, were he to act in that way, God would have held a different belief. Now, part of what is asserted here is obviously correct. It follows directly from the doctrine of divine infallibility that, were Cuthbert to refrain from his purchase, God would have held a different belief about what Cuthbert would do than the belief he actually does hold, namely the belief that Cuthbert will complete his purchase. But is Cuthbert free to refrain? How does Plantinga decide that he is so free? Apparently, the answer is something like this: Plantinga considers that Cuthbert is endowed with libertarian free will; he notes that Cuthbert is not being coerced and is not in any unusual psychological state that might compromise his freedom, so he concludes that Cuthbert is free in this regard.[20]

Considered as an answer to the argument for theological incompatibilism, however, this blatantly begs the question. For that argument asserts that Cuthbert lacks freedom *precisely on account of God's prior, infallible belief about what Cuthbert will do*. But this assertion *is not considered at all* when, following Plantinga's procedure, we decide that Cuthbert is free to refrain from making his purchase. Insofar as he fails to consider and answer the main contention of his opponents, Plantinga's 'solution' is circular and question-begging, and leaves the foreknowledge conundrum untouched.

We can bring about God's past beliefs. This solution, due to George Mavrodes, comes the closest of any we have seen to claiming that we have causal power over past events.[21] But Mavrodes does not quite say this. Rather, he draws from Jaegwon Kim the point that there are things we *bring about* but do not *cause* to be the case.[22] And he affirms that some of God's past beliefs are among the things we bring about, whether or not we *cause* them to be as they are. For example by deciding to purchase the iguana, Cuthbert brings it about that God has always believed that he would purchase that iguana. Similarly are things we *prevent* from having occurred in the past – that is, we bring about their non-occurrence – and once again, God's beliefs are the key example. For instance, if Cuthbert decides to purchase the iguana, he prevents God from having believed that Cuthbert would pass up this particular iguana-buying opportunity.

But this, so far, is not enough for libertarian free will. In order for Cuthbert to be free in the libertarian sense, he must be able to bring it about that God has always believed that he will purchase the iguana, and *also* able to *prevent* God from having believed this. Mavrodes sees this quite clearly; in an example of his own, he claims that someone might have the power, in the 1980s when he was writing his paper, to do something that would prevent the coronation of Queen Elizabeth II of England, which occurred in 1953. He then goes on to say,

> When I suggest that Elizabeth's queenship may be preventable I do not mean any of the 'sensible' interpretations which might, with some straining, be attached to my words. I do not mean, for example, ... that we might now discover that a mistake had been made in the past – that her apparent coronation was invalid because of a technicality ... No, I mean that, assuming that she has been Queen for many years, we might now be able to do something which would bring it about that she has never, up to the present time, been Queen.[23]

So, to repeat, I may[24] have the power to do something now that would bring it about that Elizabeth has never Queen, in spite of the fact that she has already been Queen for many years. And Cuthbert definitely has it in his power to prevent God from ever having believed that he would purchase an iguana, in spite of the fact that from all eternity God has believed that very thing.

So far it may not be clear exactly how Mavrodes takes exception to the TI-argument. In a more recent article, however, he suggests what his answer to this question would be. His preferred option (I believe[25]) is simply to deny altogether the 'principle of the fixity of the past', which underlies the claim that *God believes at t_1 that Cuthbert will purchase an iguana at t_3* is accidentally necessary. He writes, 'People who hold this view maintain ... that the mere pastness of an event or state of affairs does not confer any necessity on it. If it does not inherit necessity from some other source then it simply is not necessary at all. It is a contingent element in the past history of the world, an even which might have been different from what it actually was'.[26]

In saying this, Mavrodes takes a bold line, one that flies in the face of our ordinary intuitions about the necessity or fixity of the past. It is one thing to suggest that a particular class of facts about the past – such as facts about God's past beliefs – are 'soft' and still open to our control. Such a claim, though it runs counter to certain intuitions, pales in comparison with Mavrodes' stronger claim that the past is not fixed *at all*. And this very strong claim, in its turn, challenges us to make more explicit the notion of the fixity of the past, or accidental necessity – a notion which, up to this point, has been left somewhat vague and imprecise. So let us distinguish the ontological status of the past from that of the future in the following way: *At any given time, there may well be a number of different ways in which the future can be, but there are never a number of different ways in which the past can be.* It seems to me that this is absolutely consistent with our fundamental intuitions on this topic. (There remains, to be sure, the task of distinguishing those propositions that are 'really about the past' from those which are not – that is, of distinguishing hard facts from soft facts.) And from Mavrodes' words, quoted above, it seems he would simply deny that this difference exists.

But does Mavrodes really believe this? There is reason to think he does not. In a letter, he elaborates on the example concerning Elizabeth by describing what it would be like for someone to delete Elizabeth's queenship from the past:

> Elizabeth has been queen of England for many years now. Suppose that I were to do something now whose effect would be that, while she has up to now been queen for many years, from now on she will never have been queen at all or at any time. I believe that it would be perfectly correct, and powerfully communicative, to say that by performing that act I had changed the past.

He observes that some people have an intuition to the effect that such an action is impossible, and continues as follows:

> I really don't know how widespread that intuition is. But so far as I can tell, *I share it fully myself.* I have no inclination at all to think that I could perform any act which satisfied the description given above (private communication).

Here Mavrodes admits that, once Elizabeth has become queen, it is *not now possible* that she should never have been queen: alternative pasts, in which Elizabeth was never queen, are simply no longer possible. But as for the future, there is no doubt (and I don't think Mavrodes would deny) that alternative futures – some, for instance, in which Prince William someday becomes king and others in which he does not – are really possible. Denying the ontological difference between past and future is not easy to do – not for Mavrodes, and not for the rest of us either. But without this denial, the present solution to the foreknowledge problem collapses.[27]

4. A new solution: Frankfurt libertarianism

The results of the preceding section do not seen particularly promising for theological compatibilism. Each of the solutions considered confronts serious problems, problems that may keep them from laying to rest what Zagzebski called 'the gripping worries that have motivated all this work' on the foreknowledge problem. However, at least one more solution – one that represents the most interesting new development in the foreknowledge controversy during the 1990s – remains to be considered. The solution results from the application to this controversy of the notorious 'Frankfurt counterexamples' against the principle of alternative possibilities. It has normally been assumed (by both compatibilists and libertarians) that, in order to be free, one must have the power to do something other than what one in fact does. (Compatibilists and libertarians, of course, disagree about the correct analysis of 'having the power'.) But Harry Frankfurt, in a famous article, devised a scenario which, he claimed, provided a counterexample to this requirement.[28] The general structure of a Frankfurt counterexample involves a controller, Black, and a subject, Jones. Black wishes to ensure that Jones performs a particular action – say, committing a murder, or voting Republican in the next election. Black prefers, however, that Jones perform this action on his own, without intereference from Black. Black, therefore, sets a close watch on Jones, looking for indicators that show Black either that Jones *will* perform the desired action on his own or that he *will not* do so. If the indicator shows that Jones will perform the action on his own, well and good; Black stands back and allows this to occur. If on the other hand the indicator shows that Jones will *not* perform the action on his own, Black intervenes (through coercion, hypnotism, neural manipulation, or some other means) to ensure that the action is performed.

The conclusion drawn from the example is that, in the case where Black does not intervene, Jones acts freely and is responsible for his action, in spite of the fact that he could not have done otherwise than as Black wished. For if Jones had been going to refrain from the action desired by Black, Black would have intervened to ensure that he performed it anyway. But if the action is done without interference from Black, Jones acts freely and responsibility *in spite of the fact that he could not have acted otherwise*. So the principle of alternative possibilities is false.

Frankfurt himself is a compatibilist about free will. But the proponents of the 'new solution' contend that Frankfurt's main conclusion is compatible with a certain type of *libertarianism* – a version that, like standard libertarianism, contends that a free action cannot be causally predetermined, but that, unlike standard libertarianism, denies that the 'possibility of doing otherwise' is essential to free action. Thus, 'Frankfurt libertarianism'.

It is evident how Frankfurt libertarianism can provide a solution for the foreknowledge problem.[29] With respect to the TI-argument, Frankfurt libertarians simply deny premise 7, the principle of alternative possibilities. And in doing so, they neatly circumvent the whole messy scene, involving argument and counterargument, principle and counterexample, that has been the foreknowledge controversy over the past three decades. Essentially all of the effort expended by theological incompatibilists has been to show that comprehensive, infallible divine foreknowledge precludes there being alternative possibilities for our actions. And theological compatibilists have invested enormous energy in arguing that foreknowledge does *not* preclude alternative possibilities. If the principle of alternative possibilities can be simply abandoned, while retaining libertarian free will, then all of this effort was unnecessary. It doesn't matter, then, whether it was really possible for Cuthbert to refrain from purchasing the iguana – what matters is only that he was not *causally determined* to do so.[30]

Perhaps, however, it is too soon to celebrate. There are substantial reasons to doubt that Frankfurt libertarianism provides a genuine solution to the foreknowledge problem. For one thing, it is likely to occur to us that the solution is just too easy. In relation to the history of this problem, the strategy of the Frankfurt libertarians could be described as: Concede the argument, and declare victory! As was noted above, all of the energy in that argument was devoted to ascertaining whether, as matter of logical fact, comprehensive infallible divine foreknowledge precludes there being alternative possibilities for action. We are now told, by the Frankfurt libertarians, that this was never the issue in the first place! So we have to ask, was the problem really an illusion all along, or is it now just being swept under the rug? Some of us will recall the exhilaration, in the heady days of linguistic analysis, of 'discovering' that all sorts of metaphysical and epistemological questions were really pseudo-problems, to be dissolved and eliminated through a proper understanding of language. In a few instances this diagnosis may have held up – but in many, many cases the old problems have reappeared, none the worse for a few decades of neglect, in the new arena of analytic metaphysics and epistemology. It is noteworthy, also, that the proponents of Frankfurt libertarianism were themselves among those who, prior to the new 'discovery', devoted immense effort to reconciling foreknowledge with alternative possibilities. So we have to ask: Is this really a solution, or an admission of defeat?

It should also be noted that the Frankfurt counterexamples, in spite of having enjoyed much acclaim (some would say, undeserved acclaim) for a number of years, are themselves under attack. One line of attack, developed by David Widerker, focuses on the relation between the 'indicator' by which Black determines what Jones will do, and Jones' subsequent action. If the connection between the indicator and the action is deterministic, then we must conclude that the action is itself causally determined, contrary to the assumptions of the example.[31] If on the other hand the connection is not deterministic, then there can still be alternative possibilities *after* the indicator has registered, which once again undermines the example.

To be sure, it would be premature to conclude that the critics of Frankfurt have won the day. The general Frankfurt scenario admits of a great many variations, depending on the circumstances involved, the type of action Black wishes either done or left undone, the indicator used by Black to determine what Jones will do, and the means Black uses in case Jones was going to do the wrong thing. Debate about these issues continues, and it is too soon to make a decisive judgement about the outcome.[32] On the other hand, it is far from clear that the Frankfurt scenarios are sufficiently secure to outweigh the powerful intuitive support enjoyed (for many of us, at least) by the principle of alternative possibilities.

It should also be noted that Frankfurt libertarianism has internal problems that are potentially debilitating. One such problem concerns the motivation for the view. It is arguable that the requirement of alternative possibilities is the most fundamental motivation for a libertarian conception of free will, and that the aversion to causal determination is itself primarily motivated by the need to preserve alternative possibilities for action. It is noteworthy that few responded to the arguments for logical fatalism by saying that fatalism doesn't matter so long as there is no causal determinism! And if alternative possibilities are given up, a hard look will need to be taken at the reasons for continuing to resist causal determinism.[33]

There is also metaphysical problem here: If there is no causal determination, *what prevents* the agent from choosing otherwise than the way God believes she will choose? In the past, those who have accepted the argument for theological incompatibilism as not only valid but also sound (such as Jonathan Edwards) have normally posited some causal process – whether natural causation, or divine decrees, or both – that necessitates the choices that are made. Since Frankfurt libertarians cannot say this, we are left with a great mystery. In view of these considerations, it is at best premature to say that the foreknowledge conundrum has been resolved through Frankfurt libertarianism.

5. A theological option?

There is little doubt that theological incompatibilism would get a better reception if it were not perceived as theologically threatening. Alvin Plantinga, indeed, once described the argument for theological incompatibilism as an 'atheological argument'.[34] It is no such thing, of course; such stalwarts of Christian orthodoxy as Thomas Aquinas and Jonathan Edwards were theological incompatibilists. But if one combines theological incompatibilism with the view that God is temporal rather than timeless, and also with the belief that humans possess libertarian freedom, one will reach the conclusion that God does not possess complete, infallible knowledge of the future. And this conclusion is quite likely to raise theological hackles.

This is not so in all theological circles, of course. Among process theologians this kind of limitation on God's knowledge of the future is taken for granted – and as a result, process thinkers have not taken a major role in the controversies discussed in this essay. But many analytic philosophers of religion are primarily concerned with a more orthodox conception of God,[35] and this prompts strong resistance against arguments (such as the TI-argument) which might otherwise be found quite compelling.

Within the past decade, however, a 'TI-friendly' theological movement has arisen in an unexpected quarter, within the evangelical segment of Protestantism. This movement is commonly referred to as the 'openness of God', movement, or as 'open theism', in consequence of the book, *The Openness of God*, that first brought that movement to the attention of the religious public.[36] This movement does not, of course, limit itself to the mere affirmation of theological incompatibilism and the consequent limitations on God's knowledge of the future. Rather, it seeks a thorough revision of the conception of God and of God's relationship with the world – a revision which will be consistent with biblical faith and with the major creeds of historic Christian orthodoxy, but which will strip away some of the accretions that, it is alleged, became attached to the concept of God through the influence of Greek philosophy on theologians of the ancient and medieval Church.[37]

Some of the revisions that are seen as being needed include the rejection of divine simplicity and timeless eternity, as well as the Aristotelian-Thomistic doctrine of God as 'pure act'. Particularly objectionable to open theists is the doctrine of divine impassibility, which implied that God is never 'receptive' in relation to the creatures, and therefore never genuinely responsive to them. In contrast, open theists stress God's active involvement with his creation, and take seriously the biblical teachings concerning divine 'repentance' and God's emotional involvement with us his creatures – teachings that are of necessity dismissed, or interpreted in ways that drain them of significance, by adherents of the classical doctrine of impassibility. (These emphases, it may be said, bring the openness movement more strongly into consonance with evangelical piety, which stresses a personal relationship with God, than is the Calvinistic theology that is often taken to be normative for evangelicalism.) Divine sovereignty over the creation is affirmed, but it is emphasized that God has deliberately refrained from exercising absolute control over the creatures, so as to leave room for a degree of autonomy as they freely decide to align themselves for or against God's purposes. In other respects, however, open theism is very much in line with the main theological tradition. The doctrine of divine omnipotence, and of creation ex nihilo, are retained, in sharp contrast with process theism.[38] Omnipotence may be defined as God's power to do anything that is neither logically incoherent nor inconsistent with God's moral perfection. Omniscience, similarly, means that God knows everything that is logically capable of being known. (Thus, open theism does not differ from more traditional views concerning God's cognitive perfection, but rather about the inherent knowability of the future – about its ontological status, as wholly determinate or as partly indeterminate.) The doctrine of divine moral perfection is affirmed without reservation – and without the conflicts that arise if one affirms, with traditional Calvinism, that God has efficaciously decreed all of the sin and evil that takes place.

At the time of this writing, early in the 21st century, it is too soon to draw conclusions about the ultimate effects of this movement, whether about its acceptance within evangelical Protestantism – where it is meeting with fierce resistance, but is also gaining significant numbers of adherents – or about its possible influence in wider circles. At the very least, the existence of the movement demonstrates that one cannot simply assume that theological incompatibilism is inimical to Christian theology. As a fitting conclusion to this essay, we may take the following description of open theism's conception of God, 'as majestic yet intimate, as powerful yet gentle and responsive, as holy and loving and caring, as desiring for humans to decide freely for or against his will for them, yet endlessly resourceful in achieving his ultimate purposes'.[39]

Notes

1. A.N. Prior, 'The Formalities of Omniscience', *Philosophy* 32 (1962): 119–129; Nelson Pike, 'Divine Omniscience and Voluntary Action', *Philosophical Review* 74 (1965): 27–46, reprinted in John Martin Fischer, ed., *God, Foreknowledge, and Freedom* (Stanford: Stanford University Press, 1989) [hereafter, *GFF*]. For a more recent overview of the controversy by Pike, see 'A Latter-Day Look at the Foreknowledge Problem', *International Journal for Philosophy of Religion* 33 (1993): 129–164.
2. Thomas P. Flint, *Divine Providence: The Molinist Account* (Ithaca, NY: Cornell University Press, 1998), pp. 36–37.
3. Linda Trinkaus Zagzebski, *The Dilemma of Freedom and Foreknowledge* (New York: Oxford University Press, 1991), p. 180 [hereafter *Dilemma*].
4. Adapted from Linda Zagzebski, 'Foreknowledge and Human Freedom', in Philip L. Quinn and Charles Taliaferro, eds., *A Companion to Philosophy of Religion* (Cambridge, MA: Blackwell, 1997), pp. 291–292.

5. It should be noted that theological compatibilism is logically independent of ordinary causal compatibilism, which assets that free will is compatible with casual determinism.
6. Jonathan Edwards, *Freedom of the Will* (Indianapolis: Bobbs-Merrill, 1969), p. 12.
7. Richard Taylor, in crafting an argument for logical fatalism, tells a story in which a book, written by God and recounting the details of a person's future life, is discovered by that person. Taylor claims that the part about God and the book is merely an aid to the imagination and is not essential for the success of the argument (see Taylor's *Metaphysics*, 2nd edn. [Englewood Cliffs: Prentice-Hall, 1974], pp. 58–71).
8. Marilyn Adams, *William Ockham* (Notre Dame, IN: University of Notre Dame Press, 1987), p. 1135.
9. *The Philosophical Review* 76 (1967): 492–503; reprinted in *GFF*. Many of the articles in *GFF* are concerned with this aspect of the foreknowledge controversy.
10. If this is denied, we get immediately the result that God does not know these truths about the contingent future, since there are no such truths to be known. But this move is controversial; furthermore, it seems not to lend itself to further argument as readily as the considerations that arise if the existence of truths about the contingent future is granted.
11. The necessity in question is 'accidental,' because it pertains to the same proposition at one time but not at another – unlike, say, the propositions of mathematics, which are always necessary.
12. I would still defend the adequacy of my own analysis, presented in *God, Time, and Knowledge* (Ithaca, NY: Cornell University Press, 1989) [hereafter, *GTK*], pp. 81–95. (A needed correction is made in the 1998 paperback edition, p. 88.) John Martin Fischer has devoted an extraordinary amount of effort to analyzing the hard-soft fact distinction; see *GFF*, pp. 32–56, and other articles by Fischer listed in the bibliography for *GFF*.
13. Edward R. Wierenga, *The Nature of God: An Enquiry into Divine Attributes* (Ithaca, NY: Cornell University Press, 1989), pp. 59–115.
14. 'Accidental Necessity and Logical Determinism', *Journal of Philosophy* 80 (1983): 268 (reprinted in *GFF*.)
15. *Dilemma*, p. 75.
16. See Luis de Molina, *On Divine Foreknowledge: Part IV of the Concordia*, trans. with introduction by Alfred J. Freddoso (Ithaca, NY: Cornell University Press, 1988), introduction pp. 53–62. Regrettably, middle knowledge cannot be treated in this essay; this theory raised many issues of its own distinct from the foreknowledge problem. However, adherents of middle knowledge do need a solution to that problem, and they are not limited to this solution of Molina's, though this is one option that may appeal to them.
17. Thomas P. Flint, 'Omniscience', in *The Routledge Encyclopedia of Philosophy*.
18. See Alvin Plantinga, *God, Freedom, and Evil* (Grand Rapids: Eerdmans, 1977), pp. 66–73.
19. Alvin Plantinga, 'On Ockham's Way Out', *Faith and Philosophy* 3 (1986): 253 (reprinted in *GFF*).
20. Admittedly, Plantinga does not *say* that this is how he decides that Cuthbert is free; he doesn't say anything at all about how he decides this. But I have been unable to come up with any other, substantially different, way in which such a conclusion could be reached.
21. George I, Mavrodes, 'Is the Past Unpreventable?', *Faith and Philosophy* 1 (1984): 131–146.
22. Jaegwon Kim, 'Noncausal Connections', *Noûs* 8 (1974): 41–52.
23. 'Is the Past Unpreventable?': 144.

24. Note: I *may* have this power; that is, it is logically coherent to suppose that I have it. Mavrodes does not commit himself with regard to what powers we *actually* have over the past, except for the power to bring about and to prevent God's past beliefs.
25. Admittedly, Mavrodes does not *say* that this is his preferred solution; he merely lists it, along with the 'eternity solution' and the 'hard and soft fact' solution, as one of the ways in which one may deny that God's past beliefs are accidentally necessary. I am fairly confident, however, that this is in fact the solution he favors.
26. 'Omniscience', in *A Companion to Philosophy of Religion*, p. 242.
27. For more on Mavrodes' proposed solution, see *GTK*, pp. 116–143.
28. Harry G. Frankfurt, 'Alternate Possibilities and Moral Responsibility', *Journal of Philosophy* 66 (1969): 828–839.
29. The principal philosophers using Frankfurt libertarianism in this way are Linda Zagzebski (*Dilemma*, pp. 154–162; 'Foreknowledge and Human Freedom', pp. 293–298), and David Hunt ('On Augustine's Way Out', *Faith and Philosophy* 16 (1999): 1–26; 'Moral Responsibility and Unavoidable Action', *Philosophical Studies* 97 (2000): 195–227). Eleonore Stump is a Frankfurt libertarian ('Libertarian Freedom and the Principle of Alternative Possibilities', in Jeff Jordan and Daniel Howard-Snyder, eds., *Faith, Freedom, and Rationality* [Lanham, MD: Rowman and Littlefield, 1996], pp. 73–88), but she is an eternalist and does not endorse Frankfurt libertarianism as a solution to the foreknowledge problem.
30. This solution to the foreknowledge problem can be seen as essentially identical with the solution discussed in Section 1 above: God's knowledge does not cause our actions, and so there is no problem. To be sure, the Frankfurt libertarians add a great deal by way of technical sophistication to this naïve solution.
31. See Widerker, 'Libertarian Freedom and the Avoidability of Decisions', *Faith and Philosophy* 12 (1995): 113–118. This argument applies if the counterexamples are used in support of *libertarian* free will. The examples might still stand up if combined with compatibilist free will – but this is no help to Frankfort libertarians.
32. Since about 1995 there has been a lively debate about the Frankfurt cases in a number of journals, including *Journal of Philosophy, Noûs, Analysis, Philosophical Review, Philosophical Studies*, and *Faith and Philosophy*. The main participants in *Faith and Philosophy* have been John Martin Fischer, David Hunt, and Eleonore Stump (pro-Frankfurt), and Stewart Goetz and David Widerker (anti-Frankfurt). For my own assessment of the Frankfurt cases, see *The Emergent Self* (Ithaca: Cornell University Press, 1999), pp. 86–94.
33. It should be noted that Frankfurt libertarians (such as Stump) may still hold that alternative possibilities are *normally* present, while denying that they are essential for freedom and responsibility. But those who use Frankfurt libertarianism as a solution to the foreknowledge problem will have to admit that there are *never* genuine alternative possibilities.
34. *God, Freedom, and Evil*, p. 66.
35. My observations suggest that this is so even for those who are not believers: the God they disbelieve in, or about whose existence they are agnostic, is more likely to be the God of traditional theism than the process deity. There are exceptions, of course.
36. Clark Pinnock, Richard Rice, John Sanders, William Hasker, and David Basinger, *The Openness of God: A Biblical Challenge to the Traditional Understanding of God* (Downers Grove, IL: InterVarsity Press, 1994). Other representative works include Clark Pinnock and Robert Brow, *Unbounded Love: A Good News Theology for the 21st Century* (Downers Grove, IL: InterVarsity Press, 1994); Gregory A. Boyd, *God at War: The Bible and spiritual Conflict* (Downers Grove, IL: InterVarsity Press, 1997); and John Sanders,

The God Who Risks: A Theology of Divine Providence (Downers Grove, IL: InterVarsity Press, 1998).
37. It should be noted that open theists need not hold that the influence of philosophy on Christian theology was harmful in every respect or even harmful on balance. The point is merely that the synthesis of philosophy and biblical religion that resulted is open to revision – and, we believe, in need of revision at certain specific points.
38. The differences as well as the commonalities between open theism and process theism are explored in John B. Cobb, Jr., and Clark H. Pinnock, eds., *Searching for an Adequate God: A Dialogue Between Process and Free Will Theists* (Grand Rapids, MI: William B. Eerdmans, 2000).
39. *The Openness of God*, p. 154.

Address for correspondence: William Hasker, Department of Philosophy, Huntington College, Huntington, IN 46750, USA
Phone: (219) 359–4237; E-mail: whasker@huntington.edu

Theology in philosophy: Revisiting the Five Ways

FERGUS KERR
University of Oxford

At least in the English-speaking world, those who study the philosophy of religion are usually introduced at an early stage to cosmological proofs of the existence of God, and in particular to the Five Ways of Thomas Aquinas. This directs them to a conception of the task of philosophy of religion in general, as well as to certain conception of how to read Aquinas, neither of which is as incontestable as is often assumed. Recent developments in philosophy at large have not always been absorbed in the philosophy of religion. Similarly, changing approaches to the study of Aquinas have not yet much affected standard expositions of his arguments for the existence of God. Now that the borders between the philosophy of religion and Christian theology are shifting, however, it seems worthwhile to stand back a little and reflect on the continued plausibility of the standard view. Certain developments outside philosophy challenge received interpretations of Aquinas.

On the standard view, the Five Ways are *a posteriori* cosmological arguments. Beginning with features of any human experience of the world (change, causation, contingency, gradation, finality), all of which are taken to be non-religious, the arguments conclude to the existence of an unmoved mover, a first cause, some *per se* necessary existent, something which is most fully in being, and some guiding hand in nature – which everyone takes to be 'God' (*Summa Theologiae* la, q. 2, art 3).

In other words, whether we think that the arguments work or not, the assumption is that Thomas is a good example of those who think that the existence of God can be inferred from natural features of the world. Bracketing out religion and morality, it seems, suspending any appeal to Christian revelation, and certainly ignoring the human subject, Thomas expects to be able to demonstrate the existence of something which everyone would call 'God' – which, indeed, 'we [Christians?] call "God"' – depending, then, entirely on non-religious, non-human, and non-supernatural features of the world in which we find ourselves.

The advantage, to those who regard the inferences as valid, is that the existence of God is a truth about the world that can be discovered independently of supernaturally revealed religion or mystical experience. Indeed, even if these particular inferences are judged in the end to lack cogency, we might still be attracted by the project, either as a way of securing a rational foundation for the extraordinary claims that Christian believers already make on other grounds or as a challenging exercise of pure metaphysical reasoning.

The inconvenience, on the other hand, for those who regard the very idea of proving God's existence by inference from supposedly religion-free features of the world as an incitement to idolatry, is that the deity whose existence is so demonstrated could never be identical with the God self-revealed in the Jewish and Christian dispensations.

One thing is not always made clear: Aquinas does not regard the Five Ways as his own arguments, nor does he regard them as arguments which might or might not work. Rather, he regards them as arguments that already *have* worked. In the parallel discussion in the *Summa contra gentiles* he takes much more time and trouble but even there it is surely plain that he is only rehearsing what he regards as ancient and familiar arguments.

Admittedly, when Aquinas spells out the First Way, based on the obviousness of change in the world, he does not explicitly refer to Aristotle; but the parallel passage in *Summa contra gentiles* (I, 13) shows clearly enough that he knows that Aristotle is the source of the argument. The Second and Third Ways, based on efficient causality and the fact that some things have the possibility of being or not being, respectively, have equally clear roots in Aristotle.

The Fourth Way, invoking degrees of being, goodness, truth, and so forth, the only one in which Aquinas cites Aristotle explicitly, is, paradoxically, as it might seem to us, distinctly Platonist in origin and inspiration. In fact, for all his involvement in the retrieval of Aristotelianism, it has been shown in the last fifty years or so that Aquinas remains profoundly indebted to Platonism.

Admittedly, again, the renewal of the study of Aquinas, specifically and in practice almost exclusively of the *Summa Theologiae*, in the late nineteenth century, was largely at the service of the determination of the authorities in the Roman Catholic Church to resist the infiltration of theology by modern philosophy. Platonism seemed as much of a threat as Cartesianism, Kantianism and Hegelianism – idealism, in short; which meant that the Platonist side of Aquinas was systematically played down while his inclination towards certain Aristotelian options in metaphysics and philosophical psychology proved sufficient to dub him an 'Aristotelian'. Indeed, in many Roman Catholic seminary and college libraries, there are shelves of forgotten books about *philosophia Aristotelico-Thomistica*. Since the nineteen sixties, as the authority of neo-Thomism waned in Roman Catholic theology, the early essays by Louis B. Geiger, Robert J. Henle and others, drawing attention to the 'metaphysics of participation' and so to the 'Platonism' in Aquinas's work, which were then so adventurous, have long become classics. Even so, the news has not always got to students of Aquinas in courses on the philosophy of religion.

No authority is cited for the Fifth Way, from design or teleology, but the brief exposition recalls the most ancient and persistently popular argument of all, dating back to Plato and the Stoics as well as to Aristotle. While of course most of Plato's texts were unavailable, and there is little sign that Aquinas knew much of the Stoic literature at first hand, it is surely clear that he takes it for granted that he is expounding a very familiar argument.

The *Summa Theologiae*, after all, is composed for 'beginners', as Aquinas says in the prologue. The Five Ways have given rise to so much debate, particularly since the nineteen twenties, that it is almost a shock to return to the text and see how very little space it occupies in the vast expanse of the *Summa*. Indeed, like natural law, which is also commonly regarded as one of Aquinas's favourite topics, the amount of attention that he pays to the proofs of the existence of God does not suggest that he believes it is so crucial as we now mostly suppose. It might even be suggested that, instead of concentrating on reconstructing the arguments to judge their validity, the interesting question is what function they are intended to play in the second question of Aquinas's exposition of 'sacred doctrine' for 'beginners'.

This may not be the merely historical question which it first appears; while of course much has happened since the thirteenth century the function of the Five Ways in the *Summa* is perhaps of much greater methodological significance than one might think.

II

Syllabuses and anthologies usually encourage students to start immediately with the Five Ways, exploring the validity of the arguments, without ever attending to where they come in Aquinas's exposition. However, if we read the previous two articles of Question 2, we may receive a somewhat different estimate of the plausibility of the Five Ways.

In article 1 of Question 2 we find Thomas insisting that God's existence *needs to be demonstrated* – that is to say, he finds himself in a Church, and no doubt in a theology faculty, in which many people regarded God's existence as self-evident. There was no need for logical argument; the presence of God was transparently displayed in the world.

We need to pause and try to recreate an approach to the world which finds the sacred or the divine unmediatedly visible in the face of things. Aquinas lists three strong arguments in favour of such a view. First, taking John of Damascus as his authority (the voice of Eastern Orthodoxy for Aquinas), it seems that an awareness of God's existence is naturally implanted in human being; God's existence is something of which we are innately aware. Second, Aquinas gestures towards what would be called the ontological argument: if we understand the meaning of the word 'God' it follows that God exists. Third, there is no doubt that we live in a world where there is such a thing as truth; God is truth, as Scripture says; so what need is there of more argument?

On the other hand, Thomas objects, nobody can even think the opposite of a self-evident proposition. Yet the proposition 'God exists' has been denied. Seemingly having no acquaintance with people who deny God's existence, Aquinas appeals to Psalm 52:1: 'The fool has said in his heart: There is no God'. Here, surely, we need to pause and consider how strange it is that Thomas needs to – anyway in fact *does* – cite divine revelation (as he would have thought) in evidence that God's existence has been – not just *may be* – denied. For us, of course, atheism, various forms of denying God's existence, are entirely familiar everyday phenomena. For Aquinas, on the other hand, it is in Scripture – the revealed Word of God – that we hear of the existence of atheism.

From the outset, then, atheism, for Aquinas, is a properly theological concept. In effect, though it will be many pages hence before he introduces the concept, it is (implicitly) a *sin*: it is the *fool* who says in his heart: 'There is no God'.

Argument is required, then. It can only be on the basis of what owes its existence to God that God can be brought to light for us by the mediation of logical argument. It is as if Thomas wants to isolate the fool's sinful subjectivity by turning our attention to the realities of the visible world.

God in Himself is utterly intelligible, Aquinas holds, giving as the reason for this that 'God is identical with His existing', a truth that he at once promises to demonstrate in Question 3. The doctrine of divine simplicity, that is to say, is being anticipated in these supposedly religion-free ways of demonstrating God's existence. This is another small, usually overlooked, indication that the question of whether God exists, though certainly preceding the question of God's nature textually is not as pre-theological conceptually as we sometimes assume.

That God's existence is something that *does* need to be argued for, Aquinas holds, is based on the fact that we do not know what God's nature is – precisely as the doctrine of divine simplicity will show. In addition, the only way that we can proceed is by working from things that we do know – things which Aquinas at once glosses as 'effects'.

In other words, from the beginning, article 1 of Question 2 is pervaded by theological assumptions. It is the doctrine of divine simplicity that spells out our inability to know what God is. This ignorance of God's nature requires us to reason to God's existence from the world. But then it turns out that 'those things of which we do have knowledge' (*ea quae sunt magis nota quoad nos*) are already describable – without argument or explanation – as 'effects' (*effectus*).

Thomas sees no need to argue or even explain that the things with which we are familiar in the world are *effects*. We might think that this is precisely what is in question. Why should we regard features of the world as 'effects'? Is that not precisely what argument for the existence of God is supposed to effect? From the outset, however, Aquinas sees the world in a cause/effects perspective. More properly, perhaps, Aquinas relies, tacitly it seems, on the doctrine of creation. And secondly, it is already taken for granted that the cause of the world is unknowable in itself – as the doctrine of divine simplicity will explain.

Thomas allows that a certain awareness of God's existence is implanted in us - but only in a very general way and pretty vaguely. 'God is the blessedness of humankind' – *Deus est hominis beatitudo* : we naturally desire beatitude, what is naturally desired by us is naturally perceived by us – but this is not awareness of God's existence *simpliciter*. Rather, as Thomas will show later on (cf. la.2ae, q2), we are easily mistaken or deceived about where our beatitude is to be found.

Secondly, since he was familiar with people who believed that God was physical (the first question that arises after the Five Ways conclude is whether God is a body, cf. q3 art.1), Thomas dismisses the thesis that, if you understand what the word 'God' means you must know what God it is who exists. And thirdly, even more briefly, Thomas insists that, though it is indeed obvious that there is such a thing as truth, it is not the case that the first truth (*prima veritas*) is 'known in itself to us' – clearly not, since it will turn out in due course that this first truth is that which arouses faith (cf. 2a.2ae, q1 art.1), in other words God Himself. And by that stage, in the *Summa Theologiae*, we can have no doubt that Thomas is discussing the God who is the author of the Mosaic Law and of the Law of the New Testament (cf. la.2ae, qq 98–108). Once again, then, if we overlook what will be made explicit only much later, what Thomas writes here in Question 2 can easily seem much less theological than it really is.

Article 1 of Question 2 discusses whether the existence of God *needs to be* demonstrated. In article 2 of Question 2 Aquinas asks whether God's existence *can be* demonstrated.

First of all, it seems, there is no possibility of logical argument, God's existence is purely and simply a matter of faith. Secondly, again citing John of Damascus, logical argument is excluded: there can be no demonstrative argument without a middle term, and since we cannot know of God what He is but only what He is not, no argument can even begin to be mounted. And thirdly, if we could demonstrate God's existence it would have to be from His effects, and His effects are obviously incommensurable with Him: God is infinite, His effects are finite, thus there can be no analogy from the finite to the infinite (*finiti ad infinitum non est proportio*).

It would not be difficult to expand these arguments. The thesis that God's existence is simply a matter of faith adumbrates the kind of fideism with which we are very familiar in the philosophy of religion today. Secondly, we might say that the nature of God is so radically mysterious, and that we can say nothing of God unless apophatically, so that there is no way for a logical argument to get a hold. Thirdly, equally familiarly, the difference between the finite and the infinite seems so unbridgeable as to rule out any sustainable argument from the world to God.

In their way, as theologians familiar with the work of Karl Barth would perhaps think, these objections to the position that Aquinas himself will adopt amount very much to 'Barthian' objections to 'natural theology'.

The key text, for Thomas Aquinas, as for the tradition before him and since, is, of course, Romans 1: 20: 'For the invisible things of [God] from the creation of the world are clearly seen, being understood by the things that are made, even His eternal power and Godhead'. Thomas thinks he has biblical warrant for rejecting fideism, specifically the view that, since it is a matter of faith that God exists, it is not something that can be demonstrated by reason from the existence and nature of the world. On the contrary, he believes that he has Paul, and thus divine revelation, on his side, in contending that the existence of God can be demonstrated by argument from the existence and structure of the world.

III

That is the standard interpretation of Romans 1:18–20, in the patristic and medieval tradition at least. It is repeated in the recent papal encyclical *Fides et Ratio* (§22) where it is taken for granted that Romans 1:20 is 'a kind of philosophical argument in popular language' developing what is already in the Wisdom literature. It is allowable to say, even, that this extremely important Pauline text affirms 'our metaphysical capacity as human beings' (*potestas hominis metaphysica*) – which (it at once turns out) our sinful condition prevents us from exercising.

Followers of Karl Barth might be expected to object to this papal celebration of our metaphysical capacity, and yet it seems not to amount to anything significantly different from the following paragraph from Barth's Commentary – beautifully translated by Edwyn Hoskyns:

Plato in his wisdom recognised long ago that behind the visible there lies the invisible universe which is the Origin of all concrete things. And moreover, the solid good sense of the men of the world had long ago perceived that the fear of the Lord is the beginning of wisdom. The clear, honest eyes of the poet in the book of Job and of the Preacher Solomon had long ago rediscovered, mirrored in the world of appearance, the archetypal, unobservable, undiscoverable Majesty of God.[1]

Thomas Aquinas would have understood that passage, even if the rhetoric is much riper than his ever is. Inveighing against the corruptions of religious arrogance, more eloquently than Aquinas ever does, Barth nevertheless allows that there remains 'a relic of clarity of sight, a last, warning recollection of the secret of God ... A reflection of this secret lies even in the deified forces of the world, even in the deified universe itself ... from time to time this bare relic of the Unknown reasserts itself in the presentiment of awe'.[2]

Recently, however, in a very challenging article, Douglas A. Campbell questions this long accepted interpretation.[3] He argues that the sequence Romans 1:18 – 3:20, far from setting our Paul's ideas, on natural theology or anything else, is rather an exposition of precisely the theological position that he is out to 'undermine' and 'savage'. This whole section is an 'ironic subversion' of a group of 'Jewish Christian "teachers" ', Campbell hypothesises, who preach 'the principle of soteriological desert': without good deeds no one will be rewarded with eternal life (cf. chapter 2: 5b–8). This is a 'fundamentally anthropocentric and meritocratic' doctrine that conflicts with Paul's own well-known theology of grace (3: 21–24). In short, the entire passage, Campbell insists with great subtlety, is 'an *ad hominem* strategy', 'a rhetorical masterstroke', which is 'perhaps of little lasting theological moment' – 'unless equivalent teachers to these Jewish Christian rhetors resurface: a possibility that, somewhat depressingly, should not be dismissed out of hand'.

Among other things, then, on Campbell's interpretation, the commitment to natural theology in Romans 1 – which Campbell is happy to acknowledge – would be just one more element of Paul's putative opponents' doctrine of salvation by works – the doctrine that he is out to discredit.

It seems to afford Campbell some pleasure, in his first footnote, to cite Thomas Aquinas as one who takes Paul here as endorsing the doctrine of general revelation and natural theology. As Campbell notes, Romans 1:20 is 'the warrant for his Five Ways'.

Moreover, when Thomas explicates the verse in his Romans commentary, he 'supplies *philosophical* proofs' (my emphasis: a bad move to make, of course, Campbell would think). While noting 'an intriguing argument' made by Eugene Rogers, reducing the distance between Thomas and Barth,

Campbell prefers Barth's famous description of how natural theology, after the rediscovery of Aristotle, got the upper hand over theology, something that finally became apparent at the First Vatican Council, 'in the canonisation of Thomas Aquinas as its supreme achievement [*Spitzenleistung*]'.[4]

Obviously, Campbell's ingenious and indeed intriguing argument in favour of reading Romans 1:20 as an element in a position which Paul opposes will give rise to much discussion, as it invites and deserves. For philosophers of religion who see themselves as in some sense in a Christian tradition, and certainly for students of Aquinas's Five Ways, Campbell's exegesis will have to be weighed. Perhaps his proposal is much too adventurous, perhaps the use of a text over so many centuries (its *Wirkungsgeschichte*) needs to be brought into the discussion, perhaps Aquinas's appeal to Scripture may after all be legitimately set aside – Campbell's intervention seems nevertheless to raise exactly the kind of questions that new theological considerations raise for philosophers of religion.

IV

The intriguing idea in the recent book by Eugene F. Rogers, Jr., is to compare how Karl Barth and Thomas Aquinas interpret the first chapter of Paul's Epistle to the Romans.[5]

Natural theology, understood as cosmological arguments for the existence of God starting from phenomena in the world from which God is bracketed out, and conducted by philosophers who have bracketed out their moral sensibility and spirituality, was, as Barth insisted, 'the invention of the Antichrist'. Whether this was ever as fair an account of the Five Ways as neo-Thomist exponents and their critics in modern philosophy have supposed is exactly what Rogers is out to examine.

Rogers begins by reminding us that the *Summa Theologiae* is an aid to reading Scripture. If influential Thomist expositors like Etienne Gilson are right, of course, the arguments can and should be extracted from their theological context and judged from the point of view of natural reason as purely philosophical conclusions. This is just how Campbell would want us to proceed. By and large, it has been how Aquinas has been read throughout the history of neo-Thomism.

On the other hand, Rogers contends, if Question 2 of the *Summa Theologiae* is read in the light of Question 1, which does not seem a particularly audacious move, Thomas turns out to be saying nothing substantially different from what we find in his exposition of Romans 1:20. It does not seems farfetched to suggest that he expected his students to have at least some idea of the kind of thing that he said in his lectures on Paul. Thus, if the natural knowledge of God which he finds in his exegesis of Scripture is the same as the natural knowledge of God whic he expounds in his guide for novice-theologians, the whole idea of purely philosophical theistic argumentation becomes a good deal less plausibly anything that Aquinas either wanted or could even have conceived.

Furthermore, if nature as it actually is is always already shot through with grace, and human reason is never entirely detachable from affectivity and sensibility, which are surely not very contentious Thomist thoughts, the kind of natural theology that Barth feared may not be rightly ascribed to Aquinas. Natural knowledge of God's existence independently of the life of grace, Rogers insists, is not something that Thomas ever imagined. The function of the cosmological arguments in the *Summa Theologiae*, he concludes, is to 'fulfil the charge of sacred doctrine to leave no part of the world God-forsaken'.[6]

Roughly speaking, as he opened his course on sacred doctrine, for students who were all to be pastors and preachers, Aquinas would have been reminding or even reassuring them that the God whose revelation they were now to spend weeks studying had left certain traces of His presence in the world around them. It is true that, compared with the rich neo-Platonic sacramentalism of the monastic theologians of the twelfth century, and even of his contemporary and colleague Bonaventure, Thomas opted for and perhaps deliberately cultivated a comparatively restrained view of the world. On the other hand, as we have noted, even such non-religious features of the world as change, contingency, and so forth, turn out to be 'effects', so that, however discreetly, the Christian doctrine of creation is always already in place, which means that Aquinas never began his considerations from the utterly neutral and theology-free world of modern philosophy.

The key point in Rogers's comparison, anyway, is a theological one. For Barth, anything moved by God must be moved by grace; grace and nature are mutually exclusive categories; thus nothing moved by God can be natural. For Thomas, however, as Rogers insists, any such conception of nature would have been unintelligible. Aquinas inhabited a world, a culture and a theology, where nature was always already graced. Modern theologians, by contrast, live in a world from which God is supposedly absent. Much of Barth's polemic, in the first volumes of *Church Dogmatics*, is directed against the very idea of an ungraced and Christless world. He has no difficulty, however, in his exegesis of Romans 1:20, in acknowledging the existence of a knowledge of God: 'Objectively the Gentiles have always had the opportunity of knowing God. ... And again, objectively speaking, they have always known [God]'.

In the end, if Barth was wrong in attributing a notion of graceless nature to him, his objections to natural theology as Thomas understood it collapse. On the other hand, Barth's admission that a certain knowledge of God has always been available to those who have not received the Gospel frees him from the standard charges of radical fideism, arguably at least.

Of course the thesis requires much further discussion; 'intriguing' it no doubt is, as Campbell says, but it is not so easily dismissed as he seems to think. While it is true that the issues at the centre of the great nature/grace controversies in the early decades of the twentieth century are much more important here, there is surely scope also for reflection by philosophers of religion.

V

'In Catholic dogmatics, which follow St Thomas', according to Karl Barth, 'the life of God was identified with the notion of pure being'. In other words, 'the idea of God was not determined by the doctrine of the Trinity, but ... shaped by a general conception of God (that of ancient Stoicism and Neo-Platonism).' 'Starting from the generalised notion of God, the idea of the divine simplicity was necessarily exalted to the all-controlling principle, the idol, which, devouring everything concrete, stands behind all these formulae'. Despite the principle that God is not in any class – *Deus non est in aliquo genere* – a principle Barth adopts from Thomas, it turns out that Roman Catholic theology 'thinks it possible at every opportunity to fall back upon a concept of being which comprehends God and what is not God, and therefore at bottom to explain all the relations between God and what is not God in the form of an exposition of this general concept [being]'.[7] This generalised notion of God, arrived at by metaphysical reasoning, is opposed to the specifically Christian doctrine of God as Trinity, historically disclosed in the Bible. Which of these conceptions of God we meet in Thomas's theology, particularly in the opening questions of the *Summa theologiae*, is a deeply contested matter. Here again, in a different way, how the text is read in philosophy of religion contexts needs to be related to certain theological claims.

In a much cited essay first published in 1960 Karl Rahner subjected to severe criticism the separation of the courses *de Deo uno* from those *de Deo trino* in the standard neo-Thomist theology curriculum, claiming even that this division and priority are not traditional but invented by Thomas Aquinas.[8]

However that may be, Rahner's is a contestable reading of Thomas. As Henri de Lavalette pointed out, in 1962, in an almost totally neglected review, this is not a marginal or secondary issue. What is involved, on his view, is the way in which Christians should read the Old Testament – not whether Aquinas's God is the God of the philosophers (post-Enlightenment at that).[9]

For Thomas, the history of God's self revelation begins with the revelation of the divine being (Exodus 3:14: 'I am Who am') and continues with the revelation of the three divine persons, prefigured (certainly) in various ways, particularly in the Wisdom literature. For Rahner, by contrast, the history of Christian revelation begins with God as a person without origin in His relationship with the world, and continues with the revelation of this divine person as the origin of the procession within the Godhead from whom the other two persons proceed.

This second view, as de Lavalette contends, is grounded on the fact that, in the New Testament, the expression *ho Theos* always designates the Father – or so Rahner maintained in a much earlier influential paper, dating to 1950/51.[10] Offered as providing a better foundation in biblical theology for the usual course *de Deo uno* – 'in most cases just philosophy with a few trimmings of Scripture' – Rahner concluded that the Greek patristic conception of the Trinity turns out to be closer to biblical usage than the Latin or Scholastic view.

However that may be, Thomas maintained explicitly, against Bonaventure, that it is wrong 'first to posit the Father as God and then later to study His paternity', giving as his reason the fact that 'the Father is such only in His relationship to the Son and the Holy Spirit: No one knows the Father except the Son'.

In effect, Bonaventure and Rahner are on the same side, advocating a thoroughly Christian and thus Trinitarian appropriation of the Old Testament. In contrast, Thomas emphasizes the difference between the Old Testament and the New: in the former, the Father has not yet been revealed as the Father of His only-begotten Son, which means that the God of the Old Testament is not to be identified as the first person of the Trinity. Rather, for Thomas, the God of the Old Testament is (implicitly) God as Trinity, and not any one of the three persons.

Thomas maintains that it is only in the Son that it is possible for anyone to know the Father, as follows:

> I say that the name of God the Father could be known in three ways: Insofar as He is creator of all things, and in this respect He was known to the Gentiles (Romans 1:19–20) ... Secondly, as one to whom alone true worship should be addressed, and in this respect He was not known by the pagans, who worshipped other gods, but only by the Jews, who alone were commanded in the Law to worship none but the Lord ... Thirdly, as the Father of His only-begotten Son Jesus Christ and in this way He

was known to no one but was made known by the Son when the Apostles believed Him to be Son of God (in Joann., 2195).

Thus, God is known as Father only to Christians; God is known as Lord, to the Jews; and God is known as 'God' to pagans who know Him as creator. Elsewhere Thomas puts it as follows:

> There are three ways of having knowledge of God – the first is through Christ, in the sense that God is the Father of the only begotten and consubstantial one, as well as the rest of the knowledge which Christ taught about God the Father and Son and Holy Spirit, as regards unity of essence and eternity of persons – this is solely a matter of faith, never explicitly believed in the Old Testament except only by minors; secondly, God alone is to be worshipped and this was also (or even: *etiam*) believed by the Jews; and thirdly that there is one God and this is known also by the philosophers themselves, and is not a matter of faith (in Hebr., 577).

Thus, on the interpretation encouraged by Rahner's essays, the God of Thomas' *Summa theologiae* is the God whose existence and nature are established by philosophical reasoning, whereas we should do better, and be more faithful to Christian revelation, to begin from God as Father.

Thomas's view, however, is more complicated. Indeed, it is entirely different from Rahner's account. His theology begins neither from the God of the ancient philosophers (certainly not from any God to whose existence modern philosophers might reason) nor from God understood as Father. He has a kind of layered conception of God: God as creator of whose existence the philosophers have knowledge; God as the Lord whom the people of the Law were commanded to worship; and God as the Trinity, of whom knowledge has been communicated by Christ to the apostles.

The decision to open the *Summa theologiae* with a treatment of God in His divine being (or essence), before moving to the distinction of persons, and then the coming forth of creatures from God (cf. la q2 prologue), is grounded in the way that the self-revelation of the triune God begins in the Bible with the revelation of the divine being (Exodus 3:14). In a way, instead of being anachronistically concerned with post-Enlightenment foundationalist apologetics (as Rahner effectively maintains), we might rather say that Thomas is engaged in very rudimentary inter-faith dialogue: the triune God whom he worshipped daily in the liturgy of the Church was the Lord God whom the people of the Law were commanded to worship, and the God whose singular being the philosophers of Athens and Rome had already discovered by reasoning from the existence of the world.

The past tenses should be noted, as regards the ancient philosophers as well as the Jews.

We have already seen that the Five Ways simply recapitulate the arguments of the ancient philosophers. With the supersessionist assumptions of Christian interpretation of the Old Testament, unquestioned until the later twentieth century, Thomas obviously had no understanding of the continuing existence of Judaism. On the other hand, as de Lavalette suggests, his approach to the God question in the *Summa Theologiae* owes just as much to his understanding of the Old Testament as of the ancient pagan philosophers.

When he argues that Jewish infants should not be baptized against their parents' wishes (3a q68, art.10), Thomas is aware of the existence of Jews and the problems this entailed. He cites Gratian's *Decreta*, the basic canon law of his day, quoting the Fourth Council of Toledo (633) to the effect that the Jews were not to be coerced into receiving baptism; but he must have been well aware of the rising hostility to the Jewish minorities. In 1215, for instance, the Fourth Lateran Council decreed the wearing of distinctive clothing by Jews. He must have known that his view, though in line with canon law, was by no means generally accepted. He must also have been aware of a certain tension between the continuing and so highly problematic existence of Jewish communities within Christendom and his theological understanding of the Old Law as prefiguring the Christian dispensation but now of course superseded. His fascination with the Old Law is attested by the lengthy (if largely unread) analysis that he provides in his treatise on law in the *Summa Theologiae* (eight questions; compared with the one question on natural law); but the tone is set at the beginning – 'There is no doubt that the Old Law *was* good' (1a 2ae q98, a1, my italics).

For all the questions that we should raise now (very belatedly) about the supersessionist assumptions of traditional Christian theology, we cannot expect Thomas not to take them for granted. He was convinced, having inherited the scheme that goes back at least to Origen, that the Old Testament (Hebrew Bible but with the Hellenistic Greek Wisdom books) prefigures both the New Testament dispensation and the final consummation of both Old and New Testaments in the beatific vision. When the divine mysteries were disclosed to the people of the Old Testament as it were veiled by means of figures, *sub quodam figurarum velamine*, that gave them an implicit knowledge of these realities (cf. 1a 2ae q101, a2).

With the supersessionism built into this prefigurative-Christological interpretation, the sacred writings of the people of Israel were certainly appropriated by the Church. On the other hand, with the continuity as well as discontinuity built into the practice of prefigurative hermeneutics, it was easy for Thomas to take the self-revelation of the divine being attested in the Old Testament as the first phase of this divine being's self-revelation as triune in the Christian dispensation – and that, in turn, as the anticipation of the beatific vision of the triune God in heaven.

VI

Thus we have two past tenses. When he provides arguments for the existence of God, Thomas is only recalling arguments that he takes to have been accepted as valid since ancient times. He does not think of them as new arguments which he was, or should have been, defending as if from scratch. He was not trying to convince an atheist by arguments which he or anyone else would have regarded as controversial, exploratory, innovative and so on. Thomas thought that God's existence could be demonstrated by philosophical argument simply because it *had been* – long ago. And the problem with the fool who denied God's existence in his heart is that, in doing so, he *sins*: atheism is a theological category for Aquinas.

The God to whom Thomas introduces his readers at the beginning of the *Summa Theologiae* is the God who is 'beginning and end of everything', *principium rerum et finis earum*. To say this much is, of course, already to think of the world as having an origin which is also governing, and a goal which is a destiny. Whether he was aware that the Greek *arche*, in Plato and Aristotle, combines inception with domination, Thomas takes the word *principium* to have that double meaning. Again, whether he understood Aristotle's word *telos* to mean *finis* as well as purpose, the word *finis* in Thomas's work always has that ambivalence.

In short, Thomas inherited, and knew that he inherited, two different traditions: ancient philosophy and the Old Law. (It would take us too far afield to consider how much he recognized Moslems and Jews in his day as mediators of these two traditions.) He had no doubt that the ancient philosophers had discovered a certain amount of truth about God – about God's existence, uniqueness, and so on. Equally, he believed that this was the true God who was revealed to the people of the Old Testament and whom they were called and commanded to worship, and with whom now, since the Incarnation and Pentecost, he was himself in communion.

In other words: there never was any God but the creator of the world about whom the philosophers have discovered some truth, and that God was the God whom the Old Testament people worshipped as Lord. That is the one God with whom Thomas decided to open the *Summa Theologiae* – the very same God whom Jesus Christ taught his disciples to call 'Father', and who was thus revealed as Trinity.

The lesson we might learn from Thomas's *de Deo uno*, then, far from being how to conduct foundationalist apologetics, is perhaps rather to understand how to engage with diverse religious traditions. Indeed, the neo-Platonic/Aristotelian inheritance might well be described as religious and certainly not as remote from the Old Testament as communicated through Septuagint and Vulgate as would nowadays often be supposed.

The picture of the Lord God in the Hebrew books of the Bible is already modified by the Greek books and the Septuagint translation (from mid third century BCE) – so that, centuries before Thomas Aquinas, relying on Exod 3:14, thinkers like Philo of Alexandria could envisage God as the metaphysical first principle of the universe, a perfectly simple, unchangeable, unfathomable being. The God who is the fullness of life and energy – the Living God of the Bible – was already identified by the participle phrase '*ho on*': *ipsum esse subsistens*. The God whom Thomas worshiped liturgically and identified *in figura* in the daily Old Testament readings also raised the kind of metaphysical questions that could not be answered except by the kind of reading of Exodus 3:14 already canonised by the Septuagint.

This is no doubt a hermeneutic crux. We need not take it for granted, as on the standard view we usually do, that Aquinas's Five Ways stand at the beginning of the tradition that concludes with 'purely philosophical' ('natural theological') attempts to prove the existence of some generalised deity: no one's God but the deity rather of a certain style of philosophical speculation. Rather, Aquinas may be approached as a culminating point in the long tradition of uniting the God of the Septuagint with the Existent that dates back at least to Philo.

Thomas's approach, in the *Summa Theologiae*, may be read, as it usually is, as deliberately turning away from the Bible, choosing Aristotle, and opening the way to rationalist apologetics. In the light of much recent study, it may also be read, quite contrariwise, as continuing more than a thousand years of reading the Vulgate in the light of a certain neo-Platonism (Augustine but also Dionysius and Proclus). Far from inaugurating post Enlightenment evidentialist apologetics, Aquinas would remain indebted to and consonant with the Jewish way of thinking about God that goes back through Philo to the Hellenistic Judaism of the Septuagint. Far from being less biblical than his critics he would actually be much more biblical – meaning by this, however, Hellenistic-Jewish. The Thomas in whose work so many modern critics find the static deity of classical theism is, much more plausibly, the theologian whose God, as *ipsum esse subsistens*, is the 'sheer existence' self-disclosed in the burning bush (Exodus 3) – *ho on* – as the Jewish translators of the Pentateuch into Greek chose to say. In short, Thomism is as plausibly understood as an heir of Hellenistic Judaism as the bastard child of Aristotelian metaphysics.

Whatever the outcome, such theological considerations should be allowed to disturb the standard assumptions about the paradigmatic status of the Five Ways in philosophical theology: philosophy of religion may not be so easy to keep free of theology as is often supposed.

Notes

1. K. Barth, *The Epistle to the Romans* (Oxford: Oxford University Press, 1933), p. 46.
2. Ibid., p. 53.
3. Douglas A. Campbell, 'Natural Theology in Paul? Reading Romans 1: 19–20', *International Journal of Systematic Theology* 1 (1999): 231–252.
4. Karl Barth, *Church Dogmatics* (Edinburgh: T & T Clark, 1956–1975), II/1, p. 127.
5. Eugene F. Rogers, Jr., *Thomas Aquinas and Karl Barth: Sacred Doctrine and the Natural Knowledge of God* (Notre Dame and London: University of Notre Dame Press, 1995).
6. Rogers, p. 183.
7. Barth, *CD* II/1, p. 329.
8. Karl Rahner, "Remarks on the Dogmatic Treatise 'De Trinitate'," *Theological Investigations* 4 (London: Darton Longman & Todd, 1966). pp. 77–102.
9. H. de Lavalette, 'Bulletin de Théologie Dogmatique', *Recherches de Science Religieuse* 50 (1962): 119–123 especially.
10. Rahner, 'Theos in the New Testament', *Theological Investigations* 1 (Baltimore, Helicon Press and London: Darton, Longman & Todd, 1961), pp. 79–148.

Address for correspondence: Professor Fergus Kerr, Blackfriars Hall, University of Oxford OX1 3LY, United Kingdom
Fax: 01865278403; E-mail: 100755.1363@compuserve.com

Process philosophy of religion

DAVID RAY GRIFFIN
Claremont School of Theology

'Process philosophy' here refers to the movement that has Alfred North Whitehead at its center, with William James and Charles Hartshorne as the main predecessor and successor, respectively. It is a philosophy of *religion* primarily by virtue of seeking to show how religion and science can be fused 'into one rational scheme of thought'.[1] Process philosophy of religion is often called 'process theology', but this latter term can also refer to the use of Whiteheadian categories for articulating the doctrines of a particular religion. To speak of process philosophy of religion is to refer to process theology insofar as it is a 'natural theology' discussing general ideas that could in principle be employed by the theologians of all religions. To make this distinction does not imply, however, that process philosophy is a 'natural' theology in the sense of occupying a neutral standpoint superior to the standpoints of all the particular religious traditions. When this question is in view, process philosophy must be called a *Christian* natural theology,[2] to acknowledge the vision of reality by which it is shaped. It is, nevertheless, a *philosophy*, or a *natural* theology, because it bases its truth-claims not on the authority of any putative revelation but solely on the general philosophical criteria of adequacy and self-consistency.

To provide a historical discussion of process philosophy of religion from 1970 to 2000 would mean treating the thought of a great number of thinkers. Given the constraints of both time and space, I decided that I could write a coherent essay only by summarizing the main ways in which I myself have employed the Whiteheadian position to address two central topics: the problem of evil and the relation between science and religion. Prior to these substantive topics, I discuss the sense in which process philosophy is a type of 'metaphysics'.

1. Pragmatic metaphysics

The debate about metaphysics is greatly confused by the existence of widely disparate conceptions of what metaphysics *is*. Those who denounce metaphysics as impossible, unnecessary, or undesirable usually mean by it something very different from what Whitehead means. Many critics, for example, presuppose a Kantian conception, according to which metaphysics is the attempt to talk about things beyond the limits of possible experience, but Whitehead understands it as the endeavour to construct a coherent scheme of ideas 'in terms of which every element of our experience can be interpreted', adding that the 'elucidation of immediate experience is the sole justification for any thought'.[3] Sometimes metaphysics is understood as an approach that necessarily does violence to experience for the sake of a tidy system, but Whitehead, who praises the intellectual life of William James for being one long 'protest against the dismissal of experience in the interest of system',[4] insists repeatedly on the need to consider the 'whole of the evidence', adding that: 'We must be systematic; but we should keep our systems open'.[5] Some philosophers reject metaphysical systems on the grounds that they arrogantly claim to attain certainty, but Whitehead regards a metaphysical system as a tentative hypothesis, an 'experimental adventure', adding that 'the merest hint of dogmatic certainty as to finality of statement is an exhibition of folly'.[6] Closely related is the widespread assumption that metaphysics is necessarily 'foundationalist' in the sense now widely discredited, according to which the philosopher begins with a few indubitable basic beliefs, from which all other beliefs are deduced. But Whitehead explicitly rejected the idea 'that metaphysical thought started from principles which were individually clear, distinct, and certain'.[7]

Equally inapplicable is the rejection of metaphysics in the name of pragmatism. The classical pragmatists – Peirce, James, and Dewey – did, to be sure, reject a certain type of metaphysics. As Hilary Putnam has recently said, they denied 'that there is a "first philosophy" higher than the practice that we take most seriously when the chips are down. There is no Archimedean point from which we can argue that what is indispensable in life *gilt nicht in der Philosophie*.'[8] An enterprise called metaphysics, however, need not make such a claim. Hartshorne, for example, endorses the 'pragmatic principle' that 'what we have to be guided by in our decision-making, we should not pretend to reject theoretically'.[9] Whitehead even said that no philosophical dogma should be allowed to overcome 'the metaphysical rule of evidence: that we must bow to those presumptions, which, in despite of criticism, we still employ for the regulation of our lives'.[10]

Implicit in this statement is a criticism of Hume's fateful dualism between theory and practice, which allowed him to rest content with a philosophical theory that had no room for several 'natural beliefs' that, Hume admitted, he necessarily presupposed in his practical life, such as his beliefs in a real world and in causation as the real influence of one thing on another. Whitehead, in fact, makes this criticism explicit, saying:

> Whatever is found in 'practice' must lie within the scope of the metaphysical description. When the description fails to include the 'practice', the metaphysics is inadequate and requires revision. There can be no appeal to practice to supplement metaphysics. . . . Metaphysics is nothing but the description of the generalities which apply to all the details of practice.[11]

In light of Putnam's statement, we can say that Whitehead has produced a *pragmatic metaphysics*. In the remainder of this essay, I will show how this conception of metaphysics is central to process philosophy of religion.

First, however, I must respond to the question of why the inevitable presuppositions of practice, which I have come to call our 'hard-core commonsense notions',[12] should be taken as criteria of truth, in the negative sense that any position rejecting them can be assumed to be false. Could one not claim, in Humean or neo-Darwinian fashion, that they may simply be, in Kant's phrase, 'metaphysical illusions', perhaps programmed into us by Nature because believing them increases our chances of survival? The problem with any such argument is that the denial of any of our hard-core commonsense beliefs involves one in self-contradiction. If I verbally deny causation, freedom, or an external world, I am explicitly denying while implicitly affirming one and the same idea. Karl-Otto Apel and Jürgen Habermas make this point in terms of the concept of a 'performative contradiction', which occurs, in Martin Jay's words, 'when whatever is being claimed is at odds with the presuppositions or implications of the act of claiming it'.[13] One is thereby violating the law of noncontradiction, which is the first rule of reason.

To be sure, some extremists, in their rejection of any universal principles of reason, have denied the necessary validity of even this principle. But any such rejection is self-defeating, as Putnam has realized. Having at one time joined Willard van Quine in denying that there are any *a priori* truths different in kind from empirical truths, thereby suggesting that even the most fundamental laws of logic are in principle revisable, Putnam has more recently argued, in 'There is at least one a priori truth',[14] that the principle of noncontradiction is an absolutely unrevisable a priori truth. To violate it, even implicitly, is to renounce the basic principle of rational criticism. By acknowledging both the law of noncontradiction and the existence of a set of hard-core commonsense notions, which cannot be denied without self-contradiction, we are led to see that these notions must be employed as ultimate criteria for judging any philosophical position, so that any metaphysics, to be rational, must be a pragmatic metaphysics.

2. Panentheism and evil

Perhaps the topic on which the position of process philosophy of religion is best known is the problem of evil. John Hick, for example, has called process theodicy one of the 'three main Christian responses to the problem of evil', with the other two being the Augustinian and Irenaean. Barry Whitney, in his bibliography of recent theodicies, ranks process theodicy, along with the theodicies of Hick and Alvin Plantinga, as among the most important ones in the twentieth century.[15] I will here summarize its main points.

The crucial difference between it and theodicies based on traditional theism – whether of the all-determining type, exemplified by Augustine and Calvin, or of the free-will type, exemplified by Hick and Plantinga – lies in process philosophy's *panentheism*, which combines features of pantheism and traditional theism. Like pantheism, it holds that the existence of God necessarily involves the existence of the world. Like traditional theism, it holds that God is distinct from the world, able to act in it, and that our particular world (which evidently came into existence some 10 to 15 billion years ago) exists contingently, being rooted in a free divine decision. What exists necessarily, in other words, is not simply God but God-and-a-world, and yet the 'world' that exists necessarily is not our particular world, with its electrons, neutrons, and inverse square law of gravitation, but simply some world or other. The idea that a realm of finite actualities has always existed means that our particular world was not created *ex nihilo* in the strict sense, meaning out of a situation with a complete absence of finite actualities.

The doctrine of *creatio ex nihilo* in this strict sense has always been connected with the idea that none of the principles exemplified in our world, whether called 'natural laws' or 'metaphysical principles', are really 'natural' in the sense of existing naturally or really 'metaphysical' in the sense of obtaining necessarily. Rather, they are all 'arbitrary' in the sense of being rooted in the divine will. Having been freely created, furthermore, they can be freely interrupted. These ideas are part and parcel of the traditional doctrine of omnipotence, which led to the traditional problem of evil, with its questions: If God is truly good, why did God make the world such that so much evil is possible? And, having done so, why does God, who could unilaterally prevent any particular tragic event, permit so much unbearable suffering?

Process philosophy returns to the Platonic view according to which *our* world was created in time but *the* world, in the sense of a multiplicity of finite actualities, has always existed. This position provides the basis for a distinction between *cosmological* principles, which are distinctive of our particular cosmos, and *metaphysical* principles, which would necessarily be embodied in any world that God could create. According to process philosophy, one of these metaphysical principles is that the actualities making up a world have their own power. This is because the formless stuff of which all finite actualities are composed is not passive 'matter', as Plato said, but active 'creativity', which means the twofold power of self-determination and efficient causation. The doctrine, more precisely, is that any actual entity is a momentary 'actual occasion,' which first exercises a degree of self-determination in creating itself out of the causal influences it has received from prior actual occasions, then exerts efficient causation on future occasions. This twofold creativity of each actual occasion can be influenced but not completely determined by divine power, this being the principle that lies behind process philosophy's well-known dictum that divine power is persuasive, not coercive. Whereas traditional theism says that all creative power belongs essentially to God alone, so that any creative power in the world is a loan that could be withdrawn at any time, process philosophy says that creative power is inherent in the world as well as in God.

This idea, which means that God is not omnipotent in the traditional sense, provides the first element in a process theodicy. It implies that God simply cannot occasionally interrupt the basic causal principles by which the world usually operates. Because traditional theism says that God *could* interrupt these principles, it is rightly called 'supernaturalism'. Process theism, by rejecting this supernaturalism, is a form of *naturalistic* theism. God is 'all-powerful' in the sense of having all the power that one being could possibly have, but not in the sense of essentially having literally *all* the power, because that is (by hypothesis) impossible. To ask why God does not (unilaterally) prevent various evils implies, therefore, a false metaphysics.

Another metaphysical principle, besides the necessary existence of a word with partially self-determining creatures, is that any such world would embody a set of variables of power and value that are positively correlated such that if any of them increases, the remainder of them must increase proportionately. These variables are: the capacity to experience intrinsic good; the capacity to experience intrinsic evil; the power to the extrinsically good – that is, to contribute positively to the experience of others; the power to be extrinsically evil; and the power of self-determination, which in its higher forms we call 'freedom'.

It is obvious that these variables are positively correlated in our world: Creatures with more capacity for intrinsic value, such as human beings, also have more freedom and more power to influence others, for both good and ill, than lower-level creatures, such as organelles, mice, or even chimpanzees. Process theodicy is based on the idea that these correlations are not merely empirical but also metaphysical, so that they would necessarily obtain in any world that God could have created. We do not need to ask, accordingly, various standard questions, such as why God did not create human beings as 'rational saints', meaning beings with all the capacities we have for realizing values but guaranteed not to sin, or why God did not make us much less capable of inflicting suffering on others. Process theodicy maintains that to ask these questions is like asking why God did not make round squares. This process view leads to the conclusion that the only way God could have guaranteed the absence of the kinds of evils created by human beings would have been not to have created human-like beings at all. From this perspective, one could indict God for the evils of human history only if one could honestly say that these evils are so great that God should have rested content with creatures at the level of dolphins and chimpanzees.[16]

It is widely recognized that a position such as that of process philosophy can avoid the traditional problem of evil. For example, John Mackie, in his well-known argument that the world's evil makes the existence of God highly improbable, adds that theists who believe in a deity who is 'though powerful, not quite omnipotent, will not be embarrassed by this difficulty'.[17] Those who make such admissions, however, usually add the caveat that such doctrines 'are not really theism' because the putative deity is not worthy of the name 'God'.

Process theists give three rebuttals. The first rebuttal is that we do *not* affirm the idea, suggested by Mackie's phrase 'not quite omnipotent', that God has less power than some conceivable being might have. We hold that power is a relational concept, so that the traditional doctrine of omnipotence, according to which all power essentially belongs to God alone, is incoherent, which means that it provides no standard by which to regard the deity of process theism as imperfect in power.

The second rebuttal involves pointing out that process theism affirms all the elements in what can be called 'the generic idea of God in Western civilization', namely, a personal, purposive, holy being who is perfect in love, goodness, beauty, wisdom, knowledge, and power; who is creator and sustainer of our universe, providentially active in nature and history, and experienced by human beings; who exists necessarily, everlastingly, and all-prevasively; and who is the ultimate source of moral norms, the ultimate guarantee of the meaning of life, and the ground of hope for the victory of good over evil. It would be strange to claim that an actuality with all of these characteristics would not be worthy of the name 'God'.

Some critics do, nevertheless, make this claim, because they hold that process theism denies one of the most important ingredients in the meaning of 'God' in all biblically-based religions, which is the kind of omnipotence correlative with *creatio ex nihilo*. A third rebuttal by process theists, made in response to this claim, involves pointing out that historical scholars have now shown the doctrine of *creatio ex nihilo* to be postbiblical: Besides not being present in the Hebrew Bible, it is also not present in inter-testamental literature (including 2 Maccabees), a fact that undermines the old argument that it would have been presupposed by the authors of those ambiguous New Testament passages that have often been said to imply it. The doctrine of *creatio ex nihilo* in the strict sense was first articulated by Christian theologians, in response to Marcion's gnostic theology, in the latter part of the second century. Prior to that time, Christian as well as Jewish theologians had accepted the idea, suggested by both the Bible and Plato, that our world was created out of a primordial chaos.[18] Process theism, accordingly, involves a return to the biblical idea of creation.[19]

Although the preceding discussion simply presupposed process philosophy's idea of God, I have also argued that *natural theology* in the sense of 'arguments for the existence of God' can be much more convincing within the context of *naturalistic theism* than it can when philosophers are trying to prove the existence of the God of traditional theism. For example, Richard Swinburne suggests that a number of arguments constitute a cumulative case showing theism to be *somewhat* more probable than not and that with the addition of the argument from religious experience it becomes 'significantly more probable than not'.[20] But there is also a cumulative case *against* (traditional) theism, as Caroline Franks Davis points out, and John Hick concludes, largely because of the problem of evil, that the world is religiously 'ambiguous', meaning that theism *cannot* be 'shown to be in any objective sense more probable than not'.[21] Presupposing instead the God of process theism, I argue that there are many reasons to affirm the existence of a deity something like this and *no* evidence against it, so that the truth of (naturalistic) theism is '*overwhelmingly* more probable than the truth of atheism'.[22] The arguments, of course, have their full force only within the framework of process philosophy's ontology and epistemology – which brings us to the relation between science and religion.

3. Science and religion

At the very heart of process philosophy of religion is its way of overcoming the conflict that has been widely perceived to exist, especially since the middle of the nineteenth century, between science and religion. This solution involves three points: (1) the realization that the conflict is not between science as such and religion as such but between the supernaturalism with which religion is often associated and the form of naturalism with which science has been associated; (2) the realization that this form of naturalism is less adequate for science than is the kind of naturalism provided by process philosophy; and (3) the realization that religion does not need supernaturalism and is, in fact, better supported by the theistic naturalism supplied by process philosophy. I begin with a discussion of the first point. The second point will then be illustrated in terms of a number of hard-core commonsense assumptions to which the currently dominant kind of naturalism cannot do justice. The direction the argument for the third point would take is illustrated in terms of some ways in which this position can affirm ideas usually assumed to require supernaturalism.

The nature of the apparent conflict between science and religion

Although the so-called rise of modern science in the seventeenth century was associated with a supernaturalistic worldview, the scientific community quickly moved in a naturalistic direction – toward, that is, the denial of any supernatural interventions in the world. This complete denial was achieved in the middle of the nineteenth century, most notably in David Friedrich Strauss in biblical criticism and Charles Darwin in evolutionary theory. While affirming naturalism in this sense, however, Strauss and Darwin both retained belief in a divine reality – a Hegelian *Geist* for Strauss, a deistic creator for Darwin. In the following decades, the naturalism of the scientific community came increasingly to be framed within an atheistic, materialistic worldview. The term 'naturalism' is, in fact, now widely used to designate a worldview that, besides accepting the sensationist doctrine of perception formulated by early modern empiricists such as Locke, rejects Locke's theism and mind-matter dualism in favor of atheism and materialism.

It is important to see, however, that two distinguishable meanings are involved. The basic, minimal meaning of naturalism, which is simply the denial of supernatural interruptions, can be called 'naturalism$_{ns}$' (for 'nonsupernaturalistic'). Naturalism in this minimal sense is now one of the scientific community's most fundamental ontological assumptions, which it is unlikely to relinquish. The present conflict between the worldviews of the religious and the scientific communities cannot be overcome unless the religious communities relinquish supernaturalism in favor of a worldview embodying naturalism$_{ns}$. Whiteheadian panentheism, we saw in the previous section, provides such a worldview.

The maximal meaning of naturalism can be called 'naturalism$_{sam}$' (for 'sensationist-atheist-materialist'). Naturalism$_{sam}$ is incompatible not only with supernaturalistic religion but with any significantly religious outlook whatsoever. Its atheism and materialism mean that there can be no Divine Actuality, no place for moral norms to exist, no freedom, and no life after death, while its sensationism means that there could be no experience of moral ideals or a Divine Reality, even if they existed. The present conflict between the worldviews of the religious and the scientific communities cannot be overcome unless the scientific community decides that it should reject naturalism$_{sam}$.

The next step in the argument is that the scientific community should do just that, because naturalism$_{sam}$ is far less adequate for science itself than the kind of naturalism provided by process philosophy, which can be called 'naturalism$_{ppp}$', with 'ppp' standing for 'prehensive-panentheist-panexperientialist'. It replaces sensationism with a *prehensive* doctrine of perception, according to which the fundamental form of perception is nonsensory prehension; it replaces atheism with panentheism; and it replaces materialism with panexperientialism. 'Panentheism' has already been explained; the meaning of the other two terms will be made clear in the ensuing discussion of a number of issues for which naturalism$_{ppp}$ can be seen to be more adequate, for both science and religion, than naturalism$_{sam}$.

Scientific categories: Time, causation, and actual existence

Each aspect of naturalistic$_{sam}$ creates problems for science as well as for religion. The present section deals with problems that arise from its sensationism, which is the doctrine that perception can be exhaustively equated with *sensory* perception. Although this doctrine is widely thought to be both presupposed and confirmed by science, Whitehead argues that 'science conceived as resting on mere sense perception, with no other source of observation, is bankrupt'.[23] His contention is that although all *exact* observation is based on data from our sensory organs, '[t]he scientific categories of thought are obtained elsewhere'.[24] Whitehead means categories such as actuality (traditionally called 'substance'), causation, and time.

This problem was implicit in the earlier discussion of Hume's dualism between theory and practice. Hume insisted on *conceptual empiricism*, according to which we allow in our theory only concepts that are based on direct experience. According to his analysis of sensory experience, however, its data consist exhaustively of universals, such as colors and shapes, rather than telling us of the existence of a world of actually existing things. Therefore, although Hume knew that in practice he inevitably presupposed the existence of an 'external world', he in theory, *qua* philosopher, had to be a solipsist, not knowing whether anything beyond his own experience actually existed. He also argued that sensory perception provides no knowledge of causation, in the sense of one thing actually influencing another thing, so that there would be some necessary connection between them. At the outset of the twentieth century, Santayana extended Hume's analysis to argue that the philosopher, *qua* philosopher, must affirm 'solipsism of the present moment',[25] because sensory perception does not reveal the existence of the past or the future, which means that it cannot provide us with the category of time.

Science could not exist without the categories of time, causation, and actual existence, and yet the data provided by our sensory organs do not provide these categories. It was Kant's realization of the seriousness of this problem that led to his empiricism-rejecting 'Copernican revolution', according to which these (and other) categories are inherent in the mind. As a supernaturalist, Kant could understand this inherence in terms of divine implantation. Within a naturalistic framework, however, science is in the awkward position of advocating empiricism while being devoid of any empirical justification for its own basic categories.

Unlike many philosophers, Whitehead believes that the empiricist ideals should be retained. He accepts 'Hume's doctrine that nothing is to be received into the philosophical scheme which is not discoverable as an element in subjective experience', which means that 'Hume's demand that causation be describable as an element in experience is ... entirely justifiable'.[26] Whitehead is able to accept these ideals, however, only because he rejects Hume's own superficial empiricism, which is actually unempirical,[27] in favor of what William James called *radical* empiricism. Although Whitehead does not follow James's doctrine in every respect, he does develop James's contentions that we have nonsensory as well as sensory perception and that, therefore, the data of perception are not limited to isolated sense data but include relations, especially *causal* relations. Whitehead, in fact, calls the nonsensory mode of perception, which is the more fundamental mode, 'perception in the mode of causal efficacy', thereby emphasizing the fact that in this mode we directly perceive the causal influence of other actualities on our own experience. I am aware, for example, that I see the computer screen in front of me *by means of* my eyes – that is, by virtue of the causal efficacy of my eyes for my experience.[28]

The point is that sensory perception involves two distinct modes of perception. The mode emphasized by Hume, which involves the perception of sense data such as colored shapes, Whitehead calls 'perception in the mode of presentational immediacy' because, as Hume and Santayana emphasized, its data are simply present to the mind, giving no information about the past or the future or even about an actual world beyond the perceiver's own present experience. Although Humean empiricism has equated sensory perception with this mode of perception, full-fledged sensory perception also involves 'perception in the mode of causal efficacy', through which we derive the category of causation. Whitehead also refers to this mode as 'physical prehension': the term 'prehension' indicates that what is involved is a real *grasping* of some object, whereas the term 'physical' means that experience begins with the prehension of other *actualities*. It is through this mode of perception, therefore, that we get the category of other actual existents. And it is from this mode that we get the category of time, because the separation of the world 'into past and future lies with the mode of causal efficacy and not with that of presentational immediacy'.[29] Thanks to what I am calling Whitehead's prehensive doctrine of perception, therefore, process philosophy can do justice to our hard-core commonsense convictions about causation, the external world, the past, and time, thereby providing a more adequate basis for philosophy of science.

Religious experience

The way in which this nonsensationist doctrine of perception is most obviously relevant to philosophy of religion involves the controversy about religious experience. Sensationism has led to the widespread assumption that religious experience could never by *genuine*, in the sense of really involving a perception of a Holy Reality, at least without supernatural intervention. For example, J. J. C. Smart, stipulating that ' "getting in touch" involves response to physical stimuli,' says that physics and physiology enable us to explain 'how we can get in touch with rabbits or even with electrons' but that 'no naturalistic account could be given of mystical cognition of [a nonphysical Holy Reality]', so that 'if mystical experiences are not mere aberrations of feelings, ... then they must be in some way miraculous'.[30]

This conviction that mystical experiences, along with religious experiences more generally, are never genuine is widely shared among social scientists. In *Explaining Religion*, Samuel Preus says that the existence of religion must be explained on the assumption that 'God is not given'.[31] In *Explaining and Interpreting Religion*, Robert Segal says that social scientists are correct to assume that 'believers never encounter God'.[32] The social scientific tradition to which Preus and Segal refer, which includes Marx, Comte, Tylor, Frazer, Durkheim, and Freud, concluded, says Segal, that 'religion is false on philosophical, not social scientific, grounds'.[33] What kind of philosophical grounds were involved is suggested by Tylor's statement, quoted by Preus,[34] that Hume's *Natural History of Religion* 'is perhaps more than any other work the source of modern opinions as to the development of religion'.

Besides lying at the root of this tradition, Hume's sensationist doctrine of perception has also exerted tremendous influence through Kant, who said that to affirm a 'feeling of the immediate presence of the Supreme Being' would be a 'fanatical religious illusion' because it would be to affirm 'a receptivity for an intuition for which there is no sensory provision in man's nature'.[35] Kant, of course, assumed that there could be no cognitive intuitions that are not sensory. This Kantian assumption continues to influence many philosophers of religion and theologians, such as Gordon Kaufman, who, in response to the question as to what the word 'God' might refer, replies: 'Certainly not to anything we directly experience'.[36]

Whitehead's prehensive doctrine of perception, combined with his panentheism, provides a naturalistic account of how we could be 'in touch with' a Holy Reality, so that the term God *could* refer to something 'we directly experience'. It follows from panentheism, according to which the world is in God, that God is an omnipresent actuality. As such, God would be present to be experienced through our nonsensory mode of perception. This perception of God requires no special faculty, as often assumed, but falls simply under the category of 'physical prehension'. *Physical* prehensions, it must be remembered, are not limited to those whose objects are 'physical' in the ordinary (dualistic) sense of the term but include all prehensions whose objects are *actualities*. One's prehension of previous moments of one's own experience, which we call 'memory', is an example of physical prehension. Another example is the telepathic prehension of another person's mind, which Whitehead, like James before him, accepted. From the perspective of Whitehead's naturalism$_{ppp}$, accordingly, religious experience, understood as involving the direct experience of a Holy Actuality, is completely natural. We are perceiving God all the time. The only thing unusual about a 'religious experience' is that this perception, which usually occurs in the unconscious depths of experience, has risen to the level of consciousness.

Besides overcoming the presumption against the possibility of genuine religious experience generated by naturalism$_{sam}$, Whitehead's philosophy, with its panentheism, provides a new way to respond to the 'conflicting claims challenge' to the belief that religious experience involves a genuine experience of ultimate reality. This challenge is generated primarily by the fact that some people report an experience of communion with a *personal* ultimate reality, whereas others describe an experience of identity with an *impersonal* ultimate. John Hick, summarizing the skeptic's rhetorical question, asks: 'If religious experience constitutes an authentic window onto the Real, why does that reality look so different when seen through different windows?'[37] Or, as Caroline Franks Davis formulates the challenge: 'How can "ultimate reality" be both a personal being and an impersonal principle, identical to our inmost self and forever "other," loving and utterly indifferent, good and amoral . . . ?'[38] Most attempts to solve this problem, such as Hick's, have been based on the conviction that these diverse experiences all involve experiences of one and the same ultimate reality, with that conviction being rooted in the assumption that, in Hick's words, 'there cannot be a plurality of ultimates'.[39]

As John Cobb has emphasized, however, Whitehead's worldview has two ultimates: God and creativity. They are not in competition because God is an actuality whereas creativity is the formless reality embodied in all actualities. God, accordingly, can be called the 'personal ultimate' and creativity the 'impersonal ultimate'. We can say, accordingly, that the two basic types of religious experience, theistic and nontheistic, are experiences of different ultimate realities, with each description of ultimate reality being basically correct.[40]

Mathematical and moral objects

Another problem created by naturalism$_{sam}$ involves the fact that physics presupposes the existence of mathematical objects and our capacity to perceive (intuit) their existence. The traditional view, usually called 'Platonic realism', is that 'mathematical entities exist outside space and time, outside thought and matter, in an abstract realm'.[41] Most mathematicians in practice, virtually all commentators agree, presuppose this Platonic view.[42] According to the sensationist doctrine of perception, however, we can perceive things solely through our physical sense organs, which are suited to perceive only other physical things. Reuben Hersh charges mathematicians who accept the Platonic view with being 'unscientific', asking rhetorically: 'How does this [alleged] immaterial realm ... make contact with flesh and blood mathematicians?'[43]

One famous mathematician and logician, Kurt Gödel, solved this problem by simply rejecting sensationism. Arguing that 'we do have something like a perception ... of the objects of set theory', he added that he could not 'see any reason why we should have less confidence in this kind of perception, i.e., in mathematical intuition, than in sense perception'.[44] Most philosophers of mathematics, however, have not been able to countenance this rejection of the sensationist doctrine of perception. Hilary Putnam, for example, called Gödel's Platonism 'flatly incompatible with the simple fact that we think with our brains, and not with immaterial souls', adding that we 'cannot envisage *any* kind of neural process that could even correspond to the "perception of a mathematical object".'[45]

The atheism of naturalism$_{sam}$ makes the problem even more severe, as illustrated by Paul Benacerraf's 'Mathematical Truth',[46] in which he argued that true beliefs can be considered knowledge only if that which makes the belief true is *causally* responsible for the belief in an appropriate way. Summarizing the resulting problem for the Platonic view of mathematical entities, Penelope Maddy says: 'But how can entities that don't even inhabit the physical universe take part in any causal interaction whatsoever? Surely to be abstract is also to be causally inert. Thus if Platonism is true, we can have no mathematical knowledge.'[47] This problem is created not simply by Platonism, however, but by Platonism without God. As Hersh points out: 'For Leibniz and Berkeley, abstractions like numbers are thoughts in the mind of God [but] Heaven and the Mind of God are no longer heard of in academic discourse'.[48]

What is the mathematician or philosopher of mathematics to do? The most popular solution, according to Maddy, has been to continue presupposing Platonic realism in practice while publicly affirming 'formalism', according to which mathematics is just a game with meaningless symbols. The unsatisfactory nature of this solution is pointed to by Quine's emphasis on, in Putnam's words, 'the intellectual dishonesty of denying the existence of what one daily presupposes'.[49] But Quite adopts an equally problematic position. On the one hand, no one has insisted on sensationism more forcibly. Quine says, for example, that the 'stimulation of his sensory receptors is all the evidence anybody has to go on, ultimately, in arriving at his picture of the world'[50] and that 'whatever evidence there *is* for science *is* sensory evidence', which means that 'our statements about the external world face the tribunal of sense experience'.[51] On the other hand, as a 'physicalist', meaning one who takes physics to be the arbiter of what is real, Quine affirms the existence of mathematical entities simply on the ground that they are indispensable for physics. This means that Quine's physicalism 'is materialism, bluntly monistic *except for* the abstract objects of mathematics'.[52] Putnam, who accepts Quine's indispensability argument, says approvingly that Quine simply 'ignores the problem', created by his sensationism, 'as to how we can know that abstract entities exist unless we can interact with them in some way'.[53] Quine and Putnam also ignore the problem of how such entities can exist in an otherwise materialistic universe. These are examples of the irrationalism to which naturalism$_{sam}$ has led some of our prominent philosophers.

Closely parallel is the problem that naturalism$_{sam}$ creates for moral philosophy, because moral norms are in the same boat as mathematical objects. Given naturalism$_{sam}$, there is no place for moral norms to exist, and even if they could exist we would not be able to perceive them, both because they could exert no agency and because our sensory organs are equipped to perceive only physical objects. These arguments are applied to moral objects, in fact, by Princeton's Gilbert Harman and Cambridge's Bernard Williams.[54] Oxford's John Mackie, who bluntly says that '[t]here are no objective values',[55] rests part of his case on his atheism, part of it on the argument that if we could be aware of objective moral values, 'it would have to be by some special faculty of moral perception or intuition, utterly different from our ordinary ways of knowing everything else'.[56] On the basis of these considerations, many philosophers hold that morality is concerned, in the words of J. J. C. Smart, 'with evoking feelings and recommending actions, not with the cognition of facts'.[57]

The main problem with this view is that we all presuppose in practice that there really is a distinction between better and worse actions and states of affairs. Whitehead, in observing that 'the impact of ... moral notions is inescapable',[58] implies that the existence of objective moral norms is a hardcore commonsense notion. Even Mackie points out that objectivism about values has 'a firm basis in ... the meanings of moral terms' and that his own denial of this objectivism 'conflicts with what is sometimes called common sense'.[59]

Whitehead's affirmation of the existence of God is closely related to these issues. One important point is his rejection of the modern tendency, insofar as Platonic entities are affirmed at all, to limit them to purely mathematical entities. Referring to Platonic forms as 'eternal objects', Whitehead affirms the existence not only of 'eternal objects of the objective species', meaning 'the mathematical Platonic forms', but also 'eternal objects of the subjective species', which include moral norms.[60]

The next issue is how 'eternal objects' of any sort, which are not *actual* entities but merely possible ones, could exist and exert efficacy in the actual world. The key idea here is what Whitehead calls the 'ontological principle', which says both that only *actual* entities can *act* and that everything non-actual, such as eternal objects, must exist *in* something actual. This twofold point led Whitehead to affirm the old idea that 'the Platonic world of ideas' can exist because it 'subsists' in 'the primordial mind of God'.[61] The eternal objects can be efficacious in the world because God envisages them with appetition that they be realized in the world.[62] This appetition is effective because creatures not only prehend the divine appetitions but do so with initial conformation of feeling,[63] so that the divine appetition for that possibility to be actualized may become the creature's own appetition.

Viewed from the side of the creatures, even if a Platonic world of forms could exist on its own, it could not be prehended, because every experience must begin with *physical* prehensions of other actualities. But if the eternal objects are in the Divine Actuality, we can prehend them by means of prehending God. Accordingly, having said that we have 'experiences of ideals – of ideals entertained, of ideals aimed at, of ideals achieved, of ideals defaced', Whitehead concludes that the universe must include 'a source of ideals', adding that '[t]he effective aspect of this source is deity as immanent in the present experience'.[64]

Consciousness, mental action, and freedom

Naturalism$_{sam}$ has also resulted in an insoluble mind-body problem, as I have documented extensively in a book on the subject.[65] Although the sensationism and atheism of this form of naturalism contribute to the problem, the crucial element is its materialism, which includes two theses: (1) the claim that the ultimate units of nature are what Whitehead calls 'vacuous actualities', meaning that they are completely devoid of experience and thereby internal spontaneity; and (2) the claim that the mind is somehow identical with the brain. The second thesis – which constitutes materialism's difference from Cartesian dualism, with which it shares the first thesis – is defended primarily on the grounds that dualists cannot explain how mind and body can interact, at least now that the appeal to supernatural assistance, to which Descartes, Malebranche, and other dualists resorted, is no longer acceptable.

Materialism, however, turns out to have even more problems, being unable to do justice to at least three of our hard-core commonsense presuppositions: (1) mental causation, meaning that our decisions influence our bodily behavior; (2) freedom, meaning that our decisions are not wholly determined by antecedent factors but involve an element of self-determination in the moment; and (3) consciousness itself. With regard to *consciousness*, materialists not only share with dualists the problem of explaining how it could have emerged out of things completely devoid of experience, but they also, assuming that conscious experience is identical with a brain consisting of hundreds of billions of cells, have the additional problem of explaining its unity. With regard to *freedom*, some thinkers have assumed the problem to be mitigated by quantum physics' denial of complete determinism. As John Searle and others point out, however, any indetermination in the ultimate units of the world is canceled out in aggregates of such units by the 'law of large numbers'. The equation of the mind with the brain means, therefore, that the brain/mind must operate as deterministically as a rock. Finally, *mental causation*, even if not assumed to involve freedom, has proved impossible to conceive, given the fact that materialism assumes 'bottom-up' causation, according to which the behavior of all large things is entirely a function of the causation occurring at the micro-level. Some philosophers use these problems to recommend a return to mind-matter dualism, but its problems are equally insoluble.

Process philosophy, with its panexperientialism, provides a third alternative. The basic units of which the body is composed have a primitive form of experience. All actual occasions, out of which enduring individuals such as electrons are formed, are 'occasions of experience'. Because all occasions of experience are internally related to other ones by virtue of their prehensions of them, higher-level occasions of experience can arise, with the result that lower-level individuals, such as electrons and protons, can give rise to increasingly higher-level individuals, such as atoms, molecules, macromolecules, prokaryotic cells, eukaryotic cells, and animals. Rather than being mere aggregates of subatomic particles, these creatures are 'compound individuals', which means that they have a *regnant* or *dominant* member and thereby a unified experience.

According to this view, human beings and other animals do, as dualism said, have a soul or mind that is distinct from the brain. But dualism's problem of interaction between unlikes does not arise, because this soul is not ontologically different in kind, only greatly different in degree, from the actualities – the cells and their constituent parts – composing the brain. Process philosophy provides, therefore, a *nondualistic* interactionism. On this basis we can understand in principle not only how a mind with conscious experiences could arise out of the brain, but also how the decisions of the soul's occasions of experience can influence the brain and thereby the rest of the body, so that the 'mental causation' that we all presuppose in practice is intelligible.

This position also explains how it can be, as we constantly assume, that these decisions involve a degree of freedom, so that we are *responsible* for our bodily actions. In a compound individual, the more complex experience enjoyed by the regnant member includes a greater capacity for self-determination. Because the human being is not simply an aggregational society, but a compound individual, the spontaneity existing at the level of subatomic particles is, far from being canceled out by the law of large numbers, greatly amplified. Our presupposed freedom is no illusion.

Theistic evolution

Running short of space, I will discuss two other issues more briefly. For many intellectuals today, the crucial issue with regard to the relation between science and religion, especially theistic religion, is evolution. It is widely thought that neo-Darwinism really has, as its propagandists claim, explained how we and the rest of today's species could have evolved from inorganic matter without any theistic guidance. Among those who do not believe that neo-Darwinism's evolutionary naturalism provides an adequate explanation, it is widely thought that its deficiencies can only be overcome by affirming a supernatural creator.

My own reading of the literature has led me to the conclusion that neo-Darwinism is, as both 'young-Earth' and 'progressive' creationists claim, woefully inadequate, especially with regard to the apparent jumps in macroevolution. The problems, however, do not require the rejection of naturalism$_{ns}$, given the fact that naturalism$_{sam}$ is not the only or even the best form in which it is today embodied. Process philosophy's naturalism$_{ppp}$ provides a basis in which theistic guidance could, without any supernatural interventions, account for the developments left mysterious by neo-Darwinism. This conclusion does not, however, mean rejecting neo-Darwinism *tout court*. The position commonly referred to as *Darwinian* (meaning *neo-Darwinian*) *evolution* involves, I have pointed out,[66] at least fourteen distinguishable dimensions, so that it need not be taken or rejected wholesale. One can, for example, affirm the basic ideas of Darwin – that not only microevolution but also macroevolution occurs, that all complex organisms have descended from prior species, and that it all has occurred without supernatural intervention – while rejecting the more tendentious claims of neo-Darwinists, which are based more on deductions from naturalism$_{sam}$ than on empirical evidence and which are precisely the claims that appear to make evolutionism incompatible with any significantly religious view of the universe.

Parapsychology and life after death

Finally, part of my work as a philosopher of religion employing process philosophy has been to argue that it provides a framework that, while doing justice to what is usually understood to be *normal* experience and science, also allows for the 'paranormal' types of occurrences studied by parapsychology. In so doing, I mean to be carrying forward the work of William James, who said that science, so far as it denies paranormal occurrences, 'lies prostrate in the dust for me', adding that 'the most urgent intellectual need which I feel at present is that science be built up again in a form in which such things may have a positive place'.[67] I have argued that Whitehead's philosophy provides the basis for such a science.[68]

I have also sought to illustrate James's conviction that radical empiricism, understood as including psychical research, can provide important support for various religious convictions.[69] For example, telepathy provides an analogy for the kind of nonsensory perception that must occur if (theistic) religious experience involves a direct awareness of a Cosmic Mind. Psychical research also provides multiple types of evidence for continued life beyond bodily death. Although most modern philosophies, presupposing sensationism and mind-brain identism, have ruled all such evidence out of court *a priori*, Whitehead's version of naturalism allows it in principle to be veridical. And when looked at from this perspective, I have concluded, the evidence is quite strong.[70] Although most philosophers have assumed that all this 'evidence' could be safely ignored on the grounds that parapsychology is merely a pseudo-science, I have argued that none of the arguments for this contention hold up.[71] Process philosophy is thereby able to support, and be supported by, genuinely scientific evidence.

Notes

1. Alfred North Whitehead, *Process and Reality*, corrected edition, edited by David Ray Griffin and Donald W. Sherburne (New York: Free Press, 1978), p. 15.
2. John B. Cobb, Jr., *A Christian Natural Theology: Based on the Thought of Alfred North Whitehead* (Philadelphia: Westminster, 1965).
3. *Process and Reality*, pp. 3, 4.
4. Whitehead, *Modes of Thought* (New York: Free Press, 1968), p. 3.
5. Whitehead, *Science and the Modern World* (New York: Free Press, 1967), p. vii; *Modes of Thought*, p. 6.
6. *Process and Reality*, pp. 8, 9, xiv.
7. Whitehead, *The Function of Reason* (Boston: Beacon Press, 1968), p. 49.
8. Hilary Putnam, *Words and Life*, edited by James Conant (Cambridge: Harvard University Press, 1994), p. 154.
9. Charles Hartshorne, 'A Reply to My Critics', *The Philosophy of Charles Hartshorne* (The Library of Living Philosophers, Vol. 20), edited by Lewis Edwin Hahn (LaSalle, IL: Open Court, 1991), pp. 569–731, at 676, 624.
10. *Process and Reality*, p. 151.
11. Ibid., p. 13.
12. 'Introduction', Griffin et al., *Founders of Constructive Postmodern Philosophy: Peirce, James, Bergson, Whitehead, and Hartshorne* (Albany: State University of New York Press, 1993), pp. 1–42, at 26–29; *Unsnarling the World-Knot: Consciousness, Freedom, and the Mind-Body Problem* (Berkeley: University of California Press, 1998), Chap. 3.
13. Martin Jay, 'The Debate over Performative Contradiction: Habermas versus the Poststructuralists', *Force Fields: Between Intellectual History and Cultural Critique*, by Martin Jay (New York: Routledge, 1993), pp. 25–37, at 29.
14. Putnam, *Realism and Reason* (New York: Cambridge University Press, 1983), pp. 98–114.
15. John Hick, *Philosophy of Religion* (Englewood Cliffs: Prentice-Hall, 1983), p. 41; Barry Whitney, *Theodicy: An Annotated Bibliography on the Problem of Evil, 1960–1991* (Bowling Green State University, Philosophy Documentation Center, 1994), p. 135.
16. I developed this position in *God, Power, and Evil: A Process Theodicy* (Philadelphia: Westminster Press, 1976; reprinted with a new preface, Lanham, MD: University Press of America, 1991), then clarified and modified it in *Evil Revisited: Responses and Reconsiderations* (Albany: State University of New York Press, 1991).
17. John Mackie, *The Miracle of Theism: Arguments for and against the Existence of God* (Oxford: Clarendon Press, 1982), p. 151.
18. Jon D. Levenson, *Creation and the Persistence of Evil: The Jewish Drama of Divine Omnipotence* (San Francisco: Harper & Row, 1988); Gerhard May, *Creatio Ex Nihilo: The Doctrine of 'Creation out of Nothing' in Early Christian Thought*, translated by A. S. Worrall (Edinburgh: T. & T. Clark, 1994).
19. I argue this point, employing Levenson and May, in 'Creation out of Nothing, Creation out of Chaos, and the Problem of Evil', *Encountering Evil*, edited by Stephen T. Davis, 2nd edn (Philadelphia: Westminster/John Knox, 2001).
20. Richard Swinburne, *Is There a God?* (Oxford: Oxford University Press, 1996), pp. 138–139.

21. Caroline Franks Davis, *The Evidential Force of Religious Experience* (Oxford: Clarendon Press, 1989), pp. 113, 140–142; John H. Hick, *An Interpretation of Religion: Human Responses to the Transcendent* (London: Macmillan, 1989), p. 211.
22. Griffin, *Reenchantment without Supernaturalism: A Process Philosophy of Religion* (Ithaca: Cornell University Press, 2001), p. 203.
23. Whitehead, *Modes of Thought*, p. 154.
24. Whitehead, *Adventures of Ideas* (New York: Free Press, 1967), p. 225.
25. George Santayana, *Scepticism and Animal Faith* (New York: Dover, 1955), pp. 14–15.
26. *Process and Reality*, pp. 166–167.
27. Ibid., p. 316.
28. *Process and Reality*, pp. 118, 171; *Symbolism: Its Meaning and Effect* (New York: Capricorn, 1959), p. 51.
29. *Process and Reality*, p. 170.
30. J.J.C. Smart, 'Religion and Science', *Philosophy of Religion: A Global Approach*, edited by Stephen H. Phillips (Fort Worth: Harcourt Brace, 1996), pp. 217–224, at 222–223. (Reprinted from Paul Edwards, ed., *Encyclopedia of Philosophy* [New York: Macmillan Press, 1967], Vol. 7.)
31. J. Samuel Preus, *Explaining Religion: Criticism and Theory from Bodin to Freud* (New Haven & London: Yale University Press, 1987), p. xv.
32. Robert A. Segal, *Explaining and Interpreting Religion: Essays on the Issue* (New York: Peter Lang, 1992), p. 72.
33. Ibid., p. 16.
34. Preus, *Explaining Religion*, p. 142.
35. Immanuel Kant, *Religion within the Limits of Reason Alone*, translated by Theodore M. Greene and Hoyt H. Hudson (New York: Harper & Row, 1960), p. 163.
36. Gordon D. Kaufman, *In Face of Mystery: A Constructive Theology* (Cambridge: Harvard University Press, 1993), p. 415.
37. Hick, *An Interpretation of Religion*, p. 104.
38. Davis, *The Evidential Force of Religious Experience*, pp. 172–173.
39. Hick, *An Interpretation of Religion*, p. 249.
40. Cobb, *Beyond Dialogue: Toward a Mutual Transformation of Christianity and Buddhism* (Philadelphia: Fortress, 1982); Griffin, *Reenchantment without Supernaturalism*, Chap. 7, 'The Two Ultimates and the Religions'.
41. Reuben Hersh, *What is Mathematics, Really?* (New York: Oxford University Press, 1997), p. 9.
42. Ibid., p. 7; Y. N. Moschovakis, *Descriptive Set Theory* (Amsterdam: North Holland, 1980), p. 605; Penelope Maddy, *Realism in Mathematics* (Oxford: Clarendon Press, 1990), pp. 2–3.
43. Hersh, *What is Mathematics, Really?*, pp. 11–12.
44. Kurt Gödel, 'What is Cantor's Continuum Problem? Supplement to the Second [1964] Edition', *Collected Works*, Vol. II, edited by Solomon Feferman et al. (New York: Oxford University Press, 1990), pp. 266–269, at 268.
45. Putnam, *Words and Life*, p. 503 (the statement is from 'Philosophy of Mathematics: Why Nothing Works', which was originally published in 1979).
46. Paul Benacerraf, 'Mathematical Truth', *Philosophy of Mathematics*, edited by Paul Benacerraf and Hilary Putnam, 2nd edn (Cambridge: Cambridge University Press, 1983), pp. 403–420.
47. Maddy, *Realism in Mathematics*, p. 37.
48. Hersh, *What is Mathematics, Really?*, p. 12.

49. Putnam, *Mathematics, Matter and Method* (Cambridge: Cambridge University Press, 1979), p. 347 (the statement is from 'Philosophy of Logic', originally published in 1971).
50. Quine, *Ontological Relativity and Other Essays* (New York: Columbia University Press, 1969), p. 75.
51. Ibid., p. 75; *From A Logical Point of View* (Cambridge: Harvard University Press, 1953), p. 41.
52. Quine, *From Stimulus to Science* (Cambridge: Harvard University Press, 1995), p. 14; emphasis added.
53. Putnam, *Words and Life*, p. 153.
54. Gilbert Harman, *The Nature of Morality: An Introduction to Ethics* (New York: Oxford University Press, 1977), pp. 9–10; Bernard Williams, *Ethics and the Limits of Philosophy* (Cambridge: Harvard University Press, 1985), p. 94.
55. John Mackie, *Ethics: Inventing Right and Wrong* (New York: Penguin, 1977), p. 15.
56. Ibid., pp. 48, 38.
57. Smart, 'Religion and Science', p. 223.
58. Whitehead, *Modes of Thought*, p. 19.
59. Mackie, *Ethics*, pp. 31, 35.
60. Whitehead, *Process and Reality*, pp. 291–293.
61. Ibid., p. 46.
62. Ibid., pp. 32–33.
63. *Adventures of Ideas*, p. 253.
64. *Modes of Thought*, p. 103.
65. *Unsnarling the World-Knot* (see note 12, above).
66. Griffin, *Religion and Scientific Naturalism: Overcoming the Conflicts* (Albany: State University of New York Press, 2000), Chap. 8, 'Creation and Evolution'.
67. William James, *The Will to Believe* (Cambridge: Harvard University Press, 1979), p. 236.
68. I have argued this most fully in 'Parapsychology and Philosophy: A Whiteheadian Postmodern Perspective', *Journal of the American Society for Psychical Research* 87/3 (July 1993), pp. 217–288; see also *Parapsychology, Philosophy, and Spirituality: A Postmodern Exploration* (Albany: State University of New York Press, 1977).
69. James, *Essays in Radical Empiricism*, edited by Ralph Barton Perry (New York: E. P. Dutton, 1971), pp. 270–271.
70. *Parapsychology, Philosophy, and Spirituality*, Chaps. 3–8.
71. *Religion and Scientific Naturalism*, Chap. 7, 'Parapsychology, Science, and Religion'.

Address for correspondence: Professor David Ray Griffin, Claremont School of Theology, Claremont, CA 91711-5401, USA
E-mail: davraygrif@aol.com

The temporality of God

KEITH WARD
University of Oxford

Introduction

The concept of God as the idea of one supreme being, omniscient and omnipotent and possessing all possible perfections, is a relatively recent development in human history. The gods of Sumer and Egypt, of early Indian and Mediterranean cultures, were many and limited in attributes. The idea of one supreme God was a natural development, most ancient historians think, from earlier tendencies to rank one's own favoured god as more powerful than the gods of other people. The philosophical development of the monotheistic idea of a self-existent being of supreme value can, so far as written evidence is concerned, be dated to the time of Plato and Aristotle in Greece. In Europe it was especially Aristotle's discussion in book 12 of the 'Metaphysics', coupled with Plato's discussions in the *Republic* and the *Timaeus*, that helped to define the classical theism which is common to Judaism, Christianity and Islam.

The flowering of that classical tradition came between the eighth and thirteenth centuries CE, when the Greek philosophical concept was integrated into the mainstream semitic religious traditions. At roughly the same time in India, the classical schools of Sankara and Ramanuja developed a view which was also concerned with a self-existent being of supreme value, though one which was represented as non-dualist – in a more or less qualified manner – in a way that the semitic tradition was not.

In this paper I shall examine the way in which both semitic and Indian traditions developed remarkably similar ideas of God, a similarity which is disguised by differences of philosophical terminology. And I shall suggest that the classical concept needs amendment, though not rejection, in view of the new post-Enlightenment emphasis on the irreducible value of the individual and historical, in contrast with a more classical emphasis on the universal, the changeless and eternal.

It may seem strange that this was a new emphasis, given that both Judaism and Christianity are strongly historical faiths, and that Indian traditions see temporal reality as in some sense identical with the divine reality, Brahman. But in each case the philosophical development of religious ideas promoted the idea that the immutable is the fundamental reality, and that the temporal is in the end only a 'moving image' of, or even an illusory misidentification of, what is in fact the timelessly eternal. However, all these traditions allow of, and even invite, a more positive interpretation of the temporal as a true, even a necessary, expression of the eternal. It is such a more positive interpretation that I shall explore.

The convergence of semitic and indian traditions

In the great classical traditions God is beyond time. God is 'eternal', in the sense of being without either internal or external temporal relationships. This is true of the great Indian philosophers Sankara and Ramanuja. It is true of the Muslim Al Ghazzali and the Jew Maimonides. And it is true for most of the classical Christian tradition, which is epitomised in many ways by Thomas Aquinas.

Why should God be thought of as timeless? One simple consideration is that God is defined as the one and only self-existent reality, which generates from its own reality everything else that exists. The idea of one self-existent reality which generates all other beings by a conscious act of will (that is to say, being aware of what it is doing and intending to do it) is almost definitive of the classical theistic traditions in religious thought. Even Sankara, who is sometimes regarded (though I think wrongly) as a non-theist, holds that the universe is generated from Brahman by an act of will – or at least that this is the way we least misleadingly think of it.[1]

All the beings of which we are aware through the senses are in the one unified space-time which we call the universe. So it is natural to think that space and time are forms of the material universe, properties which all its material constituents possess. Take away the material universe, it might be thought, and space and time disappear with it. For is not space the way in which different material realities can co-exist one time, and is not time the way in which different material realities can co-exist in one space? If there are no material realities, there is nothing to co-exist, and so space and time would only exist as possible forms of relationship, not as actual entities. Now God is the cause of all material realities. As creator, God cannot be identical with what God creates. Therefore God must be different from any material reality, and the divine existence must be logically anterior to, and therefore independent of, the existence of any material reality. It follows that God must be independent of space and time, insofar as they are forms of relationship of material realities. Thus God as creator is not either in space or in time. God is an immaterial (non-spatial) and eternal (non-temporal) being.

For most people this argument intuitively goes through with regard to space without any difficulty. Few believers in God think that God is extended in space. Partly this is because there is only one God, so there are no different realities to exist at the same time, and spatiality is un-necessary. Aquinas puts this by saying that God is indivisible, and thus has no spatial parts.[2] Partly it is because classical theists were able to imagine a reality consisting of pure consciousness, not dependent on matter. They were in some sense ontological dualists, holding that consciousness is different from matter and exists in a logically prior way to matter (even the Indian non-dualists think this, their non-dualism consisting in a subtle identification of God and the universe). One can imagine a pure consciousness intending the universe to exist, without being in any way a physical body. This is because one can imagine perceptions, feelings and thoughts occurring without any physical body or brain. Even if one is deceived in thinking one can imagine such things, it is fairly natural and easy to think one can. So far as intuition goes, one can think of an immaterial consciousness simply by imagining one's body disappearing, while one goes on thinking. This would, after all, just be a radical extension of dreaming. For when one is asleep, how can be sure that one's body still exists? This at least is the story native intuition tells, and it seems to make the conception of an immaterial creator not wholly implausible.

Both semitic and Indian traditions regard God as the non-spatial creator of space. The classical semitic view insists that God and the created universe are quite different in kind. The Indian view is committed, on grounds of revelation, to saying that God (Brahman) and the universe are identical. I do not, however, think this is the vast difference it is sometimes said to be. To illustrate the point, I will consider the apparently contrasting views of Aquinas and Ramanuja, the former holding that God is not 'really' related to the universe,[3] and the latter holding that the universe is the body of God.[4] These views seems very different, but closer examination will show the differences to be largely at the level of exploiting differing metaphors derived from Scripture.

There is an axiom, common (though not universal) in Western thought, that nothing can be the cause of itself. Therefore God the cause must be different from the universe, the effect. Some classical Indian schools of philosophy maintain, however, that the effect is identical with its cause (*satkaryavada*). For where could the reality of the effect come from, except from its cause? In which case, the cause must in some way contain its effects. This is one root of the division between saying that the universe is different from God, and that it is identical with God. But is the difference perhaps a mainly verbal one?

There is distinction between creator and creature, but we are certainly not speaking of two distinct realities of the same sort, two individuals which belong to a common class. Only god is self-existent and fully independent. Creatures depend wholly for their being on God, and reflect the divine perfections in diverse and limited ways. One could say that there is a huge difference between one self-existent, fully independent reality and many limited and dependent realities. The infinite, as Aquinas puts it, being without boundaries, cannot share reality with the bounded finite.[5] On the other hand, one could also say, as Ramanuja does, that, since there is only one self-existent reality, all other beings must be its dependent parts.[6] The infinite, being without limits, cannot exclude the finite. Is there really anything important at stake here?

On Aquinas' own principles, there does not seem to be strong reason for denying the identity of God and the universe, in the sense that Ramanuja asserts it. Consider, for example, the relation between Father and Son in the Trinity, as Aquinas would construe it. The Father is the only ungenerated being and is wholly self-existent. The Son is generated wholly by the Father, is wholly dependent on the Father, and is determined to be what he is by the Father. Yet these are not said to be two different beings. In the contrary, they are two hypostases, we might say two forms of being, of one and the same God.

Why should an Indian theologian not say that God and the cosmos are two forms of being of one and the same God, distinct in their forms of relation yet one in substantial being? Of course the Trinitarian will say that the Son is precisely not a creature – meaning, as classically expressed against Arius, that there never was a time when the Son was not. The cosmos, however, is brought into being, and there was a time when it was not, or at least when it might not have been.

But Ramanuja could reply that there never was a time when the universe was not, either in its manifest or in its potential – *pralaya* – state. And did not Aquinas say that the universe might have existed without beginning, as far as philosophical thought is concerned? In which case the only real difference that seems to remain is that the universe expresses a contingent decision of the divine will, whereas the generation of the Son is non-contingent, being part of the divine essence from all eternity.

Contingent creation by a necessary God

At this point we approach the core of a decisive issue for theism. Is the universe the result of a contingent divine decision, and do finite agents in the universe have the sort of distinctness which lies in their not being wholly determined by God? Both classical traditions come to very similar, subtly negative, answer to these questions, and it is that answer that is challenged by the post-Enlightenment stress on individual contingent freedom, which affirms both contingency and autonomy of the created universe.

Aquinas defends the view – a defined dogma of the Roman Catholic church – that the existence of the universe is logically contingent.[7] By that he means that it is not self-contradictory to assert the existence of God and deny the existence of the universe. We cannot determine the existence of a universe, and indeed of exactly this universe, just by arriving at a correct analysis of the concept of God. We can say, without contradiction, that God might exist without any universe. Therefore it is not an analytic truth that if God exists the universe exists. Therefore it is a logically contingent truth that God creates the universe. Whereas, just to make the difference clear, it is an analytic truth about God – it is part of the essential nature of God – that God is Trinitarian, and consists of Father, Son and Spirit, indivisibly.

This argument seems to defend the truth that the existence of the universe is not necessary to God, so that it is by a free and contingent act of will that God creates this universe, which is thereby ontologically quite distinct form God. And now a gap may seem to open between Ramanuja and Aquinas, since Ramanuja, holding that the universe is the body of God, must assert that God necessarily – not freely and contingently – manifests as the universe, which is thereby part of God.

The distinction seems clear. But what is meant by a contingent act of a necessary and self-existent God, and how it would differ from a necessary manifestation of such a God? The problem is compounded for Aquinas by his assertion that God is pure act, without potentiality.[8] It follows immediately that God could not have done anything other than God does. For that would constitute a possibility in God.

One might hold that a mere logical possibility is not a real potentiality. That is, we could frame a coherent statement that 'God might not have created this universe', and this sounds like something God could have done but did not do. But in fact God doing that thing is excluded by the divine actuality which expresses divine perfection in what God actually does. It is logically possible that I could kill my mother, but the act is excluded by my love for her, which expresses a perfection of my nature. It would not be better if there was a real possibility that I might kill her; it would be worse. In a similar way, there is no real possibility that God might have done other than God did, though there is such a logical possibility. Real, as opposed to logical, possibilities are determined through the divine actuality. In that sense, there is no potentiality in God, since God does everything that God necessarily wills to do, and that is a perfection, not a defect, in the divine nature. There is nothing lacking to the divine perfection, nothing yet to be done to complete it, nothing which is as yet unfinished in the divine plan. Remarks about what God might have done are mere logical mouthings in the air, as if to say that, if God had not been perfect, things might have been otherwise.

What all this entails, however, is that in fact, because of the supreme divine perfection, God necessarily does all that God does. Anything else would be imperfect. So God necessarily creates this universe, and it would have been imperfect to do anything else. In what sense, then, is creation contingent? Only in the sense that creation is not logically implied by the divine nature. Creation is necessary de re, but not de dicto. It follows from the divine perfection, but not from the mere definition of God.

Is this the case, however, on the theory? Surely if we knew the divine nature fully, we would be able to see that the decision to create this universe is an essential part of it (for there are no contingent parts of the divine nature). Aquinas cites a similar argument when dispensing with Anselm's ontological argument for God. He suggests that, if we could understand the divine essence, we would see that his existence does indeed, as Anselm said, follow from the divine essence. But, because we cannot understand the divine essence, we cannot frame any valid argument from that essence to actual existence.[9]

Similarly, if we could understand the divine essence, we would see that this universe is implied in the divine nature. It is because we do not understand it that we cannot see such an implication. It is there, but we cannot see it. We cannot derive the universe from God; but it does necessarily derive from God. The universe is contingent, and God is said to act contingently in creating it, only because we cannot trace the real necessities involved, and because nothing that we can discern about God entails that this, and only this, universe, should come into existence. 'God could have done otherwise' remains a logically coherent statement, and one we have to make if we are to avoid the implication that God was constrained against his will to do what God did.

Their views are even closer when one realises that by saying the universe is the body of God, Ramanuja means simply that every part of the universe is under the direct control of God, and every part of it is directly known to God.[10] Thus he does not really mean that God is extended in space, as a space-filling object. He means that every spatial thing exists by divine will, is directly under the control of the divine will, and is fully known by God. Aquinas agrees entirely on these points. It is what he means by divine omnipresence. For both theologians, God is not literally present in every space. More exactly, every place is under the direct conscious control of God, but the divine mind remains without spatial extension.

So in saying the universe is the body of God, Ramanuja is not differing radically from Aquinas, who says that God is omnipresent. Both mean that God is not located at any point in space, but that God does, or can, directly control every spatial event, and has direct knowledge of every spatial event. Both hold that the creation is logically contingent, and yet in some sense necessarily implied in the divine nature. And both hold that God in fact makes everything that is the case, including the decisions of all finite free agents, to be what it is – though that divine determination is said not to infringe finite freedom and responsibility.

In Western and Indian classical traditions there is thus a much closer agreement on the nature of God, the Supreme Lord, than is sometimes thought. It is not true that Aquinas is a dualist, in thinking that God and the universe are two distinct sorts of substances – he explicitly denies that.[11] And it is not true that Ramanuja or Sankara are 'monists', thinking that God just is the universe, as it appears to us, finite, limited and manifold. All agree that God is simple, eternal, immutable, perfect (while the created universe is not, so some sort of 'dualism' is in order), and that the whole reality of the universe depends entirely on God for its existence (so there are not two independent sorts of reality, and some form of 'monism' is correct). It is not that there are no differences, but that they are not as deep and decisive as they have sometimes been said to be. In both cases, the classical traditions posit a necessary and self-existent divine being which generates a universe whose nature it determines necessarily and wholly.

Suppose, however, that the universe is contingent in a stronger sense than this. Suppose that finite agents have the sort of autonomy which consists in their not being wholly determined either by God or by any previous state of the universe. Then God would not, by one non-temporal act, make everything to be what it is, since finite agents would partly determine its nature. And events in the universe would be contingent de re, since many of its states could in fact have been other than they are. In this case, God's knowledge of what is the case will be partly dependent on what contingently happens in the universe, and God's actions will partly depend on what finite agents have determined to be the case.

There is no reason why this should affect the non-spatiality of God. But it will entail that there is temporality in God, since both God's knowledge of and God's particular intentions for the universe will logically be subsequent to ('after') the occurrence of contingent states of the universe, which God has not determined. The idea of a non-temporal consciousness may in itself be coherent, but it necessarily lacks those elements of responsive knowledge and creative activity that are so important to finite consciousness, and that would characterise any cognitive agent which was related to a contingent and autonomous universe.

It is significant that many Buddhists, who place strong emphasis on individual autonomy and freedom to determine one's own destiny, are able to conceive a non-temporal form of consciousness. This is, however, conceived as a consciousness of unchanging bliss and unvarying knowledge.[12] Nirvana is represented precisely as such a state, and no causal efficacy is ascribed to it. That is partly because they clearly see the problem of reconciling the concept of a timeless creator with an ascription of contingent autonomy to finite agents. How can the timeless be a cause, and a cause of contingent temporal realities, without being contingent and temporal in some – if only in a 'higher' – sense (since the cause must either contain its effect in a higher manner, in the European tradition, or be identical with its effect, in many Indian traditions)? And how can there be a necessary, non-temporal cause of a truly contingent universe?

Contingency is a condition of autonomy – one has autonomy only if there are alternative possibilities of action, undetermined by any internal or external necessity. Temporality is a condition of this sort of contingency – if there are alternative possibilities, then there must be a time when possibilities are open, followed by a time when one of those possibilities has become actual. So time is a necessary condition of the sort of change from potentiality to actuality which constitutes autonomy and creative freedom. This may lead one to suspect that temporality is actually a perfection, something to be positively valued, or at least a necessary condition of something of great value, rather than an imperfection, something to be excluded from the supreme being as limiting and undesirable. It is this supposition to which I now turn.

Temporality as a perfection

Time, as Aristotle said, is the measure of change, or that which makes change possible. It is this notion of 'change' which focusses the central problem. No one denies, initially, that changes take place. Plants grow and die, and so do people. Causes have effects, and new things come into being which have never previously been. But is change inexponable, irreducible, basic? Or is it somehow illusory, reducible to something which does not involve real change?

At this point the similarity between space and time breaks down. In space everything co-exists, and one can ignore change altogether, or easily think of all processes being reversed. In time, new things continually come into existence, which have not co-existed with things past, and old things leave traces which cannot be reversed.

For a mathematical representation, it does not matter whether the co-ordinates used to define the position of an object are spatial or temporal. Both space and time are treated as extensive magnitudes within which objects can have a uniquely definable position. Material objects are definable in terms of their location in space and time, and these magnitudes can be exchanged with no mathematical difficulty – as when cosmologists like Stephen Hawking suppose that in the early universe the time co-ordinate can be gradually changed into the space-co-ordinate by a fairly simple mathematical process of quasi-geometric transposition.

But suppose change is a basic irreducible feature of finite reality. Then all things are in constant flow, always changing, always influenced by what has gone before and growing into a new future, which has never been before. This is an apparently coherent hypothesis, the basis of the Buddhist doctrine of conditioned coorigination. All events are transitory, are influenced by what went before, and generate what is always coming into being.

If that is true, then time and space are fundamentally different and untranslatable. Space is the realm of fixity, of symmetrical relationships, of the unchanging. Time is the realm of perpetual flux, of one-way asymmetrical causality, of the transient. They are both aspects of reality, necessary to the way things are in our material world, but they are not co-ordinates which might be rotated to replace one another. Their basic properties are incompatible. There is nothing literally unchanged through time, since one moment continually replaced another, however little their properties may differ. There is nothing literally momentary or transient in space, since space spreads objects out timelessly, in one fixed and unchanging set of relationships.

Space never exists without time, and so the sense of fixity is not truly basic; it is an abstraction from the flow of events in time. Time can exist without space – in consciousness – but where it co-exists with space, it gives a sense of permanence, of enduring properties, whose true character is the continuous duplication of similar or slightly varying properties in similar spatial locations.

Is the sense of continuous flow, of perpetual perishing and creativity, an imperfection? The classical theistic tradition has unhesitatingly said yes, and partly for that reason, perhaps, Buddhism has developed into a non-theistic religion. For most strands of Theravada Buddhism, there is no timeless cause of the universe, no timeless personal Lord, and the timeless state of release from perpetual perishing is simply beyond description. Classical theists have to speak of a personal creator who creates and responds to the finite processes of the world, which involve real and perhaps irreducible change, and yet is changeless. There are sophisticated ways of doing so, and yet the proposal seems deeply counter-intuitive.

If time is not an imperfection, however, there would be no need for this desperate manoevre. Some sort of change might not only be an irreducible characteristic of the finite universe; it might also be a divine perfection. So it might be worth examining the classical arguments for thinking that time is an imperfection, and for that reason must be excluded from God. Such arguments focus on the fact that in time there is always a sense of loss of the past, of the transience of the present, and of the uncertainty of the future. All these, it is said, have the character of imperfections.

All things pass into nothingness, as though they had never been, and this can seem to deprive them of value. So many good things lost, so many efforts and achievements, and all of them forgotten, never to be recalled. For the classical theist, the past is not lost. It is as real as the present to God, who sees all things in one unvarying present. That is one reason for asserting timelessness of God.

Yet that supposition carries a cost. Bad as well as good things are present to God. The torture of children is always as present to God as the happiness of the blessed. Evil is never truly destroyed, and tears are never truly wiped away. They remain as real as they ever were. That is not obviously a perfection.

An alternative possibility is that evil is destroyed, though not eliminated as though it had never been. What is required is a mind which continues with the unceasing flow of the universe, and remembers the past with discrimination. That is to say, all good things will be kept wholly in mind. But evil things will be set aside, except as the causes of later events which reconcile and harmonise them with the divine perfection, which becomes what it is because of their existence. It is rather like human memory which concentrates on the attractive, and relegates the painful to a lower grade of awareness, while nevertheless being aware that the evil has contributed to the character of that growing creative experience which is that of a temporal God. Thus the loss of the past is not an unalloyed evil. It allows what is evil to be transfigured by what is good. But all that is good in the past is retrievable by the mind of a God who experiences all things as they occur, and who may grant to finite agents a share in that infinitely extending experience.

Is the transience of the present an imperfection? The imperfection lies in the sense that we enjoy only for a short time, that all good things pass, and that we cannot hold onto happiness for more than a while. Classical theism postulates that the unchanging God is in a state of unchangeable bliss. God possesses his experience without loss and without end, and there is no danger that it will fade or be destroyed.

This seems a very desirable state, but again it has a cost. The cost is that a God without change will never have any new experiences, and will never be changed by anything that happens in the universe; God will be immutable and impassible. The cost here is that many seemingly valuable experiences will not be had by God. The experience of creating something completely new, of adventuring into uncharted territory, of achieving a worthwhile task successfully, of relating to others in mutual give and take, or sharing the experiences of others and of co-operating in their endeavours – all these experiences are unavailable to an immutable God. If God is supposed to be the supreme case of all perfections, it seems odd to deny to the divine many of the experiences which we value most.

Classical theists assumed that if God is perfect any change would be for the worse. To say that change must be for the worse (or for the better) assumes that perfection is a static condition, from which one must move up or down. But if a perfection is something which it is good to experience for its own sake, why should a particular sort of process or activity not be a perfection? Aristotle defined true happiness as lying in the unimpeded exercise of the proper capacities of a human being. Activities like walking, playing a musical instrument, writing a poem or talking with a friend express properly human capacities, and may well be considered worth doing for their own sake. Some activities are good candidates for intrinsic values. But all activities involve bringing something about intentionally and successively. They involve change and creativity. I would go so far as to say that creative activity is the highest intrinsic value – since even contemplating a work of art is a creative activity, using imagination, concentration, education and continuing attention. If some sorts of change are necessary to some of the highest values, it is odd to say that all change is for the worse.

In being creative, one does not necessarily get better or worse. When Beethoven finished the ninth symphony, he was not better than when he began it, or worse either. Something then existed which had not previously existed, but it did not make Beethoven better. It added to the number of good things which actually exist. In a sense one might say that the more good things there are the better. In that sense, the world is continually getting better, but that does not mean it was imperfect to start with, or that God is getting better. The sensible thing to say is that God remains the same – a supremely creative agent – and the number of good things continually increases. But perfection is not a static condition. It is the proper fulfilment of the nature of a being. God is always perfect in being supremely creative, and the perfection of the universe includes many sorts of creative activities.

Of course the world is always partly imperfect; it can improve in many ways. God is perfect, and if you ask what a perfect being would be like, given the existence of an imperfect world, it would seems that the perfect being should not remain unchanged by that world in any way, but should seek to remedy its defects and improve them. A perfect being might share in the imperfections of creatures if by so dong it could begin to remedy them. In this sense, though it sounds paradoxical, it is in fact not at all paradoxical to say that a perfect being might choose to share in imperfection, in order to improve it, rather than to remain unmoved by it. This would involve some change in God, as the perfect shares in imperfection, in order to shape it towards its own perfection.

It might be said, however, that all change needs explaining; there must be a good reason why it occurs. God, as the ultimate explanation, must therefore be beyond change, or God would need explaining too. But this axiom is the result of thinking that the changeless does not need explaining, whereas change does. The changeless requires an explanation of why it is as it is just as much as the changing does. The best explanation of change is that it is a necessary condition of creativity, which is a great intrinsic value. Is there a better explanation of why a changeless God should exist? If it is said that God cannot fail to exist, this could be as true of a changing as of a changeless God. And if it is said that God contains all perfections in some way, then the axiom that creativity is a great intrinsic value entails that God changes, at least in some respects. Thus the transience of the present may not be an imperfection, but the condition of the value of creativity.

Is the uncertainty of the future then an imperfection? It would be if we had no idea of where things might go, of what might happen next, and of whether things would even turn out well or not. The classical theist knows exactly what will happen in future, since God has decreed it in one timeless act. Nothing is uncertain, since the future is laid down in every detail, and can be perfectly known to God and to whomsoever God chooses. We can trust wholly in God, since God has already decreed all that is to be, and his promises can be trusted absolutely.

The cost is that such a God determines everything, and that our future is predetermined even before we are born. Nothing we can do will alter the future that God has decreed – though God has also decreed that we will, or will not, try to alter it, in accordance with the divine will. For classical theists, this is almost axiomatic, and it is another reason why Buddhists reject the notion of a creator God. We are free to determine our own lives, they say, and if we experience a heaven or a hell after this life, it is entirely our responsibility, and not any predetermined divine plan. Christians are often also eager to argue that divine predestination does not undermine true human freedom, and that we must be regarded as the causes of our own responsible actions. We are not predetermined in the sense that we are forced to do what we do by an exterior cause. We act in accordance with our own desires and intentions, and so we act freely. Yet it cannot be denied that those desires and intentions are created by God, so that God is the one ultimate cause of everything being what it is. A great many volumes have been written on this topic, and I cannot pretend to resolve the issue here. All I will say is that there is a distinction between views which in the end ascribe all causal efficacy to God, and views which give created agents a freedom to act in ways which are not sufficiently determined either by God or by any previous state of the universe. If such relative autonomy is thought to be a value, then God must permit the universe to be partly non-sufficiently determined.

This does not make the future wholly uncertain. God is still able to determine anything God will, and so, whenever God chooses, God can eliminate evil and bring the good to perfection. God knows what God intends for the universe, and will ensure that the divine intentions are realised in some form, even if God chooses to let the exact form of that realisation depend partly on the decisions of finite agents.

So a sort of controlled uncertainty about the future is not an imperfection, so long as a really autonomous freedom of finite creatures is regarded as highly desirable. It is arguable, then, that a view of God as remembering the past, creatively acting in the present, and allowing creaturely freedom in the future, actually represents the divine being as possessing sorts of perfection which a timeless God cannot possess. If it is possible for God to be temporal, that would be a preferable concept of God.

Time, relativity and simultaneity

One major problem remains. It may seem that in speaking of the temporality of God, one is supposing that God is in our time, going along moment by moment with us. So our past is God's past, and our future is God's future. If this were so, however, God would be bounded by time as we are. God would be in the time that God has created. A special problem arises here from the special theory of relativity, and the well-established fact that in our space-time simultaneity is relative. That is, with respect to two observers moving at different speeds relative to one another, what is simultaneous for one may include events which are future or past for the other. There is no such thing as absolute simultaneity throughout the universe. Where, then, is God's 'now', if there is no absolute flow of time, which God could observe or share in?

The problem is to think of time as really successive, not spread out all at once, and yet to think of God as not bounded by created time. The obvious way to do this is to think of God as making the divine being successive, constricting it, as it were, to a temporal succession, while also being beyond it.

What has often or even usually gone wrong when this has been conceived is what might be called the fallacy of timeless simultaneity. God is thought of as beyond time, but is then conceived as existing all at once, so that all times are simultaneous to God. If God is beyond time, however, then God is not simultaneous any more than God is successive. God's knowledge of time does not consist of God knowing all times at once – which they are not. It consists of God knowing successivity as it truly is, but not being limited by that.

So, for example, God can go much further than being aware of two different planes of simultaneity, relative to one another. God can create two space-time universes, which are not temporally related to one another at all. So there will be no 'now' at which events in these universes can be correlated. God will know each time successively, as it flows, but will not relate those successions to one another temporally. Thus God is not to be temporally located in one of those time-streams. God simply sees them both as they are – successive. There could be a great number of such universes, and God would apprehend the successivity of each.

God is naturally able to make any of those times what they are, and sometimes God's making that the case can (correctly) be seen as a response to what has gone before. God can enter into time, act and respond, while existing in a trans-temporal way, somewhat as I might enter into your dreams and respond to events in them, while also having a separate existence in the real world.

We cannot imagine the trans-temporality of God, but it certainly should not be conceived as a total immutability and static existence, like that of mathematical equations. It might be better conceived as a transcendent agency which acts incessantly in many temporal streams, manifesting its changeless perfection in continual creative activity, sensitive awareness and overflowing goodness.

The reality of God is beyond the space-time of the universe, but why may it not contain plurality and change of a certain sort? The classical tradition assumed that simplicity and immutability (the former entails the latter) were perfections. But the main argument for that seems to be that anything plural might fall apart into its constituent elements, so that its elements might be the ultimate existents, and the being of a plural God would be secondary.

But whatever argument there is that an ultimately simple element cannot simply cease to exist, can equally well be used as an argument that a complex of elements which are bound together indissolubly cannot simply cease to exist either. One such argument is that a simple element which was good would have no reason to cease existing. That argument works equally well for a complex being. If the simple element is timeless, so that it cannot cease to exist, then so could the complete being be timeless.

Similarly, whatever argument there is for thinking that a simple being explains its own existence – for example, in being self-existent and good – can equally be used in favour of a complex being. In fact there is a powerful argument that any self-existent and good being would be complex rather than simple.

If one asks what could make a being self-existent, one candidate for a reason is the one that I think is at least implicit in Aquinas, and that is explicitly given by many rationalist philosophers of the eighteenth century, including Immanuel Kant himself.[13] If one assumes that actuality is prior to possibility – that is, there can be no possible states unless there is some actual state – then since the set of all possible states seems to be immutably existent, there must be some actual state in which they inhere as possibilities. The self-existent being is the being which is the substratum of all possible states, including itself, and whose power of existence is therefore not derivable from anything other than itself. But if that argument is felt to be compelling, it suggests not a simple being, but a complex one – a being in which an infinite number of possibilities inhere.

Of course the self-existent being is simple in the sense that it is necessarily one unified reality which contains all possibilities as parts of itself. It is not divisible into separable parts. It is a unified consciousness, and its 'parts' are the elements of that unity of consciousness. So there can be an indivisible complex being, not seperable into distinct parts, yet consisting of many elements bound together in an inseperable unity.

Moreover, if the supreme existent is supremely good, containing in itself some archetype of the highest intrinsic goods we can conceive, theists are almost bound to think that creativity is a great intrinsic good – since God is the creator. But the most natural way to think of creativity is of the generation of the new, and that sort of creativity involves a change from conception to actualisation. Again the classical tradition might argue that if one has change, then the passage of time allows for decay or even cessation of being, which cannot be allowed for God. The obvious response, however, is that a personal self-existent being could ensure that it did not pass away against its will, and it would have no reason to will its own decease.

Conclusion

It seems, then, that a self-existent, perfect, creator could well be, and might be expected to be, complex, temporal and changing in a certain carefully limited sense. God changes in relation to each temporal universe that God creates, yet exists in an unimaginable manner beyond all those personal relationships. We might then better conceive God as the source of infinite creative and responsive activity, than as a wholly changeless reality. God is not bounded by time, but God is not bounded by immutability either. God will be immutable in those respects in which it is a perfection to be mutable. We have little idea of what those respects might be in the divine being as it exists out of relation to say universe. But in relation to this and any universe we can imagine, divine immutability will be in respect of God's changeless possession of the attributes of justice, love, benevolence, mercy, wisdom and freedom. Divine mutability will be in respect of God's actualisation of those attributes in particular acts in particular universes. God is changeless in all important perfections. God cannot cease to love, to be merciful and wise, creative and just. Yet all these perfections imply, for their perfect realization, ceaseless activity, not subject to decay and death.

I conclude that there is, beneath the differing metaphors for the divine being in differing religious traditions, a common doctrine among the major classical writers that the Supreme Reality is simple, timeless and perfect, but is correctly representable by humans as a personal Lord of omnipotent power and omniscient knowledge. What I have done is to suggest that this insight is basically correct, but that it is often warped by giving the simplicity aspect of the divine logical priority over the personal aspect. This happens if one says that God is 'really' simple, immutable and eternal, and only appears to us as complex, changing and temporal. I have suggested that there is a positive value in a temporalist conception of the divine that should be fully preserved in any comprehensive philosophical account of the concept of God. Then one can say that there are respects in which God is timeless, and indeed that God's reality transcends any created time, and is not bounded by any. Yet that God is actively creative, and therefore temporal, in other important respects.

The classical concept of God in the great traditions needs supplementing by a more temporalist, personalist concept to be true to the demands of devotional practice. Such a supplementation is not false to the traditions, but brings out what they have always presupposed, but rarely explicated in a coherent conceptual way. For god is both the 'one without a second', [14] 'being devoid of form', [15] the unlimited source of all beings, and also *Isvara*, the supreme Lord of unlimited perfections, manifested in a multitude of names and forms, who meets devotees with infinitely responsive mercy and love. God must be both timeless and temporal, in different respects, if the divine perfection is to be adequately expressed.

Notes

1. Sankara, 'The World Originates from Brahman by Thought', *The Vedanta Sutras*, trans. George Thibaut, in Max Muller, ed., *Sacred Books of the East*, Vol. 38 (Delhi: Motilal Banarsidass, 1962), p. 48.
2. Thomas Aquinas, *Summa Theologiae*, 1a, qu. 3, art. 1 (London: Eyre and Spottiswoode, 1963), Vol. 2, p. 20.
3. Aquinas, 'In Deo non est aliqua realis relatio ejus ad creaturas', qu. 13, art. 7, Vol. 3, p. 74.
4. Ramanuja, 'The Entire World is a Body the Self of which is Constituted by Knowledge', *The Vedanta Sutras*, trans. George Thibaut, in *Sacred Books of the East*, Vol. 48 (Delhi: Motilal Banarsidass, 1962), p. 95.
5. Aquinas, qu. 7, art. 1, Vol. 2, p. 96.
6. Ramanuja, p. 142.
7. Aquinas, qu. 19, art. 4, Vol. 5, p. 18.
8. Aquinas, qu. 3, art. 1, Vol. 2, p. 20.
9. Aquinas, qu. 2, art. 1, Vol. 2, p. 6.
10. Ramanuja, 'Any Substance which a Sentient Soul is Capable of Completely Controlling ... Is the Body of that Soul', p. 424.
11. Aquinas, 'Deus non est in genere substantiae', qu. 3, art. 5, Vol. 2, p. 36.
12. 'The Peace Supreme and Infinite Joy', trans. Juan Mascaro, *Dhammapada* 2/23 (Harmondsworth: Penguin, 1973), p. 38.
13. The Kantian argument is given in the *Nova Dilucidatio* of 1755 (Berlin: German Academy of Sciences, 1902), Vol. 1, p. 395 ff.
14. *Chandogya Upanishad*, in R.C. Zaehner (trans.), *Hindu Scriptures* (London: Dent, 1966), p. 105.
15. Sankara, Vol. 34, p. 307.

Address for correspondence: Professor Keith Ward, The Regius Professor of Divinity, Christ Church, Oxford, OX1 1DP, UK
E-mail: keith.ward@theology.oxford.uk

Some reflections on Indian metaphysics

KEITH E. YANDELL
University of Wisconsin – Madison

Introduction

The paper that follows explores some structures and rationales in (South Asian) Indian metaphysics. While occasional references to particular views are made, the focus is on certain themes and tensions in the Indian metaphysical tradition.

Metaphysical distinctness and identity conditions

Metaphysical distinctness conditions concern that in virtue of which some item x is distinct from some item y, at some time T or at (say) sequential times T1 and T2. The distinctness distinctions of most importance are those true of incomposite items. Metaphysical identity conditions of an item x concern that in virtue of which x is what it is and not another thing at some time T, and that in virtue of which x at T1 is the same item at (say) sequential times T1 and T2. The identity conditions of most importance are those true of incomposite items. The adequacy of the metaphysical distinctness and identity conditions of relevance here does not depend on how they relate, or how well they might serve as clues, to epistemological distinctness and identity conditions – conditions by reference to which we can tell what is and is not distinct from what else.

Numerical identity

There is identity and there is distinctness. What is called qualitative identity is high similarity between distinct items. It is no genuine identity. There are various criteria for lack of identity, or distinctness. Let 'property' include spatial and temporal properties as well as others. Then:

> x *existentially conditions* y if and only if x's failing to exist is sufficient for y's failing to exist and x's existence is sufficient for y's existence, and x exists

and

x qualitatively conditions y with respect to Q if and only if either x's failing to exist is sufficient for y's failing to have Q or x's failure to have some property Q* is sufficient for y's failing to have Q, and x's existing is sufficient for y's having Q or x's having some property Q* is sufficient for y's having Q, and x does exist or x has Q*.

Some criteria for distinctness follow. They are stated in terms of conditions *sufficient* for distinctness. As we shall see, they are not *fully* stated; for example, temporal matters need to be considered. Otherwise a cheap and worthless victory for replacement theory over change theory can be won.

D1. x is distinct from y if it is logically possible that x exist and y not exist or that y exist and x not exist.

D2. x is distinct from y if there is some property Q such that x has Q and y lacks Q or that x lacks Q and y has Q.

D3. x is distinct from y if there is some property Q such that it is logically possible that x has Q and y lacks Q or that x lacks Q and y has Q.

D4. x is distinct from y if there is a z such that z existentially conditions y but not x or z existentially conditions x but not y.

D5. x is distinct from y if there is a z such that, for some property Q, z conditions x with respect to Q but does not condition y with respect to Q or z conditions y with respect to Q but does not condition x with respect to Q.

D6. x is distinct from y if it is logically possible that there is a z such that z existentially conditions y but not x or z existentially conditions x but not y.

D7. x is distinct from y if it is logically possible that there is a z such that, for some property Q, z conditions x with respect to Q but does not condition y with respect to Q or z conditions y with respect to Q but does not condition x with respect to Q.

I suggest that, whether or not this list is exhaustive (a matter on which I make no claim), each of these seven criteria is such that (once temporal considerations are factored in) satisfying it is sufficient for an incomposite item x being distinct from an incomposite item y. Further, a bit of reflection on these criteria will show that it is true that:

D8. if it is logically possible that x is distinct from y then x is distinct from y.

This, in turn, entails a fact about identity:

I1*. If x is not distinct from y then it is not logically possible that x is distinct from y.

or equivalently and more familiarly:

I1. If x is identical to y, then it is not logically possible that x is not identical to y.

These are *metaphysical* criteria, or criteria for *metaphysical distinctness* – not criteria for telling whether two items are distinct (they may or may not be helpful for that purpose) but criteria for how distinctness goes, independent of our thought and belief.

Consider the claim that (i) if x is distinct from y, then it is logically possible that, for some property Q, it is the case that x has Q and y lacks Q, or that x lacks Q and y has Q. This (with temporal considerations factored in) seems plainly a necessary truth. If it is a necessary truth, so is: (ii) if it is not logically possible that, for some property Q, it is the case that x has Q and y lacks Q, or that x lacks Q and y has Q, then it is not the case that x is distinct from y. Thus the sheer possibility of difference in property between x and y is sufficient for x and y being distinct. If the sheer possibility of difference in property between x and y is sufficient for x and y being distinct, then if x and y are distinct, they are necessarily distinct. If sheer possibility of existential distinctness between x and y distinguishes them, then identity between x and y is a matter of these possibilities not obtaining. These possibilities fail to obtain only if the identity between x and y is necessary. Hence if x and y are identical, they are necessarily identical.

Existence and permanence

There is a tendency in Indian metaphysics (as well as elsewhere) to think in terms of what exists permanently or everlastingly as really existing and of what exists only for a time as existing defectively or not at all. There is also a temptation in Indian metaphysics (as elsewhere) to think of change as an all-or-nothing affair – to think of perfect qualitative similarity over time as a condition (necessarily if not sufficient) for numerical identity, and hence to view any change in quality as change in identity. Nothing, of course, can strictly change in identity, and recognition of this leads to an ontology of change being replaced by an ontology of replacement. The appearance of an item x gaining or losing a property Q is treated as an experience of one item x that has or lacks Q coming and ceasing to be, with x being followed by another item y that lacks or has Q. Composite things then are viewed as being composed of items that are incomposite and momentary. This tendency is worthy of rejection and this temptation is worthy of resistance. It is perfectly possible that something really exist but only exist for a time. The argument that if x at time T has Q and y at time T1 lacks Q, then x and y cannot be identical is invalid. It is worth making the effort to see why these things are so.

Substances

A full-blown substance is an item that has properties, is not itself merely a collection of properties, has a nature or essence, and endures over time. A state or mode is a matter of a substance having some property. An event is a matter of some substance coming to have a property it did not have or coming to lose a property it did have. Events are changes in substances, matters of states coming to be or ceasing to be in substances that endure.

Whether there are, or can be, eternal (entirely timeless) substances or not I will not consider here. Our concern is with substances, if any, that are either *temporary continuants* (substances that come to exist, endure through some time, and then cease to exist), what we might call *beginningless continuants* (substances that do not come to be but cease to exist), *endless continuants* (substances that come to be but do not cease to exist), or *everlasting continuants* (substances that exist but neither come to be nor cease to exist). Continuants endure; they last over some time.

There are strong strains in South Asian Indian thought that think of selves or persons as everlasting substances. Monotheistic Hinduism thinks of God as an everlasting substance who everlastingly creates human persons as mental substances and who everlastingly creates physical simples which are the non-conscious items of which middle-sized objects are composed. Jainism thinks there are everlasting persons and physical simples but that they are uncreated entities that depend for existence on nothing whatever. With some qualifications, Indian Buddhism rejects the claim that there are substances of the sorts described here. (E.g., I will not deal with Buddhist Personalism or with the view that there are everlasting states that once momentarily are active.)

Reincarnation, karma, and continuants

It is typical of Indian religions/philosophies (the distinction is more important than indigenous), materialism aside, that they either accept a literal version of reincarnation and karma or offer a non-literal account that replaces a literal version. The most straightforward way to understand a literal version of reincarnation and karma is to suppose persons to be continuants, incomposite enjoyers of numerical identity over time. A single life is a matter of a person, so construed, being embodied in a single body; a single incarnation is comprised by such embodiment. One's body, one might suggest, is that part of the physical world that satisfies these conditions: (i) one can move it without first moving some other part of the physical world; (ii) one can be affected by its being affected without some other part of the physical world being affected first. Reincarnation theories, literally construed, hold some such view of bodies. Reincarnation occurs when a conscious continuant that is capable of self-consciousness comes to be in a body in which it was not previously embodied.

The account given thus far comes closer to Hindu monotheism, as represented by Ramanuja and Madhva, and to Jainism, than it does to the Buddhist tradition. As noted, Hindu monotheism, in Vsistadvaita and Dvaita, and Jainism eschew incomposite continuants that are not everlasting. A crucial difference between these perspectives is that monotheism allows for the existence of dependent everlasting continuants, and Jainism does not.

The possibility of temporary continuants

An Indian monotheist typically claims that (i) there can be dependent everlasting continuants, items that always do exist but exist only insofar and so long as Brahman sustains them in existence, and (ii) there being such items is the result of a choice by Brahman that Brahman could have refrained from making, so that there might not have been everlasting dependent continuants after all. In effect he holds that *There are dependent everlasting continuants* is a logically contingent proposition. Then there is a distinction between *always being true* and *being necessarily true*. Further, even if there is no possibility of existing in such a way as not to either be Brahman or to be dependent on Brahman, there is a distinction between *existing always* and *existing dependently*. But then something might have the property of *existing dependently* and not have the property of *existing always*. Even if there is an entailment between *always existing and not being Brahman* and *always existing dependently*, it does not follow – nor is it true – that there is an entailment between *existing dependently* and *existing always*. So consider the proposition *There is a continuant which never begins to exist but ceases to exist*, or *There is a continuant which never ceases to exist but begins to exist*, or *There is a continuant that both begins and ceases to exist*. These propositions are logically contingent. Whether they are true is not something decidable by reference to either formal or semantic necessity. Further, since they are logically contingent, Brahman can make any of them true. Thus it is perfectly possible that temporary, beginningless, or endless continuants exist.

Incontinuants and conditioning

It is as close to standard Buddhist doctrine as anything is that, with certain exceptions, everything dependently co-arises. What this amounts to is this: for any item y, there is some item x that existentially and qualitatively conditions it. This is to be so interpreted that 'y' may refer to a single item or more than one item.

Varieties of existential and qualitative conditioning

Existential conditioning comes in two varieties, simultaneous and successive. Strictly, this requires that the notion of *is sufficient for* be understood in a slightly complex manner. If x at T1 existentially conditions y at T2, let us say that x is *priorly sufficient for y*; x is all that exists at T1 that is requisite for y at T2. If x at T2 existentially conditions y at T2, let us say that x is *contemporaneously sufficient for* y at T2; x is all that exists at T2 that is requisite for y at T2. That y exists at T2 and is conditioned by both x* which exists at T1 and x which exists at T2 does not entail that y is overdetermined, but merely that y is multiply dependent – dependent on items both prior to and simultaneous with y's own brief appearance as an incontinuant. In what follows, this complexity of *is sufficient for* will be left implicit.

Thus x*, which exists at T1, may existentially condition y, which exists at T2, in that x*'s failure to exist at T1 is sufficient for y not existing at T2, x may also existentially condition y, which exists at T2, in that x's failure to exist at T2 is sufficient for y's failure to exist at T2, and x's existing at T2 is sufficient for y's existing at T2. Similarly, conditioning with respect to quality Q comes in two varieties. Thus X*, which exists at T1, may condition y, which exists at T2, in that x*'s failure to exist at T1 or x*'s failure to have property Q* at T1, may be sufficient for y's failure to have Q at T2, and x*'s existence at T1 or x's having Q* at T1 may be sufficient for y's having Q at T2. But x, which exists at T2, may also condition y, which exists at T2, with respect to Q in that x's failure to exist at T2 or failure to have some property Q* at T2 may be sufficient for y's failure to have Q at T2, and x's existing or x's having Q* at T2 may be sufficient for y's having Q at T2. This is a lot of conditioning for y to undergo. On the view in which they are only incontinuants each of which is conditioned by at least one prior and one co-existing incontinuant, with no exceptions, every incontinuant undergoes at lot of conditioning. There is no Unconditioned Incontinuant, let alone any Unconditioned Continuant, that is an exception to this rule.

Strictly speaking, this is an enumeratively pluralistic world. There are as many distinct items in this world as there are momentary incontinuants in this world. The world is viewed as beginningless, and a single eye-blink is said to cover thousands of successive incontinuants. So overall the world contains lots more incontinuants than Bill Gates has pennies.

In one version, this world is pluralistic with respect to primitive kinds. There are non-conscious incontinuants and conscious incontinuants, and so two kinds of incontinuants. This does not make the world nearly as pluralistic regarding kinds as it is regarding members, but it makes it more pluralistic regarding kinds than a kind-monist could sanction. In another version, there are only conscious incontinuants.

On the other hand, this is a tight-knit world. It is easy to see how one might be tempted to think of it as very much one thing, both at a time and over time. One with even a slight tendency to think of incontinuants as states, and to think that states must be states of something, might easily come to think of this world as really a matter of one massive substance beginninglessly having an incredible quantity of very short-lived states – as a sort of frenetic Spinozean Nature living a fast-paced life.

Incontinuants and impermanence

The doctrine that (nearly) everything is impermanent also has the status of near orthodoxy in Buddhist tradition. What it amounts to for an item to be impermanent depends on the nature of time. If time is atomic, being composed of temporal atoms or minima, then for an item x to be impermanent is for x to exist for just one atom of time. If time is continuous, a flow without intrinsic discrete parts, then for an item x to be impermanent is this: every temporal unit is conventional (none corresponds to any amount of time that time is mind-independently divided into), and for any conventional unit you please, x lasts for less time than that unit measures. If time is atomistic, what 'the present' refers to is composed by a single temporal atom. If it is continuous, what 'the present' refers to is whatever of the continuous flow then exists. (I waive considerations concerning different temporal frames here.)

It is claimed that the view that nothing has its own-nature or that everything is void follows from the doctrine of co-dependent arising. The doctrine that everything lacks its own-nature or is void is at least in part the doctrine that everything lacks an essence – a set of essential properties in virtue of which it belongs to a kind. This is a puzzling claim. Why think that:

(i) for all x, there is some y that conditions x (that determines that x exists and has the properties it has)

entails:

(ii) for all x, x lacks an essence,

or anything like that?

If one claims that (i) plus:

(ia) for all x, x is impermanent

entails (ii), it remains unclear why anyone should suppose that this entailment holds.

The basic idea is clear enough. It is that *having an essence* and *not being impermanent* are necessarily connected – that nothing lacking the latter feature can have the former feature. But why think that?

The Buddhist tradition has, as a sort of theme, the idea of taking the middle way whenever possible. Relative to things existing, the middle way is typically taken to be the doctrine of co-dependent arising, this being as it were a compromise between everything being permanent and there not being anything at all. But of course one favoring a middle way theme can hold a middle ontological ground that is quite different, maintaining that the middle way is between radical impermanence of the dependent co-arising sort and radical permanence of the *never changes* sort (Nirvana, on some conceptions thereof; Advaita Vedanta's qualityless Brahman) and that this ground is occupied by Jain substances which are permanent in the sense of everlastingly existing and possessing essential properties and impermanent in the sense of their non-essential properties forever coming and going. Or one could hold that the middle ground is found in the view that there are continuants, items that exist for a lot longer than a temporal minimum but a lot shorter than forever. Middle ground considerations aside – what the middle ground is shifts depending on the perspective from which you reflect on it – why think that only a permanent item or a continuant can have an essence? (It is worth noting that even between the same extremes, it is unclear what the middle way is. Consider the view that whatever exists, exists necessarily versus the view that nothing exists at all; is the middle ground that there are contingently existing incontinuants? that there are contingently existing continuants? or something else.)

Consider a single thought – a thought, say, of a Euclidean triangle. It seems plainly true that x is a thought of a Euclidean triangle if and only if x is a thought of a three-sided closed plane figure. This is its essence. If we ask what a thought is, one answer is that a thought is a representational mental state, a state of consciousness that represents its being the case that so-and-so, where its being so-and-so is not logically impossible. So we can expand our definition thusly: x is a thought of a Euclidean triangle if and only if x is a conscious state whose representational content is of there being a three-sided closed plane figure. Arguably, it is also the case that any thought must be someone's thought – that if there actually is any such conscious state as the one just described, it must be someone's conscious state. But this is not a move that most of the Buddhist tradition will be anxious to make.

There are different accounts of what a thought is, and accounts of what a thought is on which the present account is true of some thoughts but not of others. For present purposes, this simply amounts to there being other examples one could use to make the present point, which is that an x being a thought of a Euclidean triangle can have an essence even if it is conditioned and even if it is momentary. The answer to the question as to whether (i), or (i) plus (ia), entail (ii) seems to be that they do not. Then the answer to the question as to why one should think they do is that one shouldn't, and the answer to the question as to why anyone thinks otherwise will come in terms of either explaining mistaken reasoning or else offering social science explanations of the belief that the entailment in question holds.

One relevance of this to Buddhist metaphysics is this. It is very tempting to think of Buddhist metaphysics, insofar as it accepts the doctrines of impermanence and co-dependent arising, as holding that what exists are very short-lived items that have essences or essential properties and are conditioned by other items that also have essences or essential properties. 'Very short-lived' will be understood in one or the other of the two ways noted above, depending on how the view in question thinks of time itself. The items that dependently co-arise and blip momentarily into and then right away pop out of existence are possessors of properties (i.e., qualities and relations), and some of those properties are essential and some are not. There are at least two reasons for this being tempting. One is that the entailment between (i), or (i) and (ia), and (ii) does not seem to hold. The other is that it is very hard to understand it in any other way. Whether one suggests that the relevant incontinuants are tropes, states, or events, they have properties. If they are tropes (first-order properties) they nonetheless have second-order properties. They ae property-bearers that are not themselves collections of properties. They are not construed as enduring, but it is hard to see that they can lack essences. A red image, one would think, has *being a red image* as its essence, and it may be that the assumed but non-existent connection between *having an essence* and *being an enduring item* has prevented some philosophers from seeing that their own views require that incontinuants be construed as having essences, even if they *are* incontinuants. It is, of course, incomposite incontinuants that are under discussion here, and they are not classes or bundles of anything. If incomposite incontinuants have essences, are property bearers, and are not simply collections of properties, only lack of endurance prevents them from being substances. They are, so to speak, *nearly* substances; one might even describe them as momentary substances. There is the hard question as to how one could know that such nearly-substantial items do not endure. But if even incontinuants can have, indeed do have, essences, the incontinuantist must hope that it is false that *having an essence* entails *being an enduring item*. She then will not want impermanence to rule out possession of an essence.

Maximally impermanent incontinuants

The doctrine that (nearly) everything is impermanent also has a nearly-definitive-of-orthodoxy status. What it amounts to for an item to be impermanent depends on the nature of time. If the considerations just offered are correct, the incontinuantist should hold that what exists are what we might not improperly call *substantial incontinuants* or (as before) *momentary substances*. The disagreement about whether there are substances or not – in my terms, whether there are only *substantial incontinuants* or whether there are at least *temporary continuants* – is often viewed as the, or one of the, great and deep philosophical disagreements, one of the basic conceptual divisions than which there is no deeper. No doubt it is important, just as the difference (say) as to whether there are just *temporary continuants* or whether there are also *everlasting continuants* is an important philosophical disagreement. There is a case to be made that there is a still more basic disagreement, namely as to whether there are either contnuants or incontinuants, or something else instead. The question arises as to what that might be. The short answer is something like 'The Absolute Being' or 'The Absolute State', but these are either labels without packages or else names for something in need of explication.

The pluralist-pluralist line

The pluralist-pluralist line holds that there are two kinds of simple things, conscious and non-conscious. Each conscious simple depends for existence on some other simple, some conscious and some not. The same holds for each non-conscious simple. There are lots of simples, each of which is conditioned relative to existence and properties by other simples. Nothing whatever is existentially independent. Simple A can be distinct from simple B due to various considerations: A has different properties from B, A and B exist at different places, or A and B exist at different times. Of course A and B may be existentially or qualitatively conditioned by different items, but being existentially or qualitatively differently conditioend by (say) C and D leads to the question as to what it is by virtue of which C and D are distinct, and sooner or later one must refer to differences that are not merely matters of being differently conditioned.

The conditioning relationships

Suppose x existentially conditions y; x's non-existence is sufficient for y's non-existence. This relationship need not be necessary. Suppose x's conditions y with respect to Q; x's non-existence, or else x's lacking Q*, is sufficient for y's lacking Q. This relationship need not be necessary.

Suppose, for every x, some y conditions it, and there is no y that conditions everything. (The comments regarding conditioning here apply to both existential and qualitative conditioning.) To be more precise, consider the case in which x conditions y and y conditions z and z conditions x. Let us say that x conditions y *directly* if there is no z such that x conditions y only by virtue of conditioning z, and x conditions y and x conditions y *indirectly* if there is some z such that x conditions y only by virtue of conditioning z, and x conditions y. Suppose that, for every y, some x conditions it; that for no x is it the case that x directly conditions every y; that for every x it is the case that it indirectly conditions every y. Call each such conditioned and conditioning item a *condituant* and a collection composed only of such items a *condituant world*. If each condituant is impermanent, we have a world of momentary condituants. Is it, as the description thus far suggests, a world of distinct items? Is it a single item whose apparent parts are simple modes or states? How is one to think of such a world?

One could argue that, since everything at least indirectly existentially conditions everything else, there is just one thing. The obvious premises behind this conclusion are that if x's non-existence is sufficient for y's non-existence, then y is not distinct from x, and everything indirectly existentially conditions everything else. But it is false that if x's non-existence is sufficient for y's non-existence, then x and y are identical. My body exists as a living organism only if there is sufficient oxygen in the neighborhood; it is not identical to the oxygen in the neighborhood. God is not identical to the world which depends for its existence on God.

The argument, however, can appeal to mutual conditioning – in the sort of world envisioned, every item indirectly existentially conditions, and is existentially conditioned by, every other. If x and y mutually existentially condition one another, are they distinct? Consider two items that are sensitive to loneliness to such a degree that if they are lonely they will literally cease to exist. They will be lonely in the absence of another member of their species, and they are its only members. Thus each depends for its existence on the other. This will not prevent them from being distinct.

If they are distinct, what sort of distinct items are they? Distinct states of one thing? Distinct events? Or something else? Is a world of condituants a whole composed, each moment, of momentary parts? On one view, there are conscious incontinuants. It is possible to imagine a karma and reincarnation scenario that operates only among non-conscious incontinuants. One might think of laws of nature that are true of non-conscious incontinuants. These laws, let us say, cover the sequential connections between non-conscious incontinuants in such a manner that the state a non-conscious incontinuant is in at T1 conditions the state a successor incontinuant is in at T2 where the 'goal' is that each incontinuant be a member of a bundle which flourishes. A rose bush, on the incontinuantist account thereof, is at a time a bundle of particular sorts incontinuants and over time a series of such bundles. It seems right that a bush is not simply a matter of essenceless incontinuants being placed in the right order, but of the right kinds of incontinuants being placed in the right order. Rose bushes, presumably in contrast to individual incontinuants, can flourish – can be healthy, free from bug and rose bush plague, blooming in season, and the like. One could image a world of incontinuants, each of which was a condituant, composing something like as organism, and one could imaging its sometimes flourishing as such a whole, and sometimes not. One could also imagine something like a karma account of such flourishing.

The standard reincarnation and karma doctrine, though, concerns persons and enlightenment. Indian philosophical perspectives, materialism aside, either take the doctrine of reincarnation and karma, in some version, literally, or else replace it by some non-literal version. The non-literal versions, as H. L. Mencken said of the 1920s liberal Protestant account of the resurrection of Jesus, interpret it so that it so that it never occurs. Here we stick to the literal understanding of reincarnation and karma.

Suppose an item x is made up entirely of incontinuants. When these incontinuants (of the right sorts) collect in a certain pattern, or in a sufficient number, the resultant package of incontinuants comes to have properties that no single continuant, and no package of continuants of another pattern or a lesser number, has. (It does not matter whether there is only one recipe for the construction of incontinuants that have the relevant properties or whether there are two or more. Thus I choose the simplest version.) Then it becomes natural to think of a package at a time as having a unity all its own, and to speak of each such unit as an organically complex item. If each such item has the capacity, at least in some environments, to give rise to a like item, and if this actually sometimes happens, it is natural to identify each series of such items in which one produces the next which produces the next, as also possessing a unity of its own, this time the unity obtaining between successive rather than simultaneious items. Those inclined toward fancier speech will speak of synchronic and diachronic unity. The important point will be that there now exist units that have properties not possessed by their simple incontinuant parts.

These properties – and this is the crucial point – are not simply the logical consequences of some simple incontinuants simply coming together. If two incontinuants come together, the result is a composite of incontinuants, and the composite *has parts, is even-numbered*, and the like, whereas each component incontinuant lacks these features. Such properties are logical consequences of the combining of incontinuants. But the properties of current interest are not logical consequences of the combining of incontinuants. They are such things as *being alive, being conscious, being self-conscious, making inferences, choosing*, and the like, as these are features of what are conceived as, as it were, organically connected bundles of conscious incontinuants.

There are severe problems with the idea of a person being composed of incontinuants. Presumably Chandra at time T1 is, not a single conscious incontinuant, but a bundle thereof. There are lots of incontinuants at T1 that are no part of the bundle that is Chandra. What so relates the Chandra-composing-incontinuants so that they do compose Chandra? One can say that it is the kinds of contemporaneous conditioning that go on between just those incontinuants and do not go on between any of them and any others, save as those others constitute their own bundles. This is more the promise of an answer than an answer. Why think there are, or can be, any such distinctive causal connections? If there are such, what are they? To merely claim that they exist is to offer an unsigned black check. Perhaps a more promising answer is this. Chandra in fact can be aware of his being at a meeting and of his wishing that he weren't; his consciousness is unified. What unifies it?

One answer is that conscious incontinuants come in two varieties, namely first-order conscious states (being aware of being in a meeting, being discontent) and second-order conscious states (being aware of being aware at a meeting, and of being thereby discontent). First-order incontinuant states are tied together by being objects of a single second-order-state. There is no need to hold that there are third-order states; worry about infinite regresses here is groundless paranoia. This is probably the best determinate answer to the question as to what ties incontinuants into a bundle. But it complicates incontinuant theory in a direction that will not displease continuantists. The idea that there is a second-order state that resembles a substance save in the time it hangs around not only in virtue of having properties, being incomposite, and having as essence, but in virtue of being aware of first-order states is the best way of explaining the unity of a bundle of conscious incontinuants over time is enough to give an incontinuantist philosophical nightmares.

What ties bundles together into a series? Appeal to genuine memory won't help here. What incontinuantist genuine memory amounts to is the occurrence at T1 of an incontinuant I1 and the occurrence at some later time T* of another incontinuant I2 such that I2 represents sufficiently accurately the occurrence of I1 and is caused by I1 (typically through a causal chain involving other incontinuants). But a 'memory' of this sort does not establish anything like personal identity. If you so vividly tell me of an event before my birth that I can picture it accurately, I still don't remember that event. If you add the requirement that both I1 and I2 be in the same sequence of bundles, you use same-sequence considerations to define memory and cannot then turn around and use memory to define same-sequence-of-bundles. Appeal to some uniquely series-of-bundles-producing causal connections here is no better than before.

These remarks give at least a little sense of some of the questions an incontinuantist about persons faces. I suspect that the best attempt to answer them successfully appeals to the sort of account of incontinuantism noted above – to say that a bundle of incontinants that constitutes Chandra at time T1 has emergent properties. There will be problems about what happens to Chandra during sound sleep on this view, and perhaps the answer will have to come in terms of the alleged Chandra-series always having bundle members, many of which do not cause any 'memories' later in the series. In any case, the resulting view is of an emergent individual – of something composite that, even in its compositeness, at least seems a genuine individual. (I think it still is not, but that is another story. If it isn't, the best incontinuantist answer to what ties bundle of incontinuants together, and perhaps part of the best incontinuantist account of what ties incontinuants into a bundle – namely a combined second-order state thesis plus emergent property view – goes by the boards.)

It is as well to be fully explicit here. Let us say that if a bundle B of conscious incontinuants at time T1 is composed if incontinuants so related that B possesses properties that are not simply those *entailed* by the mere fact that there are those incontinuants in causal concourse with one another, it has *emergent properties*. Such properties, let us suppose, contain *being alive, being self-conscious, acting, acting in such a manner as to be responsible for one's action, making choices, holding beliefs, making inferences, having a unified consciousness*, and the like. It is far from clear that a bundle of incontinuantists can be so characterized, but waive that for now. (Laws are perhaps most plausibly viewed here as truths about the causal powers and liabilities of incontinuants, supposing incontinuants can have these; if they can, that too argues for their having natures or essences.) Let us also say that a bundle of the sort described is an *emergent bundle*. Then consider a series of emergent bundles, and call this an *emergent series*. An emergent series looks suspiciously like an emergent individual, a whole more than the sum of its parts, something not reducible to its members, and so on. To the degree that there being emergent individuals alleviates the problem of how to make sense of literal reincarnation and karma doctrine, in which there must be agents and actions and in which the doer of a deed must in all justice be the one who receives the karmic consequences thereof, there being emergent individuals challenges the doctrine that there are only incontinuants and no continuants.

Some tendencies toward monism

Various aspects of Indian metaphysics tend toward the view that there is but one qualityless being or state (what would distinguish a qualityless being from a qualityless state is at best murky). The criticism (by Ramanuja among others) that it is logically impossible that anything both exist and be propertyless (quite independent of whether existence itself is a property) seems entirely correct, but set it aside for the moment. The idea that individual mental items are individuated by the individual physical items that sometimes embody them, but that otherwise they are without distinguishing characteristics is easily challenged; what, in their unembodied states, distinguishes one such mental item from another? The answer seems to be 'nothing' with the result that they are not distinct after all. The notion that mind is a sort of sixth sense to be distinguished from soul, so that the beliefs, preferences, hopes, fears, character, choices, and the like are not characteristic of the soul *per se* or in itself, and that the soul as everlasting continuant exists distinct from all of these as well as from perceptions, introspections, and physical characteristics drives one in the same direction. Then there is the notion that nothing that appears to exist really does exist – that all is illusion. The criticism that an illusion must be an illusion to someone, and the criticism that just as the world cannot be convention all the way down it cannot be illusion all the way down, also seems correct, but let us put it aside too. Still further, there is the suspicion that if everything is fully conditioned, there is something arbitrary, conventional, and superficial about the distinctions we ordinarily make pulls in the direction of downgrading those distinctions until pluralisms are replaced by monisms. These various tendencies of course are not decisive. They can be resisted, and the fact that they exist does not justify them. The question remains as to whether there is good reason to accept them. One way of arguing that they are on the right track is to argue that in fact there cannot be continuants. Then one will only need an argument to show that there cannot be distinct incontinuants either.

Two arguments against continuants: Argument One

There are conscious items, human persons among them; let Chandra be such an item. The question is how such items are to be construed, as continuants or as incontinuants. Here is an argument in favor of the existence of incontinuants as opposed to continuants.

1. If it is logically possible that x exist and y not exist, then x is distinct from y.

Assume:

2. Chandra exists at T1.
3. Chandra exists at T2.

It is the case that:

4. It is logically possible that Chandra exist at T1 but not at T2.
5. It is logically possible that Chandra exist at T2 but not at T1.

Hence:

6. It is logically possible that 2 be true and 3 be false.
7. It is logically possible that 3 be true and 2 be false.

Hence:

8. That which makes 2 true is not identical to that which makes 3 true.

So:

9. Chandra at T1 is not identical to Chandra at T2.

Given this, the arguer reasons, it becomes reasonable to think of Chandra at T1 as an incontinuant and Chandra at T2 as another incontinuant. Chandra overall, so to speak, is thus reasonably thought of as a series of incontinuants. Thus ends argument one.

Two arguments against continuants: Argument Two

Here is a second argument in favor of incontinuants over continuants.

1*. If x has quality Q and y lacks quality Q, then x is distinct from y.

Assume:

2. Chandra exists at T1.
3. Chandra exists at T2.

It is then the case that:

4*. That which makes 2 true has the property *existing at T1*.
5*. That which makes 3 true has the property *existing at T2*.

Hence:

6*. That which makes 2 true is not identical to that which makes 3 true.

Premises 4* and 5* might instead appeal to the fact that Chandra at T1 may be thinking of Delhi and not of Ramanuja, and at T2 of Ramanuja and not of Delhi. Then the T1 item has the property *thinking of Delhi* and the T2 item has the property *thinking of Ramanuja*, but not conversely. Or if Chandra is thinking of Ramanuja throughout, the T1 item will have the property *thinking of Delhi* and the T2 item has the property *thinking of Ramanuja*, but not conversely. Or if Chandra is thinking of Ramanuja throughout, the T1 item will have the property *thinking of Ramanuja at T1* and the T2 item will have the property *thinking of Ramanuja at T2*. Or one could replace 1* by:

1**. If it is logically possible that x has quality Q and y lacks quality Q, then x is distinct from y.

and replace 4*. and 5*. by something like:

4**. It is logically possible that that which makes 2 true have the property *thinking of Ramanuja at T1* and that that which makes 3 true not have the property *thinking of Ramanuja at T1*.

5**. It is logically possible that that which makes 3 true have the property *thinking of Ramanuja at T2* and that that which makes 2 true not have the property *thinking of Ramanuja at T2*.

These and similar alterations will not change the comments to follow, save for the details of their statement.

Argument One, roughly, concerns Chandra the person *per se*, once at T1 and again at T2. It claims that what exists at the one time and what exists at the other time, insofar as each is incomposite or a bundle of incomposites, must be distinct incomposites or distinct bundles. Argument Two, roughly, concerns certain properties of the person Chandra, and contends that however we think of the person Chandra (and *a fortiori* any person) should be constrained by the fact, allegedly established by the argument, that the Chandra-relevant properties borne by something at T1 and the Chandra-relevant properties borne by something at T2, must be borne by different somethings, or that the Chandra-relevant states at T1 and the Chandra-relevant states at T2 cannot both be states of a single thing or incomposites in a single composite bundle. (Bundles exist at a time; what can exist over exist over time is a series of bundles, which on the doctrine safest for the incontinuantist is really nothing more or other than one bundle after another.)

Both lines of argument seem at least initially attractive.

Philosophical inelegancies of the second Argument

The continuantist has a quite satisfactory reply to Argument Two. She can reply that the second argument, in its original formulation here and in its relevant alterations, succeeds in distinguishing between distinct properties states of an item. It does not show that the item in those states is not numerically the same continuant at T1 and T2. It does not show that Chandra is a series of incontinuants rather than a continuant. Continuantists will grant that states of continuants come and go. Whether they come and go as fast as momentary-incontinuantists claim is, from a continuantist point of view, not of great interest. Suppose that they do. Nothing follows about the continuant that has those states.

One can put the matter like this. The second argument treats of items that the continuantist thinks of as states of a continuant, modes of a continuant, or properties of a continuant. These are not, even according to the continuantist, enduring items. They come and go, exactly how quickly really does not matter much. Continuants don't come and go, at least nearly as quickly as states, modes, or properties (where properties are construed as tropes). Further, the astute continuantist will not hold that there is some trope the possession of which is essential to Chandra. Perhaps Chandra has an an essential feature *being conscious* and even *being continuously conscious so long as Chandra exists at all* and *being capable of self-consciousness and being sometimes self-conscious*. Still there is no particular manner or degree of consciousness that Chandra must always have; he may sleep so soundly that his degree of consciousness elicits no memories of his restful hours. He may think long and hard about a single abstruse matter or his mind may flit about like a robin in springtime. But his being conscious is always a matter of *Chandra's being conscious in some manner or other* and only thereby is it true that the more abstract *there is a conscious state* or *consciousness occurs* apply, in their less concrete and illuminating manner, to actual Chandrian phenomena.

Or one can put things in these terms. The locutions 'that which makes 2 true' and 'that which makes 3 true' is, for a continuantist, Chandra's having one property or being in one state, and then Chandra's having another property or being in another state. So Chandra changes by reason of losing one property and gaining another or being in one state and then in another. What continuantist thinks this not true of such as Chandra? But, with perfect consistency with this recognition, she also holds that the self-same Chandra is bearer of one property at T1 and another at T2, or is in one state at T1 and another state at T2. Change in properties or states is not incompatible with, and indeed entails, numerical identity of the changer over time. It is the view that change never occurs, and apparent change is really replacement, that is problematic here.

Argument One and philosophical inelegance

The second argument, then, does not do what the incontinuantist wants. It leaves the continuantist unscathed. Even if the incontinuantist accepts the reply, she will contend that the first argument concerns, not properties or states of Chandra, but Chandra himself. Thus (the incontinuantist claims) the continuantist strategy for dealing with the second argument will not work regarding the first. An incontinuantist is a composition ontologist regarding items that the substance philosopher regards as incomposite; she thinks of alleged continuants as composed at a time of co-existing incontinuants and over time of one bundle of co-existing incontinuants after another. The continuantist takes the alleged incontinuants, not as components of continuants, but as states, modes, or properties thereof. The first argument is intended to show that, in this dispute, the incontinuantists are right. The continuantist cannot here say something like this: even if you are right in the first argument, you prove nothing that I dispute and disprove nothing that I deny. If the first argument is successful, something that the continuantist disputes is proved and something that the continuantist asserts is disproved. So argues the incontinuantist.

The first argument in effect endeavors to turn the fact that it is logically possible that a continuant which does not exist with logical necessity last a second less long than it does, into an argument for the conclusion that there are no continuants. It seems to be logically possible that the continuant Chandra live for (say) ninety years. If he lives just this long, he is a temporary continuant. According to Ramanuja and Madhava there are not incomposite temporary continuants and Chandra is incomposite; he is a dependent everlasting continuant. But whether everlasting or given but fourscore years and ten, the continuant asks, why cannot Chandra be a continuant even though it is logically possible that Chandra have not been everlasting or have lived but eight-nine years? To this question, among others, the first argument is intended to provide an answer: it is logically impossible that there be continuants.

What makes 2 be true is that Chandra exists at T1. What makes 3 true is that Chandra exists at T2. It is plainly logically possible that Chandra exist at T1 but not T2. (We need not go into the question as to whether the same person could begin existence later than he in fact did.) The necessity of metaphysical identity entails that if the item x that makes it true that Chandra exists at T1 is identical to an item y at T2, there is nothing else at T2 that x could be identical to, and nothing but y that x could be identical to. But does the argument prove that Chandra is not a continuant?

The core question here concerns what makes 3 true. On the incontinuantist account, the answer is: existence of a particular incontinuant at T2. The incontinuant might not have existed at all. On the continuantist account, the answer is: the existence of a continuant at T2. The continuant might not have existed at all or have stopped existing at T1. The problem with the first argument is this. Its first premise is:

1. If it is logically possible that x exist and y not exist, then x is distinct from y.

The idea expressed here is more perspicuously (and fully) expressed as follows:

1a. For all x, y, and T, if it is logically possible that x exist at T and y not exist at T, or logically possible that y exist at T and x not exist at T, then x is distinct from y.

So stated, it is true but it does not, together with the argument's other premises, entail the required conclusion. In order to get a perspicuously (and fully) expressed premise that together with the other premises of the first argument entail the required conclusion, something like this is needed:

1b. For all x, y, T1, and T2, if it is logically possible that x exist at T1 and y not exist at T2, or x not exist at T1 and y exist at T2, then x is distinct from y.

Suppose it is logically possible that x, which exists at T1, continue to exist at T2. Then 1b. is false. Thus 1b. is false unless it is logically impossible that there be continuants. But the first argument was supposed to prove that it is logically impossible that there be continuants. Hence the first argument fails to prove its point. The proposition *There exist continuants* seems neither formally nor semantically inconsistent, and the first argument does nothing to show otherwise. The two arguments discussed here, then, will not justify the dismissal of continuants.

In fact, then, so far as any of the arguments considered here are concerned, there seems no reason whatever to be suspicious of the notion, or of the existence, of continuants that, in contrast to such incontinuants as momentary substances, are genuine continuants, and, in contrast to everlasting continuants, are temporal, beginningless, or endless continuants.

Address for correspondence: Keith E. Yandell, Professor of Philosophy, University of Wisconsin, Madison, WI 53706, USA
Phone/Fax: (608) 263-5335; E-mail: kyandell@facstaff.wisc.edu

Gender and the infinite: On the aspiration to be all there is

PAMELA SUE ANDERSON
University of Sunderland

1. Introduction

Twentieth-century philosophers of religion made strides forward in advancing sophisticated arguments about religious knowledge, language, experience and arguments for the existence of the theistic God. However, by the end of the century Anglo-American philosophers in particular tended to treat philosophy of religion as synonymous with a Christian account of the divine. Male and female philosophers assumed an uncritical familiarity with, and so unquestioning acceptance of, the classical model of traditional theism as the subject matter for philosophers of religion. Nevertheless, before the turn of the century a number of feminist philosophers of religion had begun to challenge this account for its gender-bias; and non-western philosophers criticized the ethnocentrism or racism of western claims to neutrality in philosophy of religion. Feminist philosophers directed their criticism to the traditional theistic conception of God for its idealization of exclusively male attributes.[1]

Whether theist or atheist, twentieth-century philosophers of religion in the Anglo-American world too readily accepted the theistic frame of reference, failing to notice the uncritical – and in this sense unphilosophical – nature of the traditional conception of God as a personal being who is the omnipotent, omniscient, omnibenevolent, eternal creator and sustainer of all creation. Why should the overall conception itself remain while endless debates centre on each of the divine attributes, especially in relation to the frequently debated philosophical problem of evil? Feminist philosophers were not alone in arguing that it would be far more constructive to try to alleviate suffering than to justify the existence of evil *and* a good, all-knowing, all-powerful, eternal God? This would change the nature of the philosophical problem. The radical question is, whose conception is the God of contemporary philosophy of religion? If not our own, or if a male projection of who we are, why focus philosophical debate exclusively on it?

So the familiarity and neutrality of philosophical claims about the divine have been challenged. For some, a new starting point for philosophy of religion is now necessary. At least a more inclusive focus for philosophy of religion in the twenty-first century would seem to be crucial to the future of the field in a world with ever-interesting diversity, including diverse practices of religion. Both the particularity of beliefs as embodied in religious practices and the generality of religious yearning must be addressed. In this essay I would like to offer a feminist rethinking of a core topic for a more inclusive philosophy of religion. I advocate a gender-sensitive approach to the topic of the infinite. To articulate this approach I would like to begin with a fundamentally corrupt aspiration and see how it has taken both masculinist and feminist forms. I will, then, consider a conception of the incorrupt form of 'craving infinitude'. This is conceived to be essentially expansive for men and women.[3]

Building critically upon the differently gendered accounts of the infinite in A. W. Moore and Grace M. Jantzen, I will argue that the masculinist philosopher runs the danger of aspiring to be infinite, while the feminist philosopher runs the danger of seeking to become all (there is) in nature.[4] I will maintain that two forms of a fundamentally corrupt aspiration have followed the traditional dichotomies of gender in philosophy.[5] My concern are two gendered forms, but I also maintain that this corrupt aspiration takes other forms depending upon its cultural manifestations in the lives of men and women of different ethnic, racial, religious, sexual and gendered perspectives. Essentially the corrupting tendency of our relations to the infinite rests in an aspiration to be or become all there is.

Feminist philosophers of religion insist that the traditional theistic conception of a personal God has appeared strange to women philosophers and to followers of non-theistic religions once they have stopped – and shifted their thinking.[6] So, have western philosophers themselves aspired to be infinite in proposing the God's eye view as the achievement of men who possess all-knowledge, all-power, all-goodness, all truth? From various perspectives the conception of the infinite implicit in a God's eye view of reality seems an outmoded ideal to which western men have aspired. Following Moore's recent account of the infinite in *Points of View*, I would like to maintain a critical distinction between *the aspiration to be infinite* and a *craving for infinitude*.[7] The latter has an affinity with what I have called (following bell hooks) yearning.[8] My contention is that yearning can continue to motivate the search for truth, love, goodness and justice without the one who craves or yearns necessarily *aspiring to be* fully rational, perfectly good and completely just; that is, without aspiring to be, in traditional theistic terms, God.[9] In focusing critically upon the gendered forms of our aspirations, I urge a distinctive shift away from philosophy's privileged western point of view.

Jantzen rejects 'a drive to infinity: an insatiable desire for knowledge' as a masculinist obsession with necrophilia.[10] She insists that this drive represents a male refusal to accept boundaries. Instead Jantzen argues for a feminist pantheism in which women seek to become divine.[11] However, a danger of aspiring to become 'pan-theist' remains implicit as the potential infinite in time. Moore contends that human beings are no more able to stop aspiring to be infinite than to eliminate evil.[12] Yet his contention could be read as male or, what Jantzen would call, masculinist. In contrast a feminist imperative seeks to *eliminate* evil, or at least the evil resulting from the *hubris* of a man's thinking that he alone exists.

Ultimately I intend to pursue the possibility of incorrupt forms of male and female relations to infinitude. A particular reading of Luce Irigaray supports this pursuit. My intention is to offer a point of contestation for masculinist and feminist philosophers of religion alike. This point lies right at the heart of how we do philosophy (of religion) and how we conceive the quest for knowledge of what cannot be said. Ineffable knowledge of how to be finite in our relations to infinitude also plays a role in the renewal of philosophy of religion for the twenty-first century. Epistemological, metaphysical, ethical and political domains meet in this more modest pursuit for the incorrupt at the point of contestation concerning infinitude.

2. Gendering philosophy of religion

For Plato in line with the Pythagorean philosophers 'the infinite' was a term of abuse. It was associated with chaos, matter and femaleness, while the finite was good and associated with order, form and maleness.[13] An early twentieth-century feminism of difference – also supported by Irigaray – proposed a return to the ancient conception of the infinite as female, while reversing its value from bad to good. In contrast, Jantzen simply rejects the infinite, assuming its association with all-power, all-knowledge and maleness. Her claim that feminist pantheism replaces the infinite of a masculinist monotheism with the finite as female seems inconsistent.

In *Points of View* Moore references Irigaray's *Elemental Passions* and 'Divine Women' without any discussion.[14] It is helpful to take up this discussion of crucial claims concerning gender and our relations to the infinite in 'Divine Women'. These are claims in Irigaray's mime, or disruptive imitation, of the philosophical argument of Ludwig Feuerbach. Her mime exposes the exclusion of woman from man's projection while acknowledging the role projection has played in man's defence of his maleness.

> Man is able to exist because God helps him to define his gender (*genre*), helps him to orient his finiteness by reference to infinity. The revival of religious feeling can in fact be interpreted as the rampart man raises in defense of his very maleness.
>
> ... The goal that is most valuable is to go on *becoming* infinitely. ... To become means fulfilling the wholeness of what we are capable of being. ... If he has no existence in his gender, he lacks his relation to the infinite and, in fact, to finiteness.
>
> ... [Women] need, we need, an infinite if they are to share a *little*. Otherwise sharing means fusion-confusion, division and dislocation within themselves, among themselves. If I am unable to form a relationship with some horizon of accomplishment for my gender, I am unable to share while protecting my becoming.[15]

This mime captures the relations between gender and infinity. Men and women as embodied are described as finite, sexed beings. Our bodies can also be interpreted as gendered by reference to that which is not finite, i.e. 'infinite'. Irigaray assumes that God has served as man's projection of infinity. This projection of infinity both creates a religious feeling and supports an exclusive relation of gender as maleness. Yet women need an infinite in order to create a horizon (or ideal) for their gender. But does this mean women need a projection?

Irigaray's writings have provoked women philosophers to rethink the nature of the divine and the relations of sex to gender. I would like to suggest the implications of this rethinking for the gendering of philosophy of religion: (i) in terms of projection and (ii) in terms of sex/gender. First, to quote again from Irigaray's 'Divine Women':

> God forces us to do nothing except *become*. The only task, the only obligation laid upon us is: to become divine men and women, to become perfectly, to refuse to allow parts of ourselves to shrivel and die that have the potential for growth and fulfilment.[16]

What is Irigaray *doing* in saying this? Feuerbach is her subtext. But does she express a duty or mime Feuerbach metaphorically and disruptively?[17] Let us consider his argument and her mime more closely.

Feuerbach assumes that the basis for religion is a projection of the self onto the divine, but the recognition of the divine as a self-projection would result in the dissolution of religion. His empirical argument that religion is based upon man's projection of his ideal attributes onto a divine being is not complete without the premise that the projection is an illusion.[18] Insofar as Irigaray mimes Feuerbach she must assume, as he did, that to understand how religion is created by way of projection is to know that there is no divine being, or non-empirical object of projection, beyond the subject. For Feuerbach, 'man' is the only subject. The divine attributes are man's. If Irigaray's mime makes space in this account for a female subject, it does not necessarily follow that she calls women to create a projection for themselves. Feuerbach is not calling for men to create a projection; he is calling for a recognition of the illusion. It would seem to follow that insofar as Irigaray's mime disrupts his picture by bringing in sexual difference as the interval between two subjects, it opens up a space for women to recognise their own (hidden, not projected) attributes in order to become subjects. It seems unlikely to me (at least) that we can agree, or claim, to become divine through projection.[19] Nevertheless, I contend that regulative ideals could (yet) serve to guide us toward incorrupt, gendered relations to the infinite.

Second, Irigaray has added significantly to the philosophical debate about sex and gender, including the gendered nature of traditional theism. A central issue for the gendering of philosophy of religion is whether sex and gender should be distinguished. I argue for a distinction of sex and gender which is not strictly empirical. To move beyond the limitations of the status quo in philosophy of religion, feminist philosophers need more than an empirical depiction of reality. In particular, we need to articulate the interplay of bodily, material and social differences using a revisable conception of the sex/gender distinction. To explain the importance of distinguishing between the empirical and the conceptual I will digress somewhat from my central argument.

To employ sex/gender as a conceptual, and not an empirical (i.e. biological/cultural), distinction is important on at least two counts. For one thing, it would help to distinguish a phenomenological level of description of the body as lived (i.e. as given prior to it being made empirically intelligible). This level assumes that the body is intuitively apprehended before it is understood or interpreted. Phenomenological description would, then, broaden the fields of both feminist philosophy and philosophy of religion by introducing an account of the lived body which is given as sexed. For another thing, a dual conception of the lived and interpreted body would enable greater understanding of the interrelated factors of sex/gender, including sexual, gender, racial, class, ethnic and religious perspectives. This would mean both a phenomenology of the sexed body and a socially situated epistemology (or a hermeneutics) of the gendered body. We could, then, use this distinction to interpret religious feelings and passion: first, to uncover their conditions of possibility and, second, to recognise the necessary and sufficient conditions of bodily knowledge. Without the conceptual distinction of the lived and interpreted body, empirical claims concerning the gendered body are only contingent rather than interpreted in the light of lived experience. So I assume that it is both possible and necessary to articulate a level of intuition more fundamental than the facts or norms of gender.

To do more than describe the role of gender in philosophy of religion, it is necessary to see behind or beyond the empiricism of Anglo-American philosophers of religion. Otherwise gendering will not move men and women from the status quo. For example, a teenager who grows up in a religious community where heterosexuality is assumed to be a fact yet experiences desires which are not intelligible in terms of this fact would not be able to explain such phenomena without access to a prior, lived body. If the lived body as sexed is (intuitively) accessible this allows for a challenge to the empirical facts which render it unintelligible. Without this distinction there would be no possibility for feminists, lesbians or anyone else who does not fit an established norm (e.g. compulsory reproduction or heterosexuality) to advocate change on the basis of their desires or needs.

3. A deep, pervasive and corrupt aspiration

The question guiding this section is whether a deep, pervasive and corrupt aspiration to be infinite manifests itself as male in philosophy of religion. Moore distinguishes between the craving for infinitude and *the aspiration to be infinite*. The former is incorrupt, the latter is a corruption of the former. Both the corrupt and the incorrupt relations to the infinite seem to be inevitable for humans. Yet is there something male in this corrupt aspiration?

> It is rational to want to be rational; or, more generally, to want rationality to be instantiated. But the aspiration to be infinite has a different focus. It includes the aspiration to be rational, but includes it as a residue within the distorted aspiration to be (so to speak) rationality itself.
>
> When the craving [for infinitude] is distorted, [its] perspectival character is turned in on itself in such a way that the craving becomes an aspiration *that we alone exist*, – or, in its most distorted form, that the subject alone exists. It becomes the aspiration to be a complete self-sufficient unconditioned whole, to be that which the craving for infinitude is a craving for.[20]

It is helpful to probe the philosophical anthropology implicit in Moore's account of finitude and infinitude. For this I turn to Paul Ricoeur's *Fallible Man*.[21] Although written some thirty-seven years before Moore's *Points of View*, Ricoeur's account of 'man' as fallible due to a disproportion between his finite points of view and his desire to transgress this finitude resonates profoundly with Moore's claims.[22] There seems to be a common Kantian framework. Consider Ricoeur's claim concerning finitude and points of view,

If finitude is primordially 'point of view', the acts and operations by which we become aware of point of view as point of view will reveal the most elementary connection between an *experience* of finitude and a *movement* transgressing this finitude.[23]

The movement of transgression anticipates what Moore calls our aspiration to be infinite. Ricoeur himself goes on to locate infinitude in feelings which personalise. Or, in Kantian terms, feeling is what both individuates and connects embodiments of reason. An incorrupt desire would seek a harmonious connection of happiness and virtue in the symbolic sense of belonging to a kingdom of ends. This sense of belonging renders the infinitude of feeling as eschatological (i.e. having to do with immutable 'last things', not part of the mutable space-time order of being). Desire, however, plays a corrupting role when it takes the absolute as its object. In other words, when desire takes on epistemological and ontological, instead of symbolic and eschatological, proportions it becomes for Ricoeur the corrupting force of the infinitude of feeling. Desire claims too much for itself as follows:

> ... Only a being who wants the all and who schematizes it in the objects of human desire is able to make a mistake, that is, take his object for the *absolute, forget* the symbolic character of the bond between happiness and an object of desire: forgetting this makes the symbol an idol ... This forgetting, this birth of an idol ... falls within the domain of a hermeneutics of the passions ...[24]

Ricoeur employs a hermeneutics to elucidate the corrupting nature of desire in the passions. Moore unwittingly (perhaps) presents the aspiration to be infinite as a fundamental passion which corrupts by rendering the infinite an idol rather than maintaining it as a symbol. There is a crucial difference between treating the infinite as epistemologically and ontologically constitutive (i.e. actualized in an idol) and schematising infinitude as regulative (i.e. instantiated in practical ideals). For Ricoeur at least, man can avoid the corrupt aspiration by restoring the symbol to its proper role. Arguably this idolatrous form of corruption is male insofar as it projects the dominant male view of subjectivity in western philosophy.

According to Irigaray, a projective or selfish awareness of the other rests at the heart of western philosophy as patriarchal. The male subject defines his gender by the exclusion of the female subject. This exclusion also eclipses the body from thinking. Man creates his gender in relation to his projection of a self-same subject. That is, he projects his own attributes infinitely and fails to see the other subject who gave birth to him, i.e. the female subject. If we consider Ricoeur's awareness of finitude as embodied in a place, the maleness of his anthropology becomes apparent. (However, this awareness also suggests that his thinking is not 'disembodied' to the degree to which Irigaray's male subject generally seems to be.[25])

> ... only the displacements of my body as a totality denote a change of place and, thereby, the function of the place as a point of view. To account for this unique privilege of global movements to constitute the notion of point of view, even when this point of view is particularized by sight, hearing or touch, we must add a further point to this analysis. ... I ascribe the diversity of the operations to the identity of a subject ... these diverse silhouettes appear *to me*, that is, to this unity and this identity ... the self as an identical pole of all acts is where the body, taken as a whole, is.[26]

In addition to the above awareness of the particularities of place (including the particularized nature of bodily sensations), Ricoeur is aware to a certain degree of the significance of his birth:

> ... I was born somewhere: from the moment I am 'brought into the world' I perceive this world as a series of changes and re-establishments starting from this place which I did not chose and which I cannot find in my memory.[27]

Irigaray's mime works to uncover the difference in a male awareness of finitude. Sexual difference is not explicit in Ricoeur's awareness of place and birth. As a difference between two subjects, sexual difference emerges in yearning for 'a place of place'.[28] This is a place where an incorrupt desire (or craving) for infinitude finds expression within the finite. As Irigaray argues, 'If we are to have a sense of the other that is not projective or selfish, we have to attain an "intuition of the infinite." '[29] Arguably Irigaray seeks to subvert a corrupt conception of infinity which defends maleness as primary by excluding the female subject. She speaks playfully to a male subject – 'you' – in order to uncover the hidden and excluded 'I' who is female. For example, listen to her dialogue in *Elemental Passions*.

> The whole is not the same for me as it is for you. For me, it can never be one. Can never be completed, always in-finite. When you talk about Infinity, it seems to me that you are speaking of a closed totality: a solid, empty membrane which would gather and contain all possibilities. The absolute of self-identity – in which you were, will be, could be.
>
> For me? A fluid expansion, never enclosed once and for all. Not even by projects or projections ...[30]
>
> ... Your order freezes the mobility of relations between. It produces discontinuity. Peaks, pikes, fissures. Energy no longer circulates. Is hoarded in forms that create closure. Is saved up in phantasies: captivating some, exhausting others. Whoever has stolen it cannot dispose of it at will.

It is taken, circumvented in a morphology whose outlines are overvalued. An appropriation that resists the possessor himself and in its struggle for liberation will necessarily bring about aggression, violence and rape.[31]

Reading Irigaray's words, as she struggles to free herself and 'you' from the grip of violence which is patriarchy, we glimpse her new language. To move beyond a male (corrupt) conception of infinity she struggles to embody a fluid language. Movement can be imagined in her words. As if in a dance, she mimes the divine, while still bearing the burden of the patriarchal order of language.[27] For Irigaray, the incorrupt (female) relation to the in-finite would never be static. Our exchanges would not end with, or return to, the certainty of belief in an authoritative, all-powerful, eternal word of God. This latter represents a deep, pervasive and corrupt aspiration which Irigaray identifies as male.

Irigaray's ideal of an incorrupt horizon (for sexual difference) is the infinite as an unending potential or a movement (of the senses, of touch, voice, smell, sound and sight) in time. As a property, infinitude would not be there all at once; it would never be wholly present; infinitude describes the process of dividing endlessly the space, in motion, between us. For Irigaray, desire which moves us infinitely (in time) can preserve sexual difference as an interval.[33] Does this movement constitute an incorrupt craving for infinitude? If so, is there a female form of a corrupt aspiration? Whatever answer are given, can the corruption be avoided? In the next section (4) I explore the relations of finitude and sexual difference. Sections 5 and 6 address the other questions by considering the incorrupt instantiation of the ideals for infinitude.

4. Knowing how to be finite and sexual difference

I propose that the female subject offers insight on knowing how to be finite in *showing* the relation of gender to the infinite. 'Showing' derives from Moore's accounts in *The Infinite* and *Points of View*.[34] The latter employs the formula, 'A is shown that x' as equivalent to A has ineffable knowledge, and when an *attempt* is made to put what A knows into words, the result is x. What ever words are put in place of x will be nonsense, or mere verbiage. Moore establishes that there is ineffable knowledge, for example, states of knowledge which do not answer to how things are (i.e. they are not representations); and, then, that there is such a thing as *attempting* to express some of this knowledge.[35] So when Moore claims that knowing how to be finite is a paradigm of ineffable knowledge, he implies that this knowledge can be shown. This is crucial for the process of coming to terms with the aspiration to be infinite:

> Knowing how to be finite, the desired outcome of this process, is a paradigm of ineffable knowledge. It has nothing to answer to. It is knowledge of how to be finite *in accord with our craving for infinitude*. But there is no independent right or wrong about it.[36]

Moore's account of finitude and infinitude (as above) owes a debt to Kant and post-Kantian philosophy in recognising a limit to what we (say we) know. As suggested in the previous section Ricoeur gives us an explicitly Kantian account of infinitude. He describes our desire to transgress finitude by seeking, in Kant's words, 'a view into a higher immutable order of things ... in accordance with the highest vocation of reason'.[37] Like Kant before and Moore after him Ricoeur maintains that the rational finite being seeks the unconditioned, despite self-consciousness of its own finitude. *Fallible Man* articulates an account of finitude that virtually anticipates Moore's claims about finitude and representations of reality in *Points of View*.

> Kant was not wrong in identifying finitude and receptivity: according to him the finite is a rational being that does not create the objects of its representation but receives them. ... the world is primarily not the boundary of my existence but its correlate ...[38]

Finitude is a fundamental characteristic of man according to western philosophy in general. It is also argued that man's awareness of finitude presupposes an *a priori* idea of infinitude. Western philosophers have offered various arguments concerning man's awareness of finitude (in the light of an idea of infinitude). Charles Taylor presents a classic argument, turning to Augustine to distinguish two sorts of relation to the infinite.[39] On the one hand, Augustine has an awareness of himself as finite and (his 'heart') longs to be eternally at rest, in this sense to be infinite. On the other hand, Augustine's argument is that he would not have his awareness of finitude without the idea of the infinitude of a perfect being, i.e. God.[40] Taylor cites Augustine's *Confessions*,

> O God, You are the Light of my heart, and the Bread of my inmost soul, and the Power that weds my mind and the thoughts of my heart.[41]

Furthermore, Taylor argues that Augustine's reflections represent an important shift in the history of western philosophical thinking about the infinite. In Augustine, 'the route to the higher passes within ... [and] radical reflexivity takes on a new status, because it is the "space" in which we come to encounter God, in which we effect the turning from lower to higher'.[42] He insists that Augustine is the originator in western philosophy of the strand of thought which has sought God as the infinite within man. Yet Moore suggests that a corrupt aspiration to be infinite leads the subject 'to try to situate the infinite whole within itself'.⁴³ Feminist philosophy with the help of, in this case, Irigarayan mime can shed light on the gendered nature of the development of what I have referred to as a classic argument concerning man's finitude and the infinite.

The question in Irigaray's terms of sexual difference emerges in recognition of the corruption of man's relation to the infinite. Irigaray employs her feminist form of mime in order to disrupt the patriarchal accounts. Positively Irigaray exposes infinitude as the crucial characteristic of the divine.⁴⁴ Yet Irigaray's mime of a corrupt male version of the desire to be infinite is both provocative and subversive.⁴⁵ Consider her reading of the nostalgia for security, unity and infinity as a (male) desire to return to the place of the womb:

> The womb, for its part, would figure rather as place. Though of course what unfolds in the womb unfolds in function of an interval, a cord, that is never done away with. Whence perhaps the infinite nostalgia for that first home? The interval cannot be done away with?
>
> ... The boundary of the 'containing body' can be understood of the womb. If it has no outside, desire can go on to infinity. Is this the way with the desire for God that does not know the outside of the universe?
>
> But sexual desire that goes toward the womb and no longer returns to it also goes toward infinity since it never touches the body that contains it *hic et nunc*, it goes toward another container. Instead of moving across the actual container in the direction of the other through porosity, it remains nostalgic for another home.⁴⁶

In the above Irigaray provokes reflection on desire (for the maternal) which goes on infinitely and desire which constantly goes toward infinity never reaching the container (or God) beyond. Neither desire touches the bodies in space.⁴⁷ Irigaray imitates in order to disrupt these two (male) dimensions of, on the one hand, going to infinity endlessly in time and, on the other hand, moving toward infinity never traversing the actual container. Her implicit criticism is that this male longing for something beyond touch (i.e. beyond space – and time) misses the infinitude within the finite. Irigaray insinuates that this double, time-space relation to infinity has characterised the religious feeling of an European man.⁴⁸ In contrast, for her only in time in the interval between two subjects, for instance, in touch is infinitude found as a trace. This is perhaps a trace of an eschatological (or regulative) ideal.

Listen to Irigaray's provocative language on sexual difference:

> Not in me but in our difference lies the abyss. We can never be sure of bridging our gap between us. But that is our adventure. Without this peril there is no us ...

> ... The outline engendered between my lips is never once and for all. Reserve, excess, source of movement – my lips could never be reduced to subject or object, instrument of use or function. Our exchanges? An engendering through rare and always infinite fortune.[39]

The above passage exhibits how Irigaray conceives a role for the infinite within her account of sexual difference. In contrast, Jantzen's feminist philosophical theology misses the fact that the infinite exists within the finite: as in 'an engendering through rare and always infinite fortune'. In missing the possibility in this fact, a corrupt aspiration to become all-nature is a danger.[50] Jantzen's feminist conception of pantheism cannot avoid the dangers of the infinite as unlimited and corrupting; nor is it clear that her pantheism preserves difference. Yet a feminist philosopher of religion can still confront infinitude's corruption. I would like to confront this with the help of Moore's account of regulative ideals.

5. The instantiation of regulative ideals: Infinitude as incorrupt

Moore explains the incorrupt possibility in craving infinitude as follows.

> ... Infinitude ... includes ideals of representation, conation and agency. These are regulative ideals involving unconditionedness. To satisfy them would mean thinking what is true, wanting what is right and doing what is required. It would mean being perfectly rational. A craving for infinitude, in an incorrupt form, would be largely a craving for the instantiation of such ideals.

I maintain that for an ideal to be instantiated as regulative it would have to remain symbolic and eschatological, not epistemological and ontological. To aspire to instantiate these ideals epistemologically and ontologically would be to forget the real (incorrupt) significance in the perspectival nature of our knowledge. Both the relativist and the absolutist philosopher fail to grasp the necessarily regulative nature of the ideals of infinitude. Instead they would claim to possess their own knowledge of the true, the right and the good. The philosopher (whether relativist or absolutist) who aspires to be infinite treats the point of view from which he or she exists as the whole of reality. This distorts reality and can corrupt the knower. Remember in Moore's words,

> Our craving for infinitude has a perspectival character corresponding to the point of view from which alone we exist ... When the craving is distorted, this perspectival character is turned in on itself in such a way that the craving becomes an aspiration *that we alone exist*.[51]

Consistent with what Moore would agree is the perspectival nature of knowledge Ricoeur draws the following distinctions between the infinite and the finite:

> ... the will [as practical reason], freedom and the infinite [are] on one side, and the understanding, truth and the finite on the other.[52]

So truth and knowledge are finite; and for Ricoeur finitude implies being limited by perspective. Yet it should also be remembered that Ricoeur accounts for infinitude by giving an eschatological role to feeling. This is not explicit in either Kant or Moore. Yet Ricoeur proposes,

> ... The *infinitude of feeling* emerges clearly from the fact that no organized, historical community, no economy, no politic, no human culture can exhaust its demand for a totalization of persons, of a Kingdom[53] in which, nevertheless, we now are and 'in which, alone, we are capable of continuing our existence'.[54]
>
> ... Feeling anticipates more than it gives, and so all 'spiritual' feelings are feeling of a transition toward ...[55]

Ricoeur's reference to a kingdom in the above remains Kantian. Yet he is more explicit than Kant about the spiritual role of feelings. Nevertheless, Ricoeur offers the philosophical tools to avoid a corrupt aspiration: he maintains the regulative role for the ideals of infinitude and employs hermeneutics to interpret man's passions. This is as far as Ricoeur goes. He remains unaware of the maleness of his perspective on human disproportion. For this next step I have already turned to Irigaray. As seen in section 3, Irigaray's mime endeavours to elucidate and disrupt the male form of a corrupt aspiration.

At this point it is my turn to make a further proposal. Both the male and the female philosopher can and should seek to cease aspiring to situate the infinite whole within himself (or herself). This would seek to do more than Moore with his crucial distinction below:

> Whereas the *incorrupt* craving for *infinitude would be essentially expansive*, leading the subject to try to situate itself within the infinite whole, the aspiration to be infinite is essentially inert, leading the subject to try to situate the infinite whole within itself. And, again by its own lights, it (the aspiration to be infinite) is bad. There is an irrationality in wanting to be that which makes anything rational. It is a revolt, and an offence, against that which truly makes anything rational: rationality itself.[56]

Bearing in mind Moore's description of the incorrupt craving for infinitude as essentially expansive recall the words of Irigaray's female subject who describes the in-finite: 'A fluid expansion, never enclosed once and for all. Not even by projects or projections'. Violence – not justice – is a result of conceiving infinity as a closed totality: 'a solid, empty membrane which would gather and contain all possibilities'.[57] Irigaray's description represents male morphology – i.e. a male body or sexual organ alone – as violence itself. So the resistance to eliminate evil or to stop the aspiration to be infinite creates an unresolvable problem for the male philosopher who fails to see sexual difference in a relation to a differently gendered subject. Why do philosophers fail to seek the means to eliminate evil or to cease trying to be infinite? Irigaray suggests that an answer rests in a specifically male failure to recognise their gender as well as that of another, female subject.

However, to articulate the possibility of two incorrupt relations of gender to the infinite, I have built on Moore's conception of a craving for infinitude. What is craved, or yearned, for? A list of possible answers would include craving for the infinity of power, of knowledge, of beauty, of goodness, of truth, of meaning, of security, of justice. But Moore's Kantian claim that we crave the instantiation of certain regulative ideas in seeking to think what is true, to want what is right and to do what is required is incomplete. What about seeking to give each another what is due (to her)? Justice is the desire to live well – and we might add – with and for others in social institutions.[58] Justice has also been called 'the first virtue of social institutions'.[59]

A common danger has appeared in masculinist, feminist and more radical attempts to (better) orientate our finiteness – including race, class, gender and sexual differences – by reference to infinitude. To confront this danger of aspiring to be/become all there is I do not advocate the status quo in philosophy of religion. Instead I propose an additional ideal – of justice – which would be regulative for the relations to infinitude of every man and woman. This means every person who acknowledges their differences according to the interrelated factors of gender, racial, class, religious, ethnic and sexual perspectives.

6. A fourth regulative ideal: Justice

Generally justice as a regulative ideal is absent from masculinist philosophy of religion. *Justice* would demand recognising *a necessary relation to infinitude for each differently gendered point of view*. If philosophers of religion could admit that all of our relations, whether spiritual, sexual, ethical or political, involve power, then they would also have to face issues of justice. An influential philosopher of discourse on sex/gender, Michel Foucault proclaims that 'power is everywhere'.[60] Power does not have one source; nor is it one structure of domination. Instead power 'comes from everywhere'; and so every relation is recognised as having political significance. In Foucault's terms, relations of power are not in a position of exteriority with respect to other types of relations, including sexual and spiritual relationships; they are immanent and infinite! So they have a directly productive role to play in everything, including our religious thinking, feeling, acting and giving.[61]

In exposing the male specificity in human relations to the divine, Irigaray stops short of the further question of justice concerning sexual difference. What about the men and women who only know a male or female relation to infinity, or unity, second-hand as a sense of powerful security which belongs to someone superior to them? This is someone whose security is at their expense as the other. Not everyone can recall a secure image of the mother's womb or imagine the infinitude of a loving, all-powerful and all-protective divine. Women and marginalized others, especially those others who have suffered the total denigration of self in slavery, are used as the pretext for a yearning which eclipses them as other. The flip side of the strong erect image of powerful, privileged European [white] men is violence. Violence is the result of excluding from this picture the one who contains[62] *and* also the ones who are alienated from the domain in which Irigaray finds sexual difference preserved! Non-dominant people can be alienated from the white male sense of, on the one hand, the place of the maternal (womb) and, on the other hand, the place within a perfectly created universe. Recognition of this alienation can move us to a radical feminist conception of gender and infinitude. A radical feminist conception informs my own proposal to place *yearning* at the heart of feminist philosophy of religion. It attempts to capture what Ricoeur calls the infinitude of spiritual feelings (or what I have called the eschatological and symbolic order) beyond the idolatrous and exclusive desire for the absolute.

Yearning constitutes a place where differences can meet in the desire to live well for and with others. As the African-American feminist bell hooks explains,

> under the heading *Yearning* . . . I looked for *common* passions, sentiments shared by folks across race, class, gender, and sexual practice, I was struck by the depths of longing in many of us. . . .
>
> The shared space and feeling of 'yearning' opens up the possibility of common ground where all these differences might meet and engage one another.[63]

Justice is the implicit goal of gaining greater knowledge from those others in the cultures that shape us. Again hooks explains this in terms of yearning,

> ... Much ... engagement with culture emerges from the yearning to do intellectual work that connects with habits of being, forms of artistic expression, and aesthetics that inform the daily life of writers and scholarsas well as a mass population. On the terrain of culture, one can participatein critical dialogue with the uneducated poor, the black underclass who are thinking about aesthetics. One can talk about what we are seeing, thinking, or listening to; a space is there for critical dialogue.[64]

hooks's writings serve as a critical supplement to my conception of yearning which brings together a Kantian account of seeking the unconditioned and Irigaray's account of sexual difference. hooks's understanding of culture and the implicit search for justice can shape a gender-sensitive approach to the infinite for philosophy of religion.[65] Her understanding of race works to transform sexual difference.

Irigaray mimes a nostalgic longing for infinity which exists before birth and beyond the sexual act as equally corruptible. She describes the male form of this longing as characterized by its place(s) of fulfilment. The (white) male awareness lacks an interval between subjects. Irigaray's mime of patriarchy shows women do not have a specific place of their own (*genre*). In the male account, women are both the place (like a womb) for men and the pretext for their need of God (protective like the mother) conceived as powerful and transcendent. What about a divine for women? Irigaray finds it a diabolical thing that women do not have a god to secure a *genre* of their own.[66] Instead women constitute the unacknowledged condition of the male God. Yet what would a 'god' of women's own look like?

Ellen Armour tackles the danger in having Irigaray's 'Divine Women' project an essentialist account of the white woman subject. In her words,

> Uncovering a differing and deferring subject at the base of the race/gender divide when explored from both sides confirms, chastens and supplements whitefeminism's move toward woman as multiple. ... It chastens whitefeminism's confidence that approaching multiplicity through sexual difference is sufficient to disrupt race's double erasure. It supplements whitefeminism's turn toward multiplicity in doubling sexual difference and deferral with racial difference and deferral. ... building on this (non)foundational foundation requires first going backward into history rather than forward into the future.[67]

Exhausting white solipsism's invisibility theology moves [Armour] toward realizing feminism's (im)possible telos of providing a platform for resistance to the multiple oppressions women face.[68]

The woman subject who constantly differs in relation to other women subjects (according to race, gender, etc) is also constantly deferred in time because she is never completely (liberated as) herself. Armour establishes women's difference(s) and deferral in relation to African American women authors and so provides an important argument to support my turn to the writings of hooks. African American feminist writings confirm that the western woman, like man, is a site bounded by race. Armour demonstrates the role of black writing in contesting the white boundaries of race and the content of woman that they protect.[69] With Armour's subversions of the race/gender divide with the differing and deferring subject in mind I have rethought the role of aesthetic representations by African-American and other feminists in communicating ineffable knowledge.

The powerful synthetic representations of yearning in works of art (e.g. literature, music, sculpture, dance) attempt to grasp the political nature of our relations to the infinite. Yearning shapes and is shaped by the power for change which can be channelled into rational (including moral) and aesthetic forms.[70] Irigaray's image of the place where bodies embrace gives an appropriate expression of the divine in the sense of a divine coupling.[71] This Irigarayan image also offers a point of contact with hooks's yearning to work with words. hooks's yearning moves her towards the infinite 'in a dance with the divine'.[72] hooks's poetic expressions mediate the meaning of the divine as a radical political gesture of solidarity. If women and men are to achieve change, community and, according to hooks, 'the sacredness of words,' then the truth of what has been, according to Irigaray, 'the overbearing power' of God must be told.[73] hooks and Irigaray each seek a space for infinite movement; Irigaray seeks the divine as infinite potential between two subjects; and together their pair, black-white women, creates a crucial tension. We can imagine the seductive atmosphere of pleasure and danger which surrounds an African-American realisation of 'a writing life'. hooks plays with language in order to create 'a redemptive practice' in writing (her) life; she aims to redeem the past denigration of self at the heart of the history of slavery.[74] Ultimately she gives memory a future in redeeming our raced/gendered relations to infinitude.

Compatible with Irigaray, hooks arouses her readers to touch the pleasures of the body, mind and soul. Yet unlike Irigaray, hooks exposes the wounds of social oppression due to racism and white supremacy. She performs words in writing, in order to create a passionate place of personal, social and racial transformation. Her act of writing is a gesture of political solidarity in a standpoint that is always restless. hooks's claims, 'As a writer, I seek that moment of ecstasy when I am dancing with words, moving in a circle of love so complete that like the mystical dervish who dances to be one with the Divine, I move toward the infinite'.[75] The challenge is for this movement to maintain the regulative ideals necessary for the gendered transformations of philosophy of religion.

Conclusion

It is important to keep in mind Moore's claim that knowing how to be finite is a paradigm of ineffable knowledge which is equivalent to (claiming that) we are shown how to be finite. Feminist philosophers such as Irigaray and hooks contribute examples of ineffable knowledge, as well as new practices for communicating knowledge in philosophy of religion. New strategies for exploiting words in the infinite play of language, in art or dance, reflect endeavours to express ineffable knowledge. Normally these are linguistic practices, but as Moore admits music and other aesthetic practices are different manners of showing.[76] Ineffable knowledge is shown in Irigarayan images of female subjectivity, of song and dance, in miming the texts of mystics and in other creatively subversive ways.

My concluding argument goes beyond Moore. If infinitude confronts us with ineffable knowledge then philosophers of religion can only try to communicate this knowledge. In Irigaray's terms we know that we are in-finite. We are shown this in the infinite play of language about the divine. We are also shown a craving for infinitude. So our knowledge of regulative ideals of infinitude is ineffable; it answers to nothing. Yet we are shown that certain ideals motivate us and politicize the nature of our relationships. There are dangers for men and for women in these claims about infinitude. On the one hand, the danger is evident in the male aspiration to be infinite. On the other hand, there would seem to be a similar danger in the female aspiration to become divine. With an aspiration to be *all there is* a subject eclipses others. A critical embrace of bodies would reform this aspiration and our thinking. It should also challenge our physical, sensual and material relations with others.

hooks's conception of yearning is compatible with the political intent of contemporary feminist philosophy to develop social epistemology. The core concern in feminist social epistemology is to see reality from alternative points of view, i.e. to refuse to allow inertia to blind us from the reality of other lives and so a larger social world than one's own. Moore and Ricoeur each account for the inevitable finitude of a person's point of view. Moreover, the tradition going back to Augustine exhibits two sorts of responses to this finitude. Whether the concern is ethical, epistemological or metaphysical, the possible political responses run the fine line between corrupt or incorrupt relations to the infinite. Philosophers of religion can attempt to express an incorrupt form of craving infinitude, while resisting a corrupt aspiration to be infinite.

The novelty of this philosophical topic rests in the necessary tension between the enabling and corrupting power immanent in material, personal and social relations. Relations of power are infinite. The feminist philosopher who struggles for renewal of the field of philosophy of religion performs her writing again and again, in order to move beyond any nostalgia for a secure place. The goal is, then, to express the divine anew in a shared space and feeling of yearning that can transform all gendered forms of a corrupt aspiration into a mobile dance toward the infinite.

Notes

1. The criticism could be explored further in terms of a problem of the *imago dei* as man's own self-image. Here and generally in this essay 'man' refers to the male subject.
2. Later in this essay I criticize A. W. Moore for seeking merely 'to come to terms with a deep, pervasive and corrupt aspiration': like evil, he insists it cannot be eliminated. However, this stops short of seeking to eradicate a corrupt (male) aspiration which perpetuates injustice.
3. See Luce Irigaray, *Elemental Passions*, trans. Joanne Collie and Judith Still (London: The Athlone Press, 1992), p. 89. A. W. Moore, *Points of View* (Oxford: Clarendon Press, 1997), p. 275.
4. Grace Jantzen, *Becoming Divine* (Manchester: Manchester University Press, 1998). Jantzen argues that feminists should seek 'to become divine' as 'natals'. Yet she also claims that 'the obligation to become divine is not an obligation to become limitless' (Ibid., p. 154). In one sense, Jantzen is closer to the ancient Greek table of opposites than she realizes: the Pythagoreans associated the infinite with the other as a form of suspicion, as chaotic and limitless (see endnote 50 below). However, a corrupt aspiration to become infinite would need to be reigned in by something more than Jantzen's reference to limit supplies (e.g. infinite time can exist along with finite space). The crucial difference between Jantzen's conception of the male drive to be infinite and the Pythagorean conception of male-female is the equation of female with the disorderly, bad infinite. Moreover, as seen in Irigaray, the infinite (as female) can exist (as good) within certain limits.
5. For a classic statement of these dichotomies, Genevieve Lloyd, *The Man of Reason: 'Male' and 'Female' in Western Philosophy* (London: Methuen, 1984). Cf. Pamela Sue Anderson, *A Feminist Philosophy of Religion: The Rationality and Myths of Religious Belief* (Oxford: Blackwell, 1998), pp. 5–10.
6. Terri Elliot, 'Making Strange What Had Appeared Familiar', *The Monist: An International Journal of General Philosophical Inquiry* (General Topic – Feminist Epistemology: For and Against) 77/4 (October 1994): 424–433. Also see Pamela Sue Anderson, 'A Case for a Feminist Philosophy of Religion: Transforming Philosophy's Imagery and Myths', *Ars Disputandi: The Online Journal in Philosophy of Religion* (September 2000).
7. Moore, *Points of View*, pp. 274–279, also 105–106, 210–215, 250–251.
8. Pamela Sue Anderson, 'Yearning: A Spiritual Passion for Postmodern Times', St Mary's College 150th Anniversary Lecture (unpublished), Strawberry Hill, University of Surrey, 17 June 2000.
9. Moore, *Points of View*, p. 276.
10. Jantzen, *Becoming Divine*, pp. 154–155.

11. Ibid., pp. 265–268.
12. Moore, *Points of View*, p. 276.
13. Sabina Lovibond, 'An Ancient Theory of Gender: Plato and the Pythagorean Table', in Leonie J. Archer, Susain Fischer and Maria Wyke, eds., *Women in Ancient Societies* (London: Macmillan, 1994), pp. 88–101; and 'Feminism in Ancient Philosophy: The Feminist Stake in Greek Rationalism', in Miranda Fricker and Jennifer Hornsby, eds., *The Cambridge Companion to Feminism in Philosophy* (Cambridge: Cambridge University Press, 2000), pp. 10–28.
14. Moore, *Points of View*, p. 279; Irigaray, *Elemental Passions*, and 'Divine Women', in *Sexes and Genealogies*, trans. Gillian C. Gill (New York: Columbia University Press, 1993), pp. 55–72.
15. Irigaray, 'Divine Women', pp. 61–2.
16. Ibid., pp. 68–9.
17. Without answering this, Jantzen appropriates Irigarya's statement to argue against Feuerbach's reliance upon a binary opposition between theism/atheism in his account of projection; see Jantzen, *Becoming Divine*, pp. 88–92.
18. Ludwig Feuerbach, *The Essence of Christianity*, trans. George Eliot (Buffalo, NY: Prometheus Books, 1989), especially pp. 12–19 and 270–278.
19. Jantzen rejects Feuerbach's argument as masculine oppositional thinking (i.e. privileging belief and truth over desire and adequacy) in order to reconceive 'projection'. Yet she could give up this term completely for a regulative ideal which would be less problematic; a regulative ideal is not the same thing as a projection, despite her claim that it is (Jantzen, *Becoming Divine*, p. 92).
20. Moore, *Points of View*, pp. 275–276.
21. Paul Ricoeur, *Fallible Man*, revised translation by Charles A. Kelbley, with an Introduction by Walter J. Lowe (New York: Fordham University Press, 1986).
22. Moore claims that there are three foundational principles: We are finite. We are conscious of ourselves as finite. We aspire to be infinite. See Moore, *Points of View*, pp. 253–263.
23. Ricoeur, *Fallible Man*, pp. 25–26.
24. Ibid., p. 131.
25. For more on the 'disembodied' nature of philosophical thinking, see Anderson, *A Feminist Philosophy of Religion*, pp. 94n10, 98–9, 127–131.
26. Ricoeur, *Fallible Man*, p. 22.
27. Ibid., p. 23.
28. Luce Irigarya, 'Place, Interval: A Reading of Aristotle's *Physics IV*', *An Ethics of Sexual Difference*, trans. Carolyn Burke and Gillian C. Gill (London: The Athlone Press, 1993), p. 35.
29. Irigaray, 'Love of Same, Love of Other', *An Ethics of Sexual Difference*, p. 111.
30. Irigaray, *Elemental Passions*, p. 89.
31. Ibid., p. 90.
32. For an original reading of Irigaray and dancing, see Eluned Summers-Bremmer, 'Reading Irigaray, Dancing', *Hypatia* 15/1 (Winter 2000): 90–124.
33. I have interpreted this interval in terms of a trace, Pamela Sue Anderson, 'Tracing Sexual Difference: Beyond the *Aporia* of the Other', *Sophia: Journal of Cross-Cultural Philosophy of Religion and Ethics* 38/1 (March–April 1999): 54–73.
34. Moore, *The Infinite*, pp. 186–200; *Points of View*, pp. xii–xiii, 156–157, 195–213 and 277–278. I recall Moore's references to showing in the Conclusion below.
35. Moore, *Points of View*, pp. 156–157.
36. Ibid., p. 277.

37. Immanuel Kant, *Critique of Practical Reason*, edited by Mary Gregor. Introduction by Andrews Reath (Cambridge: Cambridge University Press, 1997), p. 90.
38. Ricoeur, *Fallible Man*, p. 20; Cf. Moore, *Points of View*, pp. 6–9, 256, 282.
39. Charles Taylor, *Sources of the Self: The Making of the Modern Identity* (Cambridge MA: Harvard University Prses, 1989), pp. 138–139.
40. Taylor, *Sources of the Self*, pp. 139–141.
41. Augustine, *Confessions*, trans. R. S. Pine-Coffin (Harmondsworth: Penguin Books, 1961), p. 34.
42. Taylor, *Sources of the Self*, pp. 139–140.
43. Moore, *Points of View*, p. 276.
44. Irigaray, 'Divine Women', pp. 61–63.
45. Irigaray, 'Place, Interval', pp. 34–55.
46. Ibid., pp. 49–50.
47. Aristotle who is Irigaray's subtext here maintains that space is finite (e.g. body is bounded by a surface) and time is potentially infinite (i.e. never wholly present and infinite by addition).
48. Irigaray, 'Divine Women', p. 61.
49. Irigaray, *Elemental Passions*, pp. 28 and 29.
50. Jantzen's view of the infinite as masculine in the history of western philosophy is ironic. Some of the earliest western philosophers, the Pythagoreans and Plato conceived the infinite as the disorderly, chaotic female. Jantzen is inconsistent when she refers to the table of opposites attributed to Pythagoras which lists female on the same side as the unlimited without seeing that this aligns the female, not the male, with the infinite. Jantzen, *Becoming Divine*, pp. 154–155 and 266–268; cf. Moore, *The Infinite*, pp. 19–29, 202. Jantzen also skirts the critical role played by the infinite in the pantheism of earlier western philosophers such as Spinoza. The essence of Spinoza's God was to exist and to be all that exists. The (male) fear of the infinite in pantheism seems compatible with the ancient Greek male philosopher's suspicion of the infinite. Jantzen, *Becoming Divine*, pp. 267, 272–273.
51. Moore, *Points of View*, p. 276.
52. Ricoeur, *Fallible Man*, p. 36.
53. This infinitude of feeling may be understood in relation to what Kant recognises as a demand for a higher order of things, in the regulative idea of the kingdom of ends (i.e. of persons), in the *Critique of Practical Reasons*, pp. 63–75. However, the only moral feeling described by Kant himself is respect for the law or for persons as ends in themselves.
54. Further on in the same text Ricoeur discusses an important passage from Kant's second *Critique*: 'We may remember that excellent text where Kant – the philosopher who began by rejecting happiness as a principle of morality – rediscovers, at the root of every dialectic and every transcendental illusion, 'a view [*Aussicht*] into a higher immutable order of things in which we already are, and in which we may, by definite precepts, continue our existence in accordance with the supreme decree of reason' [cf. Kant, *Critique of Practical Reason*, p. 90]. This text makes it very clear what the reciprocal genesis of reason and feeling can signify ... In Kantian terms, reason is my 'decree' and my 'destination' – my *Bestimmung* – the intention according to which I can 'continue my existnece'. In short, feeling reveals the identity of existence and reason: it personalizes reason' (Ricoeur, *Fallible Man*, p. 102).
55. Ibid., p. 104. Italics added.
56. Moore, *Points of View*, pp. 275–276.
57. Irigaray, *Elemental Passions*, p. 89.

58. Paul Ricoeur, *Oneself as Another*, trans. David Pellauer (Chicago: University of Chicago Press, 1992), pp. 227–39.
59. John Rawls, *A Theory of Justice* (Cambridge: MA: Harvard University Press, 1971), p. 3.
60. Michel Foucault, *The History of Sexuality*, Vol. 1, An Introduction, trans. Robert Hurley (Harmondsworth: Penguin Books, 1979), p. 93.
61. Foucault, *The History of Sexuality*, Vol. 1, p. 94.
62. Irigaray describes this exclusion provocatively as escaping the touch of the female body or skin; this is also suggested by her contrast 'instead of moving across the actual container ... through porosity', see Irigaray, 'Place Interval', pp. 49–50.
63. bell hooks, *Yearning: Race, Gender and Cultural Politics* (Boston: South Bend Press, 1990), pp. 12–13. Note 'bell hooks' is a penname written in only lower case letters.
64. hooks, *Yearning*, p. 31.
65. Also see Patricia Hill Collins, *Fighting Words: Black Women and the Search for Justice* (Minneapolis, MN: University of Minnesota Press, 1998).
66. Irigaray, 'Divine Women', p. 64.
67. Ellen, Armour, *Deconstruction, Feminist Theology and the Problem of Difference: Subverting the Race/Gender Divide* (Chicago: University of Chicago Press, 1999), p. 167.
68. Armour, *Deconstruction, Feminist Theology and the Problem of Difference*, p. 168.
69. Ibid., pp. 168–9.
70. I have explored the aesthetically and rationally shaped transformation of the world, especially of suffering and loss of love evident in Kathe Kollwitz's sculpture, 'The lovers'; see Anderson 'Yearning: A Spiritual Passion for Postmodern Times'. Kollwitz's aesthetic representation evokes the dual, active and passive aspects of, what I have called, a rational passion. Reason actively shapes a passion into a form of yearning. Cf. Anderson, *A Feminist Philosophy of Religion*, pp. 22–23, 241 and 247.
71. For elucidation of this image, see Kathleen O'Grady, 'Where Bodies Embrace: Pamela Sue Anderson's *A Feminist Philosophy of Religion*', Review Essay, *Feminist Theology*, issue 20 (1999): 99–100.
72. hooks, *Remembered Rapture: The Writer at Work* (London: The Women's Press, 1999), p. 38.
73. Irigaray, *Elemental Passions*, p. 92.
74. hooks, *Remembered Rapture*, pp. 7, 11–12.
75. Ibid., p. 38.
76. On music as an example of expressing the inexpressible, see Moore, *Points of View*, pp. 201–203.

Address for correspondence: Dr. Pamela Anderson, Department of Philosophy, University of Sunderland, Priestman Building, Green Terrace, Sunderland SR1 3PZ, England, UK
Phone: +44-91-5152170; E-mail: pamela.anderson@sunderland.ac.uk

STUDIES IN PHILOSOPHY AND RELIGION

1. E.-R. FREUND: *Franz Rosenzweig's Philosophy of Existence*. An Analysis of 'The Star of Redemption'. (Translation from the German revised edition.) 1979
   ISBN 90-247-2091-5
2. A. M. OLSON: *Transcendence and Hermeneutics*. An Interpretation of the Philosophy of Karl Jaspers. 1979   ISBN Pb 90-247-2092-3
3. A. VERDU: *The Philosophy of Buddhism*. A 'Totalistic' Synthesis. 1981
   ISBN 90-247-2224-1
4. H. H. OLIVER: *A Relational Metaphysic*. 1981   ISBN 90-247-2457-0
5. J. G. ARAPURA: *Gnosis and the Question of Thought in Vedānta*. Dialogue with the Foundations. 1986   ISBN 90-247-3061-9
6. W. HOROSZ and T. CLEMENTS (eds.): *Religion and Human Purpose*. A Cross Disciplinary Approach. 1987   ISBN 90-247-3000-7
7. S. SIA: *God in Process Thought*. A Study in Charles Hartshorne's Concept of God. 1985   ISBN 90-247-3103-8; Pb 90-247-3156-9
8. J. F. KOBLER: *Vatican II and Phenomenology*. Reflections on the Life-World of the Church. 1985   ISBN 90-247-3193-3; Pb 90-247-3194-1
9. J. J. GODFREY: *A Philosophy of Human Hope*. 1987
   ISBN 90-247-3353-7; Pb 90-247-3354-5
10. R. W. PERRETT: *Death and Immortality*. 1987   ISBN 90-247-3440-1
11. R. S. GALL: *Beyond Theism and Atheism*. Heidegger's Significance for Religious Thinking. 1987   ISBN 90-247-3623-4
12. S. SIA (ed.): *Charles Hartshorne's Concept of God*. Philosophical and Theological Responses. 1990   ISBN 0-7923-0290-7
13. R. W. PERRETT (ed.): *Indian Philosophy of Religion*. 1989   ISBN 0-7923-0437-3
14. H. E. M. HOFMEISTER: *Truth and Belief*. Interpretation and Critique of the Analytical Theory of Religion. 1990   ISBN 0-7923-0976-6
15. J. F. HARRIS (ed.): *Logic, God and Metaphysics*. 1992   ISBN 0-7923-1454-9
16. K. J. CLARK (ed.): *Our Knowledge of God*. Essays on Natural and Philosophical Theology. 1992   ISBN 0-7923-1485-9
17. H. P. KAINZ: *Democracy and the 'Kingdom of God'*. 1993   ISBN 0-7923-2106-5
18. E. T. LONG (ed.): *God, Reason and Religions*. New Essays in the Philosophy of Religion. 1995   ISBN 0-7923-3810-3
19. G. BRÜNTRUP and R.K. TACELLI (eds.): *The Rationality of Theism* 1999
    ISBN 0-7923-5829-5
20. C. SEYMOUR: *A Theodicy of Hell*. 2000   ISBN 0-7923-6364-7

STUDIES IN PHILOSOPHY AND RELIGION

21. V. S. HARRISON: *The Apologetic Value of Human Holiness.* Von Balthasar's Christocentric Philosophical Anthropology. 2000 ISBN 0-7923-6617-4
22. M. BLONDEL†: *The Idealist Illusion and Other Essays.* Translation and Introduction by Fiachra Long, annotations by Fiachra Long and Claude Troisfontaines. 2000 ISBN 0-7923-6654-9
23. E. T. LONG (ed.): *Issues in Contemporary Philosophy of Religion.* 2001 ISBN 1-4020-0167-3

KLUWER ACADEMIC PUBLISHERS DORDRECHT / BOSTON / LONDON

Accelerating the World of Research

Kluwer*Online*

A dynamic electronic journal service with over 700 research-level and scholarly journals.

Content

BENEFITS include:
- Institution-wide access via IP numbers; remote access is also available.
- No requirement to keep print journals with electronic subscriptions.
- Electronic journals can be viewed as PDF files weeks before printed versions.
- CrossRef electronically links article citations to original referenced materials.
- Boolean search engine allows for look-up by key words, titles and/or authors.
- Access available to institutions as standard subscriptions, single-site or multi-site.

SUBJECT AREAS include:
- Agricultural, Biological and Environmental Sciences
- Business, Economics, Law and Tax
- Computer Science and Materials Science
- Education, Humanities and Social Sciences
- Engineering, Mathematics and Reference
- Medicine and Health Sciences
- Natural and Physical Sciences

CONTACT one of our representatives for additional information:

In North and South America
Kluwer Academic Publishers
101 Philip Drive
Assinippi Park
Norwell, MA 02061
Tel: +1 781 871 6600
Fax: +1 781 871 6528
E-mail: kluweronline@wkap.com

In Europe, Asia, Africa & Australia
Kluwer Academic Publishers
Sales Department, Spuiboulevard 50
P.O. Box 989, 3300 AA Dordrecht
The Netherlands
Tel: +31 78 6392179
Fax: +31 78 6392300
E-mail: sales@wkap.nl

VISIT www.kluweronline.nl

 Kluwer academic publishers

A Wolters Kluwer Company

Twentieth-Century Western Philosophy of Religion 1900-2000

By:
Eugene Thomas Long
Dept. of Philosophy, University of South Carolina, USA

HANDBOOK OF CONTEMPORARY PHILOSOPHY OF RELIGION 1

This book provides in one volume a map of one hundred years of twentieth-century western philosophy of religion. Divided into four divisions approximating four chronological periods, the book begins at the turn of the twentieth-century with Absolute Idealism, Personal Idealism, Neo-Kantianism, Positivism and the Science of Religion. The period between the two world wars includes discussions of Neo-Realism, Phenomenology, American Pragmatism, Personalism and the Philosophy of History. The primary strands of philosophy of religion after mid-century are Philosophical Analysis, Existential Philosophy, Neo-Thomism and Process Philosophy. The final division, which leads to the turn of the twenty-first century, includes discussions of Analytic Philosophy, Hermeneutics and Deconstruction, Critical Theory, Comparative Philosophy and Feminist Philosophy. The primary task of the book is interpretative. However, brief remarks intended to highlight central issues and raise critical questions are included at the end of each chapter and in the concluding chapter of the book. The book should be of particular interest to persons working in the fields of philosophy of religion and theology and to persons more generally interested in the variety and scope of philosophical reflection on religion in the twentieth-century.

Contents:
Part One: Philosophy of Religion at the Turn of the Twentieth-Century.
Part Two: Philosophy of Religion Between the Wars.
Part Three: Philosophy of Religion after Mid-Century.
Part Four: Philosophy of Religion at the Turn of the Twenty-First Century.

2000 ISBN 0-7923-6285-3
544 pp./Hardbound
Price: NLG 440.00/GBP 136.00/USD 234.00

P.O. Box 322, 3300 AH Dordrecht, The Netherlands
P.O. Box 358, Accord Station, Hingham, MA 02018-0358, U.S.A.

http://www.wkap.nl

Kluwer academic publishers

Printed in the United Kingdom
by Lightning Source UK Ltd.
119403UK00009B/153